The China Factor
Peking and the
Superpowers

Edited by Gerald Segal

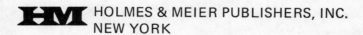 HOLMES & MEIER PUBLISHERS, INC.
NEW YORK

First published in the United States of America 1982 by
Holmes & Meier Publishers, Inc.
30 Irving Place
New York, NY 10003

Library of Congress Cataloging in Publication Data

Main entry under title:
The China factor.
    Bibliography: p.193.
    Includes index.
    Contents: An introduction to the great power triangle
/ Gerald Segal — China and the great power triangle /
Michael Yahuda — The Soviet Union and the great power
triangle / Gerald Segal — [etc.]
    1. China—Foreign relations—1949-   —Addresses,
essays, lectures. 2. World politics—1945-   —Ad-
dresses, essays, lectures. I. Segal, Gerald, 1953-
DS777.8.C45   1982   327.51   81-6897   AACR2

ISBN 0-8419-0735-8

Printed and bound in Great Britain

CONTENTS

To my colleague and friend

1   AN INTRODUCTION TO THE GREAT POWER TRIANGLE

Gerald Segal

How important is China in international relations? There is much talk of Washington 'playing the China card' or indeed China 'playing the American card' against Moscow. There are also those who discuss the great power triangle and some who even talk of China as NATO's sixteenth member. There is an increasingly widespread belief that apart from the superpowers, China is the most important power in contemporary international politics. While there is undoubtedly some truth in those assessments, the reality is, as usual, far more complex than is suggested by such international games as 'card playing' or by temporary talk of alliances of convenience.

The purpose of this book is to analyse certain crucial aspects of the contemporary great power triangle in order to begin developing a more complete picture of the role of China in the superpower balance. In order to pre-empt possible lines of criticism, it should be stated at the outset that this is not a book about general Chinese foreign policy, nor is it about all issues where China affects the policies of the superpowers. China's role in the Middle East or Africa has already been extensively analysed both in respect of general Chinese policy as well as its effect on Soviet-American relations. If this study had attempted to take in, for example, the disparate events in various Third World conflicts, the material would have become unmanageable. In any case, it is assumed that important as these developing states are, they are not part of the superpowers', or even China's, most basic strategic interests. The emphasis in this work is placed squarely on a limited, but crucial, aspect of international relations: the way in which the China factor affects the main strategic concerns of the superpowers.

This study also does not suggest that the great power triangle on strategic issues is either the most important topic in international politics, or is the only way of conceiving of the international system. There are various issues, for example concerning international energy requirements, where the great power triangle is not a useful

9

way of conceiving of global politics. Before outlining more posi-
tively what this study *is* about, a few additional clarifications should
be made.

There are several basic problems in analysing the great power
triangle, not the least of which is that the geometric designation
implies greater exactitude than exists in reality. This is a basic
problem in almost any definition, let alone model, in international
relations, as the reality is far more complex than is suggested by the
simple definition. This study acknowledges that the relations among
the three great powers that we have, for convenience sake, called a
triangle, is far from uniform. Not only does it change over time, but
it is also different depending on the place of events. It is these differences that will form a large part of the analysis in the text. We use the
term great power triangle primarily as an organizing concept. No
more precision can be expected when describing an international
reality full of ever-changing variables.

Another major problem in analysing the great power triangle is
the obvious fact that China is not as powerful as the superpowers.
This view of the importance of China is based less on a calculation of
Peking's available nuclear throw-weight, as on the tendency of the
two superpowers to treat China as the next most important force in
the global system after themselves. It would be foolish to argue that
China, even in these terms, has become an equally significant point
in the triangular relationship, but it is clearly the third most significant force in the world, both in terms of the perceptions of Moscow
and Washington and in terms of the facts of political life. China is
the only power other than the superpowers with a fully independent
nuclear force and an embryonic second strike capability. It has in
demographic and economic terms the potential to make credible its
threat to engage in a protracted people's war if attacked. It is also
largely autarkic and therefore is little bothered by the constraints of
trade dependencies.

The origins of the great power triangle lay with the emergence of
China as an important third independent actor upsetting the bipolar
equations of the cold war. Although they did not come to fruition at
the time, there were clear signs of potential tripolarity well before the
establishment of the People's Republic of China in 1949. The simultaneous negotiations conducted by Mao Zedong and Zhou Enlai in
the mid-1940s with US delegations seeking friendship with Mao's
forces, along with the Communists' continuing contacts with
Moscow, meant that even then there was potential to avoid a bipolar

post-war world. As late as 1949 there were secret negotiations led by Zhou Enlai to 'serve as a mediator' between the USSR and the US but these efforts fell victim to domestic politics and growing cold war misperceptions.

Zhou Enlai's effort to have China play an independent role was not fulfilled in the 1950s, but it was increasingly satisfied in the 1960s. In the late 1950s, as a result of growing Chinese disagreement with the Soviet Union over a wide gamut of issues, the Soviets began moderating their foreign policy in a fashion that the PRC found increasingly unacceptable. Moscow gingerly sought a middle path between the US and China, all the while emphasizing its superpower relations and attempting to quell Chinese criticisms. Although there were previous polycentric tendencies and indicators of multipolarity in the international system, the PRC stood out as the single most important factor which regularly figured in both the US' and the USSR's calculations. By virtue of being the great power with the most co-operative and least conflictive relations with the other two powers, the USSR can be seen as the pivot power in the great power triangle. The course of the 1960s was dominated by Moscow's attempt to tread the careful path between the US and China. Its early trials and tribulations, especially in the 1961-2 Laos crisis and the negotiations for the 1963 Partial Test Ban Treaty, are vivid cases in point. At various times the Soviet Union formed 'loose' alignments with one power or another, but none lasted for any length of time. Major complications existed as the US in particular, as well as the Soviets, failed fully to comprehend the new international environment. Furthermore, due to the essential disparity in power between the superpowers and China, the US and the USSR always regarded their bipolar axis as the main concern. Nevertheless, despite its lesser capability China loomed increasingly larger on the horizon for both superpowers.

The newly complicated international system began evolving its own new pattern of relations from crisis management problems to deterrence postures. Major break points in the process can be suggested, but the great power triangle should be seen as a developing course of change. The 1963 test ban, the major worsening of Sino-Soviet relations, the growing US recognition of the China factor, and the 1966 rupture of Sino-Soviet party ties, were probably crucial dates. By the late 1960s the groundwork had been laid for the most significant shift since the emergence of the Sino-Soviet split. With increasing conflict in USSR-PRC ties and tension in superpower relations, especially over Vietnam, the Kremlin was losing its position as the power with the best relations with the other two powers. As Sino-American détente rapidly evolved in the early 1970s, an entirely new phase of tripolarity began and the US assumed the crucial pivotal position in the triangle. The major strategic shift was reinforced by events in the mid-1970s and even managed to survive the death of Mao in 1976. In December 1978 the US' pivotal position was further assured when normalization of Peking-Washington relations was announced. The period since then has been dominated by the virtual abandonment of the superpower détente process and increasing talk between China and America regarding closer cooperation in the military sphere. These discussions of either Peking 'playing the America card' or Washington 'playing the China card' against the USSR, especially after the invasion of Afghanistan, has meant that tripolar politics have been a main aspect of contemporary international relations.

In the chapters that follow, the great power triangle will be analysed in general, but special emphasis is placed on the way in which the fundamental strategic interests of the three powers are affected. In order to overcome the notorious problem of lack of coherence in volumes of collected chapters by different authors, this study has been organized around several detailed sets of questions. While it is obvious that the contributors have not approached these questions in precisely the same way, they do deal broadly with similar material. The final chapter will attempt to tie these threads more tightly together. The first section of this book deals with the attitudes of the three great powers themselves towards the great power triangle.

While it is clear that only US policymakers have spoken explicitly about a great power triangle, both the USSR and China have also shown themselves to be aware of the meaning of the concept. In each chapter in this section the authors will explore the question of whether the notion of a triangle is merely an ethnocentric American one, or whether it has some relevance for the foreign policy of the Communist powers as well. Much like in the dispute among academics whether the Soviet Union has a conception of deterrence in strategic policy, so it is crucial to ascertain the non-American meanings of an evident relationship between three great powers.

The contributors will then explore the question of how important the relationship between the three powers is for the respective decision makers. There may be a recognition that the concept of a triangle is relevant, but that it is relatively unimportant. This question will be dealt with in three main areas of relations: political/ideological, economic and military. The distinctións are important ones to make as each power has different strengths, let alone varying interests around the globe. China's worldwide economic influence may not be significant, especially as compared with that of OPEC or Japan, but it does seem to affect the military and political sphere. Furthermore, when some important triangular aspect is uncovered, each area will be explored in greater detail. It is important to understand, for example, if the USSR is concerned more about arms sales to China or PLA deployments along the Sino-Soviet frontier. The centrality of the triangle alters not only depending on the place, but also with the nature of the aspect of policy.

The contributors dealing with the policy of the three powers will also be concerned with the tactics adopted in managing the triangular relationship. There is a large amount of theoretical literature in the American social sciences regarding 'three-person relationships' and there is a growing body of policy-oriented prescription from Western academics on the role of China in the superpower balance. The conclusions of both are far from similar. The contributors to this book will deal with what has happened rather than what theoretically should happen in the great power triangle. In practice the tactics adopted in the triangle do not appear to be very sophisticated, but two stand out as the most often analysed: 'card playing' and 'tilting'. Each chapter will make reference to the notion of one power leaning to another in the triangle in order to ascertain how effective it has been and whether it is part of a consistent policy. To what extent have new 'alliance' tactics developed for a tripolar world, or is the policy merely an *ad hoc* response to fast-breaking events? As we have already suggested, the role of the pivot power in the triangle is of special importance, and the contributors will also refer to the way in which policy is different for each power depending on their position and interests in the triangle. This applies pre-eminently to the question of deterrence in tripolarity. For example how do the powers cope with the necessity to deter two rather than merely one power as in bipolarity?

So far the discussion has spoken of 'the power' as if it were a unified decision maker. The contributors will all avoid the analytical pitfalls of adopting a 'black box' perspective when they cover in fair detail the problems of different strategic views in each capital. Much coverage has been given to those in Washington who want to 'play the China card' and those who find this policy too dangerous, but similar divergences of policy apparently also exist in Peking and Moscow. In a sense, in the bipolar world it is easier to talk of 'hawks' and 'doves' as basic factional groups, but in a tripolar world the range of policy options is more varied, therefore producing more policy differences. In order to end this first section on the policy of the great powers, the contributors will also draw together the strands of analysis so as to suggest likely future trends for the international system.

The second section of the book will analyse in detail the way in which triangular politics has affected the two most important regions for the superpowers: East and West Europe. Unlike the previous section, this one will emphasize the perspective of the local states. How important do they see China for their own foreign policy in general, and how does Peking affect the position of the superpowers in their area? Do these states see China as increasing their room for manoeuvre or do they provide any other benefit? As in the previous section, this question of the importance of China will be broken down into its constituent parts in political, ideological, economic and military relations. For example, the question of how important China is for the West Europeans in the military sphere would involve an analysis of both the potential of arms sales to Peking as well as the extent to which they see China as the sixteenth member of NATO. The importance of China can also be seen as only in the short term and the contributors will therefore approach the problem of whether Peking is of more than fleeting significance.

A related question to be analysed by the two contributors in this section will be whether the three powers themselves see their position as improved or harmed by China's presence in the area. For example, does China's urging of a hard West European line against the USSR serve US interests?

Much as in the previous section, the decision makers of the three powers were not seen as having a unified view, so in this second section the contributors do not treat either West or East Europe as a single bloc. The importance of diversity in both spheres will be stressed and the chapters will point out important policy disagreements. If an overall pattern does exist on certain broad issues, then they will also be highlighted. But it is expected that because of the varying interests and positions of independent states, it will be difficult to paint a general picture.

This may appear to be a large sweep of subject matter for a

relatively short book, but it should be emphasized that this is avowedly a strategic analysis. Although the documentation of each contribution may vary in comprehensiveness, the authors are essentially drawing on their detailed familiarity with their particular speciality in order to reflect in a general way on the problem. While other publications may deal in far greater detail with certain narrow areas of the subject (see Bibliography) the purpose of this book is to tie together the various specialized material in order to provide an overall view. By asking common and fundamental questions about each aspect of foreign policy, it is hoped that a more complete view of the importance of the China factor in the strategic balance will become apparent.

Part One
The Powers and the Triangle

2 CHINA AND THE GREAT POWER TRIANGLE

Michael Yahuda

The foreign policy of the People's Republic of China (PRC) has been shaped by the consideration of tripolarity far earlier and more intensively than either of the two superpowers. The independent perspectives and the experiences of China's Communist leaders and especially Mao Zedong before the establishment of the PRC in 1949 contributed to formulating this policy, but it has been sustained for more than 30 years by specific geopolitical factors of the international system affecting China in particular. China has been one of the centres shaping the bipolar relationship between the United States and the Soviet Union since the end of the Second World War. The defeat of Chiang Kai-shek and Mao's advent to power was recognized in the late 1940s as constituting a major shift in the global balance of power. Beginning with the Korean War and ending with the American defeat in Vietnam, a considerable amount of American military power, diplomatic effort and economic treasure was devoted over a 20-year period to the conflict with Communist China. To be sure for much of these two decades successive American administrations perceived these endeavours to be a component of their struggles with 'International Communism' (or more specifically the Soviet Union). It is also true that American strategic thinking and its armament programmes were directed primarily against its major adversary the Soviet Union. Nevertheless the focus on China and its periphery obviously benefited the Soviet Union in diverting pressure which might otherwise have been directed exclusively towards it. Likewise China's tilt to the West in the 1970s has been recognized as a major advantage to the Western allies.[1] Something like a quarter of the Soviet military forces are displayed against China. The old Soviet nightmare of having to face a front in the east as well as in the west has been realized.

China's foreign relations have been dominated for the last 30 years by the pressure from one or the other of the two superpowers. In practice China has tilted towards the less threatening one as a balance against the other. But insofar as China's leaders have sought to protect and promote the independence and separate identity of their country they have striven to limit that tilt from becoming a relationship of dependency. In certain respects much of Mao's initial irritation with the Sino-Soviet alliance was due precisely to the dependency that had developed.[2] Not all China's leaders showed Mao's distinctive approach but there is little doubt that on the central geopolitical and ideological issues concerning Sino-Soviet and Sino-American relations Mao was successful in imposing his will.[3] Moreover although his successors may have criticised him and moved away from many of his policies the geopolitical considerations which shape China's relations with the two superpowers are still those determined by Mao at the beginning of the 1970s.

China's relationships with the two superpowers over these three decades have been inescapably affected by its continuing relative weakness. As still very much a developing country and one that was very much damaged by the self-inflicted wounds of the ten year Cultural Revolution (1966–76), China lacks the trained personnel and the adequate level of industrial and technological development to be considered in any sense an equivalent to either of the super-powers. From its inception the PRC has been confronted by the superior military power of first the United States and then the Soviet Union. However, China's leaders have claimed that China could successfully engage either in a defensive people's war should either have the temerity to invade. It is this perhaps which has given China's successive leaders the self confidence to pursue an independent line in the geopolitical area affecting the central balance between America and Russia.

Mao's Geopolitical Perspectives

Although Mao did not address himself specifically to this theme, a very strong and insistent geopolitical strand is clearly visible in his writings. Much of Mao's writing on imperialism, for example, is concerned with its political and military aspects rather than with discourses on such Leninist themes as the political economy of advanced capitalism or changing class relations in colonies and former colonies outside China.[4] Yet Mao was not a geopolitical theorist as such, but like Lenin considerations of power and balances of forces were an important component of his political vision. His leadership of the Communist Party of China (CPC) to ultimate victory may be seen as the triumph over adversity in which the revolutionary forces moved from abject relative weakness to absolute power. His speeches and writings during this period may be seen as concerned with charting the appropriate strategies and tactics of gradually shifting the adverse balance of forces in favour of the CPC while maintaining and developing its revolutionary identity. These balances of forces included not only domestic factors but the external forces of imperialism too. At a low point in the Chinese revolution, as small red rural bases were established in the hinterland of southeast China, Mao rallied his pitifully few forces against the threat of extinction by the more numerous and apparently more powerful armies of various warlords, not to mention by the modern armies of Chiang Kai-shek. He argued that it was precisely because there were various warlord cliques and various imperialist powers vying for control and influence in China that the revolutionaries could exploit the contradictions or conflicts between them. Red political power could survive and prosper despite complete encirclement by a white regime.[5]

More widely-known examples of Mao's geopolitical political vision are evident in his major writings on people's war, principally to be found in his celebrated essays on the war of resistance to Japan.[6] Mao's independent course from Moscow is too well known to require elaboration here, at the same time it was clearly an important factor in the subsequent elaboration of the PRC's global position as a separate point of polarity in global geopolitics. Perhaps the most important statement by Mao before 1949 in this regard was his analysis of the world situation in the aftermath of the Second World War. Not only did his analysis differ considerably from that of Stalin, but it accorded a significant independent role to the revolutionary forces in China in determining the issue of peace or war in the world at large. With an ever ready eye to symbolic signalling, Mao sketched out his views in the form of an interview with the American Communist journalist Anna Louise Strong who had previously been arrested in Russia on suspicion of being an American agent.

The Soviet Union at that time was moving towards the 'two camp' thesis which argued that the world was divided into two antagonistic blocs and that the purpose of the imperialist bloc headed by the United States was to attack the Soviet Union, the head of the camp of socialism and peace. It followed therefore that every Communist movement should prudently avoid provocative acts against the

United States lest this might lead to an attack on the Soviet Union, which would spark off World War III. This was undoubtedly one of the reasons which led Stalin to press the French Communists to lay down their arms after the war, to withhold effective support for the Greek Communists in their civil war and to advise the CPC against taking up arms against Chiang Kai-shek in 1945–6. It is deeply ingrained in the attitudes of successive Soviet leaders to equate the interests of Communist parties throughout the world with the interests of the Soviet Union. However much Soviet leaders have had to adjust in practice to a multipolar world their deepest impulse enshrined by doctrine and by institutionalized experience is to view the world in bipolar terms. Although they recognize the existence of other forces and ideas in the world, successive Soviet leaders have tended to argue that in the final analysis they are subsumed within the bipolar conflict between imperialism and socialism centred on the Soviet Union.

In 1946, however, despite the anti-Communist declaratory statements by 'US reactionaries', their immediate target was not the Soviet Union:

> The United States and the Soviet Union are separated by a vast zone which includes many capitalist, colonial and semi-colonial countries in Europe, Asia and Africa. Before the US reactionaries have subjugated these countries, an attack on the Soviet Union is out of the question.

Mao acknowledged that the US had supposedly anti-Soviet bases in many countries but he asserted that their actual objective was different:

> At present, however, it is not the Soviet Union but the countries in which these military bases are located that are the first to suffer US aggression. I believe that it won't be long before these countries come to realise who is really oppressing them . . . It turns out that under the cover of anti-Soviet slogans they are frantically attacking the workers and democratic circles in the United States and turning all the countries which are the targets of US external expansion into US dependencies. I think the American people and the peoples of all countries menaced by US aggression should unite and struggle against the attacks of the US reactionaries and their running dogs in these countries. *Only by victory in this struggle*

can a third world war be avoided; otherwise it is unavoidable.[7] (emphasis added)

This analysis not only provided a rationale for carrying out armed struggle against the forces of Chiang Kai-shek, allied as they were to the United States, but in fact made it the internationalist duty of the CPC. According to Mao the issue of world peace or war would be determined in the first instance not by the direct great power conflict between the United States and the Soviet Union, but by a united front of all those 'menaced by US aggression'. In particular this would be determined by the struggles of those in the intermediate zone between the two powers. China, by implication, was allocated a central position in this zone.

This analysis also contained within it the seeds of the reasoning which underlay China's emergence as an independent polar point in the configuration of world politics following the rupture with the Soviet Union. Nevertheless neither this analysis nor any subsequent account by a CPC leader formally endorsed a tripolar vision of world politics involving China and the two great powers. All such Chinese accounts of the configurations of global politics essentially depicted the world as caught up in a struggle principally involving a struggle between two parties. On the one side stood an aggressive expansionist imperialist power and on the other side stood all the other countries and the peoples of the world.

It is this aspect of the Chinese position which helps to give their practice of power politics a certain revolutionary edge. The kind of state craft of what might be called 'Machiavellian cunning' depicted in the popular Chinese traditional novel *The Romance of the Three Kingdoms* has thoroughly familiarized Chinese with the tactics of power politics. The ever resourceful statesman Zhu Keliang of the novel has entered Chinese folklore as the epitome of the man who in the most adverse conditions is able to devise successful stratagems by exploiting divisions and weaknesses amid his apparently more power-ful adversaries. The experience of the Chinese revolutionaries under Mao's leadership may also be seen in this light as one which plucked victory against overwhelming odds. The theories and practices of the pre-1949 period may be regarded as having given the Chinese Com-munist leaders the confidence and perhaps some of the necessary skills and vision to pursue an independent polar position in relation to the two superpowers despite China's marked relative weakness. For Mao power politics was an endlessly shifting panorama in which harmony and equilibrium were relative and temporary while conflict and imbalance were absolute and long term. As seen by Mao the world was made up of countless conflicts and contradictions. He once said that without contradictions there was no life. The art was to identify at any given stage which of these contradictions was the principal one to which all the others were subordinate. Even more important was the ability to be able to perceive when the balance had shifted so that the relations between the contradictory forces changed and another one became primary. This in turn determined who was the foe and who friend. When seeking to justify China's alignment with reactionary regimes such as those of the Shah of Iran or Pinochet of Chile (begun in Mao's lifetime) Mao's successors highlighted a hitherto little noticed passage in his article 'On New Democracy' of 1940:

> No matter what classes, parties or individuals in an oppressed nation join the revolution, and no matter whether they themselves are conscious of the point or understand it, so long as they oppose imperialism, their revolution becomes part of the proletariat-socialist world revolution and they become its allies.[8]

In retrospect it is possible to point to this as being the basis on which under Mao's leadership the Chinese revolutionary forces had prospered by winning over the middle ground and isolating the enemy. But this also explains how the CPR with few apparent qualms has been able to make common ground with countries of vastly different social systems whose governments from other points of view could be regarded as reactionary.

This brief account of Mao's distinctive approach to power politics would be incomplete without distinguishing between what in his view was genuine political power and what was only a 'paper tiger'. The latter might encompass superior economic, technological and military capabilities but without genuine popular support it would be destroyed in the end by its inner contradictions. The duty of true revolutionaries who alone in the final analysis really enjoyed genuine popular support was to dare to challenge the apparently stronger paper tigers. This required a peculiar mixture of caution and boldness. In the mythology of people's war it calls for the mobility and initiative to manipulate tactical battle superiority within a framework of overall strategic inferiority. Or as a people's war aphorism once put it: 'Strategy equals 10 to 1, tactics equals 1 to 10.'

In the Maoist vision the capacity to engage in the shifting sands of power politics was ultimately dependent upon a secure domestic revolutionary base. On the eve of the Cultural Revolution in 1965–6, rather than soil his revolutionary banner in Soviet mud by a compromise with Russia because of the American threat in Vietnam, Mao chose to confront the two superpowers simultaneously. As his late friend Edgar Snow explained it after lengthy discussions with him and Zhou Enlai: 'Mao knew what he was doing. The greater threat was internal, not external. Compromising with either of the superpowers could then only lead to a split on the home front. A resolutely independent and united China could weather any storm. A China torn apart internally by factions seeking to exploit alliance with Russia could not stand.'[9]

Of course events soon proved that whatever else may be said about the Cultural Revolution a 'united China' was achieved neither during its duration or in its aftermath. Nevertheless Snow's explanation of Mao's thinking at the time still seems plausible even though the outcome was not as Mao had thought.

It has been a characteristic of Chinese foreign policy under Mao's leadership and of his successors (who in this respect at least are following him fairly closely[10]) that the mainstream of China's foreign relations has been determined by the disciplined application of the geopolitical consequences of what the leaders had identified as the principal contradiction in the world.[11] Consider for example the ruthless determination by which nearly every facet of China's foreign policy in the seventies has been shaped by the perception of the Soviet Union as the main enemy.

This sketch of Mao's geopolitical vision can best be concluded by a comparison with that of the former US Secretary of State Henry Kissinger who professed admiration for Mao and Zhou's skill in this regard. Kissinger has argued that it was only 'by the end of 1969' that 'America's relationship with the Communist world was slowly becoming triangular'. He went on to explain that the objective of the Nixon administration was 'to shape a global equilibrium. It was not to collude against the Soviet Union but to give us a balancing position to use for constructive ends — to give each Communist power a stake in better relations with us. Such an equilibrium could assure stability among the major powers, and eventual cooperation in the Seventies and Eighties'.[12]

Implied in this is that by skilful diplomacy America could bring about a relatively stable great power equilibrium to the advantage of the United States. For Mao and his successors, with experience of constant conflict and turmoil stretching back to the 1920s, great power relations have not been characterized by stability. To the contrary, their experience is of a kaleidoscopic rise and fall of powers determined to expand and gain empires. They have witnessed the demise of the great European empires, the rise and fall of Japan, the expansion and relative decline of the United States and more recently the expanding influence of Soviet power. The experience and doctrines of China's leaders suggest that imperial great powers tend to over-extend themselves and that it is only by encountering resistance and difficulties that their inner contradictions become manifest and their paper tiger like features revealed. The way to prevent global war, therefore, is not by seeking a will-o'-the-wisp great power equilibrium; it is rather by standing up to which ever happens to be the expansionist great power at the time. There is a congruity between Mao's geopolitical arguments of 1946 and those of his successors 35 years later. Then Mao argued that the United States sought to control the intermediate zone as a necessary preliminary before an attack on the Soviet Union could be contemplated. Today China's leaders hold that the Soviet Union is engaged upon a 'southern strategy' focused on the Persian Gulf but extending from Africa through to the Western Pacific as a means of outflanking Europe and commanding its vital resources. Just as Mao in 1946 suggested that a world war could be indefinitely postponed by successful resistance to the United States in the intermediate zone, so his successors today maintain the same with regard to the Soviet Union.

Tripolarity in China's Foreign Policy

In restrospect it is clear that in 1949—50 there were elements in the Chinese Communist leadership as powerful as Zhou Enlai and possibly Mao Zedong himself who sought a relatively independent third great power position for China. This would have challenged the bipolar rigidities of the Cold War which had already emerged by this stage. Zhou Enlai is known to have told American diplomats in the summer of 1949, 'we shall lean to our side [i.e. towards Russia] but how far we shall lean depends on you'. Zhou also reportedly appealed secretly to Washington for aid so that China could act as a mediator between the Western Powers and the USSR. Mao is said to have asserted in June 1949 that in the event of a US-USSR war China was not committed to joining the Soviet Union. In the event Washington did not respond to these probes and perhaps because of that and divisions in the Chinese leadership these were not pursued further.[13] The negotiations between Mao and Stalin in late 1949 early 1950 leading to the Sino-Soviet alliance were protracted and difficult. Mao later described them as a 'struggle' and claimed that Stalin distrusted him as a potential 'Tito'. The Korean War was the bench mark which finally ended such minimal prospects as existed at the time for China playing a role independent of the Soviet bloc. The war served to tie China to the Soviet Union and there is evidence to suggest Chinese resentment at the treatment meted to them by the Soviet Union then.[14] Paradoxically the war also enhanced Chinese self confidence and boosted their claims to independent great power status, so that following the death of Stalin in 1953 Mao was able to assert considerable independence *vis-à-vis* its major ally. Nevertheless while Moscow conceded China great power status on issues concerning Asia it did not do so on a general global basis. Thus China's leaders were not even informed in advance, let alone consulted, by the Soviet leaders before Krushchev's speech to the CPSU 20th Congress in February 1956 which was to change the politics of the Communist world. Similarly Chinese claims in 1954 to have become 'One of the Big Powers' were tacitly played down by the Russians when they held the first post-war summit at Geneva in 1955 with the United States, Britain and France, but without China. Far Eastern questions were discussed then and Krushchev privately expressed concern to his Western adversaries about future relations with his socialist ally, China.[15] China's leaders for their part were cultivating relations at this time with Afro-Asian countries and they were also exploring diplomatic openings to the United States. In some respects the 1955-6 period has certain parallels with the contemporary period. This was a period of great power summitry following the Geneva agreements, China was in the middle of what is often called the Bandung phase of its foreign policy and it was seeking to begin a dialogue with the United States amid statements that the PRC required international tranquillity so as to concentrate on domestic economic development. The rigid bipolar structure of the Cold War was being loosened as the Afro-Asians moved towards non-alignment and West European countries such as Britain and France explored diplomatic initiatives independently of the Americans. Not surprisingly, the independent character of China's foreign policy was being increasingly recognized. Had the United States treated China differently at this stage it is possible that tripolarity might have emerged earlier. Instead it had to wait ten to fifteen years until the rupture of Sino-Soviet relations.

If in the Kissinger view triangular diplomacy did not begin before 1969, for China's leaders the underlying issues of tripolarity were all too clear once Mao had declared to CPC conference of 7,000 cadres in January 1962: 'The Party and State leadership of the Soviet Union has now been usurped by the revisionists'.[16] This was not only an ideological challenge to Soviet leadership of the international Communist movement, but it implied a lack of faith in the reliability of the Soviet ally and it was in effect a declaration that henceforth China would be an independent factor in world politics. To be sure he was opposed within the Political Bureau. Indeed at this stage Mao was engaged in a struggle to gain political ascendancy after having been downgraded in the wake of the economic disasters following the Great Leap Forward of 1958. The struggle was to culminate in the Cultural Revolution four years later. But in foreign affairs his line gained ascendancy against those who argued for a reduction in the hostility towards America, India and Russia and against those who queried the rationality of 'a man with a swollen head' who refused to 'learn from' and 'unite with' countries 'stronger than our own'. Mao, however, explained his position in September 1962 by in effect denying the classic Soviet (and indeed American) argument on bipolarity that the principal contradiction in the world was between socialism and imperialism (or in American terms, Communist totalitarianism and the free world) as represented at the core by the Soviet Union and the United States. Mao analysed the basic conflicts which characterized the world at that time as follows:

> The contradiction between the people of the whole world and imperialism is the primary one. There is the opposition of the people of all countries to the reactionary bourgeoisie and to reactionary nationalism. There are also the contradictions between the people of all countries and revisionism, the contradictions among imperialist countries, the contradiction between nationalist countries and imperialism, internal contradictions within imperialist countries, and the contradiction between socialism and imperialism.

By placing the contradiction between socialism and imperialism last on his list, especially after having extolled the significance of what is now called the Third World, Mao was arguing in effect that the United States imperium would be stopped by the struggles of resistance in the Third World rather than by the Socialist camp headed by the Soviet Union. This also meant that henceforth the CPR sought to exclude the Soviet Union from membership of the international united front it was seeking to establish against the United States. In a sense it could be argued that the CPR was already presenting itself as a separate polar point in world politics — but not just in great power terms. The Chinese polarity was as a leading element in the struggle for Third World aspirations against the threats of intervention and dominance by the United States.

By this stage China was well on the way towards the development of an independent nuclear capability. The Test Ban Treaty of July 1963 between the United States, the USSR and Britain was immediately interpreted in China as evidence of collusion against China by the US and the Soviet Union. An editorial in the *People's Daily* outlined the Chinese view:

> It is most obvious that the tripartite treaty is aimed at tying China's hands. The U.S. representative to the Moscow talks has said publicly that the United States, Britain and the Soviet Union were able to arrive at an agreement, because 'we could work together to prevent China getting a nuclear capability' . . . This is a US-Soviet alliance against China pure and simple.

The viewpoint of the Kennedy administration was far less clear cut than as presented by Chinese statements. However, after the Cuban missile crisis the Kennedy administration tended to view the Soviet leadership as 'moderate' and 'rational' as befitted the third leadership generation after the revolution. China's first-generation revolutionary leaders tended to be depicted as extremist and irrational. It should be recalled that at this time when the American adviser team in Vietnam had been increased from a few score in 1959 to over 18,000 by the time of Kennedy's death China was regarded as expansionist and the domino theory was in vogue. The view was that the Vietnamese Communists were proxies for the Chinese and that by containing the former one was in fact containing the latter. The theory was that containment had finally persuaded the Soviet Union to adopt a more co-operative pattern of behaviour and that in time it would convince a new generation of Chinese leaders to follow a similar pattern too. Meanwhile the United States had to demonstrate that insurgency wars of national liberation could be defeated and that they did not constitute a 'magic weapon' for alleged Chinese expansionism by proxy. Liberal American scholars in the middle 1960s advanced a policy designed to elicit a more 'co-operative' Chinese attitude by calling for 'containment without isolation'. Meanwhile General Maxwell Taylor pioneered the 'special forces' and American military academies developed special courses on counter insurgency. The strategy of flexible response was also adaptable to deal with insurgencies. In short the Kennedy liberals misunderstood the Chinese position. The American strategy of relative co-operation with the Soviet Union and of relative hardness towards China may have helped to widen the Sino-Soviet divide, but it denied the United States sufficient flexibility in great power politics and it played a large part in drawing America more deeply into the fruitless war in Vietnam.

In Mao's perspective an embattled China had few options except to confront the two superpowers or enter into a kind of dependency with the Soviet Union. By this time the issue had become enmeshed with the factional politics which culminated in the Cultural Revolution. Nevertheless the day on which China tested its first nuclear device in October 1964 was the day on which Krushchev was ousted. A month later Zhou went to Moscow to see whether the new leaders had changed policy more to China's liking. But he returned with the message that Brezhnev and Kosygin were following 'Krushchevism without Krushchev'. The American escalation in Vietnam in early 1965 sparked off a complex strategic debate in Peking. For Mao, who saw himself engaged in a power struggle against opponents whom he already regarded as revisionist, a renewed association with the Soviet Union would have exacerbated the domestic conflict as well as having led to an unacceptable dependency. The earlier quotation from Edgar Snow has already explained his view.

In a sense the American escalation of the Vietnam War saved China from a combined USA-USSR partnership aimed against it. For Moscow was drawn into support for Hanoi. The continuation of the war served China's national security interests by keeping Moscow and Washington in an adversary relationship. China opposed negotiated compromises. But when Hanoi agreed to negotiate with the United States after its resolve had been broken in the wake of the Tet Offensive of 1968, the situation changed radically for China. Once again there loomed the prospect of superpower collusion against China.

The Russian invasion of Czechoslovakia (applauded by Hanoi), accompanied by a systemic build up of military strength along the Sino-Soviet border, changed the national security situation of China. By late 1968, Peking offered relations of peaceful co-existence with the USA and began to search for the broadest possible united front against the Soviet Union. Once again this new strategy was the subject of intense domestic factional struggle. There were those who prudentially sought conciliation with the Russians, still others opted for continuing the isolationism of the Cultural Revolution.[17] However the line of Mao Zedong, Zhou Enlai and Deng Xiaoping won out. Peking sought links with Third World governments (and defined China as a member of the Third World) and with Japan and Western Europe for trade for modernization as well as diplomatic and military support against the Soviet Union. The opening to the United States involved sharper domestic factional conflict and more delicate diplomatic manoeuvring.

Before considering China's role in the triangular diplomacy of the seventies it may be useful to summarize the CPR experience of tripolarity in the previous 20 years. This has taken place against the background of a framework of analysis for understanding world politics which differs from that of the Soviet Union or of the United States. It is a framework which has always accorded great significance to the essentially nationalist impulses of the peoples and countries in the intermediate zone against the threats of alien control by one or other of the two superpowers. The preferred pattern of China's diplomatic practice has been the establishment of rather loose coalitions or international united fronts whose members act out of their interests in their own particular way to resist the main expansionist power of the day. The central issues for China's leaders have not been about the establishment of a preferred pattern of global politics as such. Rather they have concerned questions vital to China's national security as a relatively weak power with great power aspirations confronted by the military and technological superiority of one or the other of the two superpowers. These foreign policy issues have impinged on domestic politics in ways as to make factional conflict an important element in the foreign policy arena. It has been persuasively argued that China's interaction with the outside world has revolved around the themes of independence, modernization and revolution.[18] China's leaders at times have disagreed deeply as to the meanings and priorities to be accorded to them. The various turning points in China's tripolar experience have been marked by intense factional strife in Peking. This was true as early as 1949 when Zhou Enlai sought an opening to the United States and it has been evident during the course of the different stages of the Sino-Soviet conflict down to the new relationship begun with the United States at the beginning of the 1970s. Another aspect of this experience has been that on the whole it is Mao's geopolitical vision which has prevailed. Mao's strategic calculations from a position of fundamental weakness have involved a refusal to be 'weak kneed' and a readiness to use military force in a limited and cautious way. Nevertheless this has been frequently seen by others as involving a high degree of risk. The American depiction of China as a highly bellicose power in the 1950s and 1960s has been matched or even exceeded by that advanced by the Soviet Union in the sixties and seventies. Careful and detailed studies of China's use of military force, however, do not sustain this image of bellicosity and recklessness.[19] Underlying Mao's geopolitical vision has been a highly conflictual view of international politics. In this view the world is depicted as continually in flux, whose patterns are determined at any point by the principal contradiction to which all the sources of conflict are subordinate. The principal contradiction in international politics has always turned around which ever happens to be the most expansionist imperial power at the time. Therefore in this view China's role has been to preserve its independent character by seeking to isolate and exacerbate the inner contradictions of the most offensive of the superpowers. Thus despite his preoccupation with the significance of the intermediate zone, most of Mao's writings and talks about international affairs have focused on the Soviet Union and the United States.[20] Moreover, despite the logic of Mao's position of siding with the weaker of the two superpowers against the other he was always numbered amongst those who at propitious opportunities tried to improve relations with the United States. Likewise his opposition to the Soviet Union in the 1960s went deeper than a concern mainly with the logic of power politics might suggest. His view of what might be called China's polarity included considerations of power politics but it included other factors too.

It is both a strength and a weakness of the application of Maoist geopolitics in China's foreign policy that nearly all aspects of the conduct of China's foreign relations have been subordinated to it. It is a strength because of the consistency of vision and purpose which underlies so much of the practical day-to-day dealings and man-oeuvrings of all facets of China's foreign relations. But it is a weakness because this very consistency underplays other important themes of China's foreign relations and it creates difficulties for establishing those coalitions or united fronts which the logic of Maoist geopolitics demand. Firstly, other countries may not perceive the threats posed by one or other of the superpowers in the same way or accord them the same saliency as China. Secondly, although the geopolitical logic of China's foreign policy may suggest an overarching consistency to its apparent changes over the last three decades, China's policies towards specific countries have been characterised by twists and turns which for the leaders of the countries concerned have seemed opportunistic at best and inexplicable at worst. Thus many of China's friends in Africa felt betrayed by China's policies regarding Angola and Zaire in the mid-1970s. China's relations with the European countries of both East and West provide clear examples of these general propositions.

By its weight in world politics and in the strategic calculations of both the USA and the USSR the CPR has been an important factor in the security considerations affecting Europe. This was true of the period when the CPR was thought of as a member of the Soviet bloc and it has been more evident in the 1970s when the Soviet Union was faced with potential simultaneous conflicts in the Far East and Europe. But the CPR has always lacked the capabilities or sufficient access to translate that general weight into specific and effective influence. Nevertheless the European countries have always figured largely in China's attempts to shape global politics. Thus in the early 1960s when China's leaders tried to build an international coalition against both the superpowers, Mao appealed to the West European leaders on the basis that they all shared or should share a common interest. Mao opined to a visiting French parliamentary delegation in early 1964: 'France herself, Germany, England on the condition that she ceases to be a courier of America, Japan and we ourselves — there is your Third World'.[21] (This was before the term acquired the very different meaning it has today.) In Mao's view these countries were chafing under superpower attempts to dominate and control them. It was at this time that De Gaulle's France recognized Mao's China, much to the chagrin of Washington. This attempt to make common cause with the West Europeans on terms which showed little understanding of the realities of the common bonds and tensions of the NATO alliance was soon lost in the new alignments arising out of the second Vietnam War and the isolation of the Cultural Revolution. In the early 1970s, when China once again reached out to Western Europe, it was on the grounds that they were jointly threatened by the Soviet Union. This time the Chinese in fact encouraged closer ties between Western Europe and the USA and they were both puzzled by and opposed to West European attempts to establish their own 'détente' with the Soviet Union as manifested by growing trade and above all by West Germany's *Ostpolitik*. For their part the West European leaders welcomed China's return to the international diplomatic community and they encouraged the growing trading opportunities with the country. But they did not wish to join with China in an anti-Soviet coalition. The stridency with which many of China's leaders proclaimed the alleged Soviet threats to Western Europe was widely regarded as serving exclusively Chinese interests. Likewise many were wary of unduly exciting Russian fears of a Western-Chinese quasi alliance. All were agreed that on the one hand Russia should not be allowed to dictate the terms of Euro-Chinese relations, while on the other China should not be allowed to use Euro-Soviet tensions to its own ends. China is widely regarded as an important, but unpredictable, factor in world politics. Indeed the more the Chinese have insisted upon the need for an anti-Soviet coalition the more difficult it has been for European leaders to endorse the idea.[22]

China's relations with the East European countries illustrate a different dimension of the problems in applying China's geopolitical principles to non superpowers. If China's leaders supported the Soviet invasion of Hungary in 1956 (indeed they claimed responsibility for pushing a reluctant Krushchev into the act) they regarded the Soviet invasion of Czechoslovakia in 1968 as the first indication that the Soviet Union had taken the path of imperialism. From that point the independent East European countries Romania and Yugoslavia became 'special friends' of China and those under Soviet control were regarded less as revisionist than as industrially developed states suffering under the yoke of Soviet imperialism. According to the doctrine of the three worlds these countries belong to the second world (i.e., they share the same status as the West Europeans). The difficulties of this classification became apparent when by the same token the Chinese placed Romania and Yugoslavia in the Third World. Moreover in the late seventies the Chinese openly considered the applicability to China of the Hungarian model of market socialism. Since 1979 the development of the Polish crisis, which has posed problems for East-West relations, has posed different kinds of problems to China. On the one hand this may be said to vindicate much of the Chinese critique on the imperialist character of the Soviet position in Eastern Europe, and on the inevitability of a nationalist based response; on the other hand the emergence of Solidarity and the domestic Polish critique of its Communist Party is embarrassing within a China whose Party has lost much of the moral authority it once had and where there is economic crisis amid calls for greater democracy.

China's leaders then have encountered great difficulties in carrying out their geopolitical principles not so much in their relations with the superpowers as with the lesser powers who actually are supposed to be China's coalition partners.

China and Triangular Diplomacy

It can be argued that in the 1950s China's incipient tripolarity was thwarted by the intransigence of the United States. In the 1960s China began to behave in a tripolar fashion. But triangular diplomacy as such only became possible in the 1970s. Yet this at once raises a paradox. China, which might be thought to be the one great power to have practiced tripolarity in earlier periods, has neither developed a theory about the great power triangle nor has it put into practice what might be called the rules of such a system. Thus Washington alone maintains high-level diplomatic exchange with Peking and Moscow. Relations between the two others have been relatively frozen despite several abortive moves aimed ostensibly at reducing the tension and hostility between them. This undoubtedly has given Washington a certain diplomatic advantage and greater opportunities for manoeuvre.

In a sense China's posture in the 1970s can be compared to that of the 1950s in that it has tilted towards the less threatening and expansionist power while trying to build up a larger coalition against the greater enemy. Chinese criticisms of Soviet attempts in the 1950s to establish modalities of co-operation with the United States especially on nuclear issues have been paralleled by similar strictures in the 1970s against the United States for pursuing détente with the Soviet Union. There are of course important differences between the two periods, both in terms of the changed international environment of the 1970s and in terms of the different quality of China's bilateral relationships with the two superpowers at the different times. But the point of the parallel is the similarity of Chinese approaches towards the two superpowers. However great Deng Xiaoping's departure from Mao and his policies may be in other respects, in terms of the geopolitical vision shaping China's foreign policy Deng's position is firmly within Mao's framework. In so far as there is continuity of purpose behind China's triangular diplomacy in the 1970s, it consists of an attempt to build up an anti-Soviet coalition so as to isolate and build up pressures upon the Soviet Union in the hope that the more it expands the greater will be its difficulties. This also serves China's national security interests by strengthening its deterrent posture *vis-à-vis* the Soviet Union.

Similarly, Chinese theorizing about the configurations of world politics also downplays the significance of what might be called the great power triangle. Officially China divides the world into three: the first world consists of the two superpowers, the second of the industrialized medium and small powers and the third of the less developed former colonies and semi-colonies. The primary conflict in the world is seen as between the first and third world with the second world as putative vacillating allies of the third. China is placed within the third world.[23] At the same time China's spokesmen in this period, but especially since the mid 1970s (the precise timing does not depend upon the power struggles in Peking of these years), have increasingly identified the major axis in world politics as between the hegemonist Soviet Union and the rest of the world, thereby classifying the American superpower as a vital component of the anti-Soviet hegemonist coalition.[24] Thus as late as 1980 Deng Xiaoping could still proclaim the continued validity of the three worlds theory while simultaneously stating that the closer relationship with the United States was a long-term strategy of China's foreign policy and that it was not a temporary tactical ploy.

It is difficult to gauge the operational significance of the three worlds theory. It is certainly sufficiently elastic as to encompass a wide range of different policies. Clearly the theory serves the purpose of providing a framework (claimed to be Leninist) for analysing world politics in non-Soviet terms (of imperialism versus socialism) which elevates the significance of two great Chinese concerns: national independence and economic development. It is interesting in this regard that some Chinese academicians have publicly put forward alternatives to the three worlds theory. In 1972 (two years before the three worlds theory was first put forward) the late Guo Moro (who was close to Mao) had suggested that the configurations of world politics might best be depicted as a 'five pointed star' made up of the USA, the USSR, Western Europe, Japan and China.[25] Little was subsequently heard from China along these Kissinger-type lines until the *People's Daily* of 2 January 1981 carried an article from a leading member of the Foreign Ministry's research institute on multipolarity. His argument was that the new multipolarity after 'the collapse' of the two major camps in the 1960s has been marked by the emergence of Western Europe, Japan, 'China and the Third World countries'. Interestingly, China is regarded as a separate pole from the Third World countries. He went on to suggest that this introduced new complexities: 'Due to their different situations and internal conflicts, countries in the West see and treat the Soviet Union differently', but at the same time growing West European unity and Japanese power would place greater constraints on Soviet expansionism. His major point was that Soviet expansionism would in itself elicit united resistance but that under conditions of multipolarity the emergence of that unity would follow a tortuous path.[26] It remains to be seen whether this greater subtlety of analysis will be reflected in a more flexible foreign policy posture able to accommodate itself to the different perspectives and interests of others.

In retrospect during the seventies the Chinese leaders cannot be said to have exploited the new triangular diplomacy as much as many Western observers thought possible. This would have involved cultivating new relations with the Soviet Union. Perhaps domestic factional strife within China during this period combined with Sino-Soviet perceptions of mutual encirclement precluded that. However there were signs during this period that both sides independently recognized the advantages to be secured from an improvement in their bilateral relations and, as we shall see, these were closely linked with triangular diplomacy. Thus at different times both sides made proposals to this end and in late 1979 inter-governmental talks were begun only to be indefinitely postponed by the Chinese side after the Soviet invasion of Afghanistan. Nevertheless by the beginning of the eighties a number of the impediments (especially with regard to ideology and trade) to improved relations had been removed on both sides so that the increased tensions in American-Soviet relations and in Sino-Soviet relations in the East Asian region need not in themselves preclude Sino-Soviet moves to reduce the levels of hostility in their bilateral relations. Indeed a case can be made within Maoist geopolitical perspectives that it is precisely at the stage in which the Soviet Union might be regarded as over extended and bogged down in costly commitments to Vietnam, Cuba, Afghanistan and to Eastern Europe that China should seek to negotiate seriously about improving relations. Because such a situation would indicate a shift in the balance of forces towards China so it would not be negotiating 'on its knees'.

But to return to an account of China's place in the triangular diplomacy of the 1970s. Following Henry Kissinger's epoch-making first visit to Peking in July 1971 the Soviet leadership immediately changed tack. In the preceding year the Soviet leaders had played what has been described as a 'waiting game' in their dealings with the Chinese and the United States, in which they simultaneously sought a kind of anti-China alliance with Washington and proposed friendlier relations to what was perceived to be an isolated China. But after July 1971 they increased the pace and scope of their bargaining with both the Americans and the Chinese. The negotiations over Berlin were rapidly completed a month after Kissinger's visit to China and a summit with President Nixon was arranged for soon after his summit with Mao and Zhou. Sino-Soviet border negotiations were resumed in 1972 and in March (just after the Shanghai Communiqué on Sino-American relations) Brezhnev revealed that proposals had been made to China for a non-aggression treaty, a border settlement and even for improving relations on the basis of the principles of peaceful coexistence.[27]

In 1973 Soviet-American relations improved markedly with the visit by Brezhnev and the moves towards the Helsinki Conference and the SALT summit of the following year. Such early token signs of improved Sino-Soviet relations, such as increased two-way trade (its value in 1970 stood at only 42 million roubles, by 1973 it came to 224 and in 1976 it reached 400) and an agreement to inaugurate Peking-Moscow civil air flights, did not lead onto a substantive improvement of relations. At the 10th CPC Congress in August 1973 Zhou Enlai took a tough line on the Soviet Union and foreclosed such hopes as the Russians might have entertained that with him in the ascendancy the prospects for better relations might be good. Meanwhile, alarmed once again at the possibility of new Soviet-American strategic understandings which might undo some of the advantages they had secured from the entente with the United States, the Chinese leaders made new proposals to the Soviet Union in November 1974. One notable feature of these was the dropping for the first time that the Soviet leaders acknowledge that their existing border was based on unequal treaties. However, these proposals were brusquely rejected by Brezhnev during a stopover in Mongolia en route to signing the SALT I Agreement with President Ford in Vladivostok.

The Chinese then indicated their displeasure with American diplomacy in public. The so-called Sonnenfeldt Doctrine, which the Chinese reported as calling for American support for increased Soviet dominance in Eastern Europe, was denounced as appeasement, as were the Helsinki agreements. Chinese commentaries began to refer to a new Munich-type appeasement and they warned against what they regarded as the 'illusions' of those who thought that the conflict in Europe might be stabilized so that the focus of conflict would shift to the East. The Chinese leaders were also highly exercised by the SALT agreement. After the Vladivostok summit Kissinger visited China for the seventh time, but this was the first occasion on which he did not meet Mao. His explanations on SALT were rejected by Chinese leaders. A month later the *People's Daily* dismissed the new agreement as merely 'new emulation rules for their next round of the nuclear arms race'. The agreement it suggested was no more than a 'scrap of paper' which involved self deception by the Americans.[28]

If in the terms of triangular diplomacy China in the early 1970s may be regarded as having been under considerable pressure, the two years 1975–6 were marked by a certain immobility as a result of the intense power struggle in Peking. But the years 1973–5 were also marked by considerable Chinese diplomacy and trade with Japan and Western Europe and by attempts to improve relations with the ASEAN countries. In tripolar terms perhaps the growth of Sino-Japanese relations and European arms sales (especially the $100 million deal of the advanced Spey jet engine) were the most significant. Sino-American trade, which had leaped to over $1000 million in value by 1974, thereafter declined until the boost it received from the normalization of relations in late 1978. Soviet attempts to establish better relations with China after Mao's death were rebuffed. By the spring of 1977 Soviet commentaries were beginning to dub China's policy as 'Maoism with Mao'.

It was not until 1978 that a deteriorating situation from the perspective of China's new leaders impelled them to act with greater urgency. The modernization programme announced in March 1978 has since been criticized for its grandiose targets, but its promise of calling for Western and Japanese trade and investment as an integral part of China's drive to becoming modern and strong has been repeatedly endorsed ever since. In the ensuing months various foreign policy invitations with an anti-Soviet motif were undertaken. These included the signing of a Sino-Japanese Treaty of Peace and Friendship in August; a tour by Hua Guofeng of Romania, Yugoslavia and Iran; a visit by Deng Xiaoping to Japan; visits by other leaders to Southeast Asian countries; and finally the normalization of relations with the United States in mid-December. These took place against the background of growing conflict with Vietnam supported by the Soviet Union and greater Soviet assertiveness in Afghanistan as well as in other parts of Asia and the Horn of Africa, leading to Chinese apprehension of a deliberate Soviet attempt strategically to encircle China. In July 1978 Vietnam joined the Soviet-dominated Council for Mutual Economic Assistance (Comecon) and on 3 November signed with the Soviet Union a Treaty of Friendship and Co-operation, which was the precondition for the Vietnamese attack on Kampuchea in late December. Under these pressures Peking made important concessions to Washington on the Taiwan issue in its haste to conclude the normalization of relations. Perhaps the most important of these was the readiness to sign the agreement despite Washington's declared public commitment to continue arms sales to the authorities in Taiwan.

As seen from the Soviet Union a dangerous conjunction of relations was emerging between China, Japan and the United States on the one side and between China and NATO (including the United States on the other). The view from China on the other hand was of a Soviet strategic encirclement. Deng Xiaoping's tour of the United States in January 1979, in which he made a point of condemning Soviet hegemony and of vowing to 'teach Vietnam a lesson', followed and American embarrassment was complete when Chinese forces engaged in their limited war with Vietnam soon after his return. Indeed an American leader who visited Peking at the time made a point of expressing the administration's displeasure in public. Nevertheless the fact of his visit and continued Western interest in expanding trade with China suggested that the main thrust of improved Sino-Western relations would continue.

Even if the Carter administration at this stage hesitated at 'playing the China card' and sought to pursue a policy of 'even handedness' towards China and Russia, China's leaders had no such qualms in leaning towards the United States. It was not until the Soviet invasion of Afghanistan that China's leaders began to express satisfaction with the American attack. A Vice Premier who visited Washington to begin the first session of the Sino-American Economic Commission noted approvingly that 'especially after the Soviet invasion of Afghanistan the present US Administration has been pursuing a more enthusiastic policy in its relations with us'.[29] In July 1980 a Chinese official commentary greeted enthusiastically the end of what it regarded as American triangular diplomacy (perhaps better regarded as 'evenhandedness') in its dealings with Russia and China.

The Soviet invasion of Afghanistan also put an end to the Sino-Soviet intergovernmental dialogue begun in 1979 following a Chinese initiative announced on the occasion of the formal ending of the long defunct Sino-Soviet alliance of 1950. Interestingly the invitation and the subsequent talks followed the Chinese Vietnam war. Deng Xiaoping calculated that the Russians would not intervene|or start up a second front on the Sino-Soviet border (presumably on the proviso that the Chinese attack should remain limited in extent and duration — which Deng took pains to declare at the time). He therefore calculated presumably that the balance of forces and the psychological balance were such that China would not be negotiating from a position of excessive diplomatic weakness. The Soviet attitude was less clear as to the suitability of the timing. But having recently strengthened considerably the combat readiness of their forces near the Sino-Soviet border the Soviet leaders were certainly not negotiating from weakness. Some of their deeper apprehensions about underlying Chinese motives for having launched the war against Vietnam were revealed by some of their comments on the tripolar implications of the war. The initial Soviet reaction was to accuse the Americans of connivance which was incompatible with American-Soviet détente. But by the last week of the Chinese attack Soviet commentaries were congratulating the Soviet and American leaderships for having resisted the alleged Chinese scheme to draw them into conflict.[30] From the early days of the Sino-Soviet conflict Soviet leaders have often accused the Chinese of wanting a Soviet-American war so that they could 'sit on the mountain and watch the tigers fight'. Regardless of the motivations and the calculations of both sides the important point is that the representatives of the two governments duly met in Moscow later in 1979 and could agree on nothing (not even the agenda) except to meet again in Peking early in 1980. The Soviet invasion of Afghanistan caused the Chinese (three weeks later) to 'postpone' (rather than cancel) the next meeting. Privately, a Chinese academician explained that China could not negotiate 'on its knees'.

Thus China's practice of triangular diplomacy during the seventies decade, although affected by the power struggles in Peking — especially until the fall of the 'Gang of Four' — suggests a persistent concern with the Soviet threat and the need to establish a common purpose with an effective countervailing power. Such attempts as have been made to establish a significant dialogue with the Soviet Union have been severely constrained by *either* a close Soviet-American détente, as in 1974 the year of the Helsinki and SALT I Agreements when Brezhnev snubbed a Chinese overture, *or* Chinese perception of relative weakness in the wake of a Soviet aggressive move, as in 1980 after the Soviet invasion of Afghanistan.

Conclusion

As the one power which has had the greatest experience of tripolarity it is curious that when triangular diplomacy finally became a recognized feature of international politics in the seventies, China's leaders seem to have practised it less than either the American or Soviet leaders. As already suggested this is undoubtedly in part a result of the intense factionalism of the prolonged struggle for political succession in Peking. Other reasons can be advanced. The major factor limiting China's leaders' capacity to seize such opportunities as may have been available in the triangular diplomacy has been the continued freeze in Sino-Soviet relations. Given China's relative weakness it necessarily lacked the international 'weight' and the freedom for manoeuvre available to the other two. The 'China factor' has doubtless been of some significance in the Soviet-American Strategic Arms Limitations Talks, but it has not been one that China could manipulate or use to its advantage. Now that China has demonstrated a solid fuel ICBM capability which in theory should enable it to reach continental America as well as European Russia, the 'China factor' will loom still larger. But it still remains to be seen how China could be drawn into arms control measures.

In many respects China's leaders may be said to have cleared part of the way for improving relations with the Soviet Union. The ideological impediments from the Mao era have gradually disappeared. This has been a consequence of domestic changes. 'Revisionism' is no longer part of China's political terminology, the 'theory of the productive forces' has ceased to be condemned. China's leaders have disowned the famous 'Nine Comments' of the CPC Central Committee of the early sixties which were the main documents of their ideological critique of the Soviet Union. China's leaders' current definition of socialism (a system in which the means of production are publicly owned and people are paid according to work) is one that could apply to the Soviet Union too. It is only Soviet expansionism which has caused Deng Xiaoping to insist that a hegemonist power cannot be socialist. But China's leaders no longer seek to explain the domestic sources of that hegemonism. Indeed Chinese social scientists have debated whether or not the Soviet Union could be described as Socialist and, interestingly, the Chinese official press stated that some of them answered in the affirmative. These changes in themselves do not mean that Sino-Soviet relations will necessarily improve. But it does suggest that the determinants for that are increasingly portrayed in China as lying in the realm of power politics. Perhaps that is one of the reasons as to why there are those in China who are beginning to depict the world not in terms of the theory of the three worlds but in terms of a multipolar balance.

A powerful case can be made for the mutual advantages to be secured by both sides from even a limited improvement in Sino-Soviet relations. The difficulties which China has experienced in its new economic policy have necessitated a cutback in many of the major projects planned previously, military expenditure has had to be reduced and the anticipated arms purchases from the West have had to be delayed indefinitely. This means that the military imbalance along the Sino-Soviet border will undoubtedly persist for the foreseeable future. China's capacity to absorb and pay for Western plants using the most advanced technology has been shown to be strictly limited. If Soviet imports were to be accorded a more significant role in China's modernization many of these difficulties would be eased: the technological level would be closer to that currently prevailing in China; the trade practices and organizational arrangements of the Soviet Union are those which are familiar in China; as this would involve primarily compensation trade China's foreign currency reserves would be unaffected; and finally, unlike the West the Soviet Union would doubtless welcome China's exports of textiles and other light industrial goods. From a Soviet perspective this trade would help to plug many of the shortages prevalent in the Soviet economy. Politically and militarily both sides would acquire greater flexibility in international politics and their mutual fears of encirclement by the other and its allies would be diminished.

As against this the two powers have a legacy of deep mutual distrust and their geopolitical interests clash in a number of areas. The problems in overcoming these in negotiations should not be underestimated. Meanwhile each side is engaged in strategic alignments which cannot but be seen as threatening to the other.

China's leaders continue to hold a conflictual model of world politics. The focus on modernization may have induced China into more co-operative patterns of behaviour — but only to a limited extent for trade purposes and for cultivating allies or potential allies in the West. But the geopolitical outlook of Mao, accompanied by its focus on primary and lesser contradictions, is still applied in Peking. This does lend itself to tripolarity but along somewhat different lines to classical Western conceptions of a triangular balance of power.

Notes

1. The fact that the United States in the fifties and the sixties maintained separate capacities to conduct a war in East Asia and another with the Soviet Union in Europe and that the Soviet Union too has the capacity to fight a war in the west without having to draw on its forces in the east does not gainsay the significance of the conflict with China as a major factor in the calculations of both respective sets of leaders.

2. See, for example, Mao's remarks of March 1958 'Talk at Chengtu: On the Problem of Stalin', in Stuart Schram (ed.), *Mao Tse-tung Unrehearsed*, Harmondsworth: Penguin, 1974, p. 98, and still later that year on the dangers of 'eating precooked food' in ibid, p. 129.

3. For example, all the evidence points to Mao as having been the main driving force on the Chinese side to the rupture of relations with the Soviet Union (which he had negotiated personally in Moscow in the winter of 1949–50). Likewise he took the initiative in the opening to the United States at the beginning of the seventies.

4. One can search in vain in Mao's writings on imperialism for an analysis of the economics of monopoly capitalism or of the economics of exploitation of colonies.

5. Mao Tse-tung, 'Why is it that Red Political Power can exist in China?', 5 October 1928, in *Selected Works*, Peking: Foreign Languages Press, 1965, Vol. 1, p. 63.

6. See especially, 'On Protracted War' and 'Problems of Strategy in Guerrilla War Against Japan', ibid., Vol. 11, pp. 113–94 and 79–112, respectively.

7. Mao Tse-tung, 'Talk with Anna Louise Strong', August 1946, ibid., Vol. IV, pp. 99–100. For a fuller and more vivid version, see A.L. Strong 'World's Eye View from a Yenan Cave', *Amerasia* (April 1947). See also the analysis in John Gittings, *The World and China 1922–72*, Eyre and Methuen, 1974, pp. 141–50.

8. See *People's Daily*, 1 November 1977, for a 35,000 word article entitled, 'Chairman Mao's Theory of the Differentiation of the Three Worlds is a Major Contribution to Marxism-Leninism'; translated in *Peking Review*, No. 45, 1977.

9. Edgar Snow, *The Long Revolution*, NY: Random House, 1972, pp. 19–20.

10. For an elaboration of this point, see Michael Yahuda, 'Modernization and foreign policy in China', *The World Today*, November 1980.

11. For an extended analysis of China's foreign policy along these lines see Michael B. Yahuda, *China's Role in World Affairs*, Croom Helm, 1978.

12. Henry Kissinger, *The White House Years*, London: Weidenfeld and Nicolson and Michael Joseph, 1979, pp. 191–2.

13. See Gerald Segal, 'China and the Great Power Triangle', *The China Quarterly*, September 1980, No. 83, p. 491.

14. Cited in Gittings, *The World and China*, pp. 185–6, and by the same author, *The Role of the Chinese Army*, Oxford University Press, 1967, pp. 119–27. See also the remarks by the 'rightist' Lung Yun published by New China News Agency, 18 June 1957, cited in R. MacFarquhar (ed.), *The Hundred Flowers*, Praeger, 1960.

15. See the account in Gittings, *The World and China*, pp. 200–1.

16. Schram, *Mao Tse-tung Unrehearsed*, p. 181.

17. For a detailed analysis see Thomas M. Gottlieb, *Chinese Foreign Policy Factionalism and the Origins of the Strategic Triangle*, Rand Cooperation R-1902-NA, July 1977.

18. Wang Gung Wu, *China and the World Since 1949: The Impact of Independence, Modernity and Revolution*, London: Macmillan, 1977.

19. For the most careful and informed account see Whiting, Allen S., *The Chinese Calculus of Deterrence*, Michigan: University of Michigan Press, 1975.

20. See John Gittings, 'New Light on Mao: His View of the World', *The China Quarterly*, December 1974, No. 60, esp. p. 765.

21. *New York Times*, 21 February 1964. See also the discussion in Yahuda, *China's Role in World Affairs*, pp. 149–54.

22. Consider for example the British government's embarrassed disclaimer of the reported remarks of Chief of the Defence Staff Air Marshal Sir Neil Cameron in Peking that Britain and China shared a common enemy with its capital in Moscow.

23. The classic statement of this position was by Deng Xiaoping (Teng Hsiaoping) to the UN General Assembly in April 1974. See *Peking Review*, Special Supplement to No. 15, 12 April 1974.

24. This was implied in the Sino-American joint Communiqué of February 1972 which agreed to oppose 'hegemony' but after the final US débâcle in Indo China in 1975 China's official press and radio began to drop direct criticism of the US as an imperialist superpower.

25. Reported interview by G. Rowbotham *East is Red*, October 1971 (York SACU), pp. 6–10, cited by John Gittings, 'China's Foreign Policy: Continuity or Change?', in *Journal of Contemporary Asia*, Vol. 2, No. 1.

26. See BBC *Summary of World Broadcasts*, Part 3, FE/6618/A1/1, 9 January 1981.

27. See the account by William G. Hyland, 'The Sino-Soviet Conflict: A Search for New Security Strategies', in Richard H. Solomon (ed.), *Asian Security in the 1980s*, Cambridge, Massachusetts: Oelgeschlager, Gunn and Hain, especially pp. 41–4.

28. See *People's Daily*, 27 November 1974.

29. *The Times*, 17 September 1980.

30. See *Soviet News*, 20 February 1979, and a *Pravda* commentary of 5 March cited in *International Herald Tribune*, 6 March 1979.

3 THE SOVIET UNION AND THE GREAT POWER TRIANGLE

Gerald Segal

As the Sino-Soviet split emerged into the open, the USSR was confronted with a major foreign policy problem: how to balance the twin conflicting pressures from a China independent of Communist bloc control, and from the United States, the other superpower. The lessons learned and the evolving pattern of triangular relations is the focus of this essay. A short review of the historical aspects of the USSR's behaviour in the great power triad will be followed by a more detailed examination of the specific aspects of tripolarity as viewed from the Kremlin. Moscow's view of triangular tactics such as 'card playing' will be considered and some comment offered on the possible differences of opinion within the USSR on the great power triangle. The conclusion will analyse the Soviet sense of future trends in the triad, and summarize the overarching concepts entailed in Moscow's view of the triangle.

The Historical Context

The two most salient shifts in the global strategic balance can probably be traced to two watersheds in the political development with the PRC. The first change, the emerging Sino-Soviet rift, was a major strategic loss for the USSR which rent its bloc and caused untold foreign policy complications. The Chinese drift out of the Soviet orbit led to the gradual emergence of the USSR as the pivot in the great power triangle. The pivot was the power with the most co-operative and least conflictive relations among the three. Moscow increasingly discovered the pressures of being caught between the opposing demands of the US Scylla and the Chinese Charybdis on such issues as the Laos conflict, nuclear weapons negotiations and the Vietnam War.[1]

As a result of these pressures the USSR began to formulate a series of responses to problems occurring in the triangle. In general however, the room for manoeuvre for all three powers was restricted and incrementalism and caution increasingly afflicted policy. Crisis management in the triad became complex as communication included trilateral signalling. Other important triadic aspects included deterrence where two powers rather than one issued deterrence commitments against the initiator and one power tended to incorporate the deterrence posture of the other.

The first phase of tripolarity, i.e. the Sino-Soviet rift and the major strategic shift of the early 1960s, lasted until the late 1960s and early 1970s. At that time, as a result of a serious widening of the Sino-Soviet rift and the nascent Sino-American détente, the US emerged as the great power with the most co-operative and least conflictive relations among the three, and hence assumed the role of pivot. Although the view of the 1960s in tripolar terms is somewhat controversial, such an analysis of the 1970s is less so. Henry Kissinger is in no doubt that Moscow understood the triangle,[2] and certain academic analysts have produced persuasive analyses of the USSR's tripolar concerns.[3] What is clear is that the tripolar events of the present have an historical precedent and whatever pattern there is in contemporary relations, it is very much tied to the process of development in tripolar politics. This process forms the backdrop to the Soviet Union's broad view of the great power triangle of recent years.

Strategic Aspects

It is notoriously difficult to substantiate that a state implicitly accepts the relevance of a concept while explicitly denying it, yet this has precisely been the Soviet Union's response to the notion of a triad. Broadly speaking, the ideology of the Soviet state postulates a bipolar clash of socialist and capitalist systems, but a more in-depth analysis, even of Soviet documentation, reveals a different perspective. For practical purposes an acceptance of the importance of at least certain aspects of the international scene as tripolar is acknowledged.[4] Although the USSR may not accept that triangular concepts are a valid way of looking at the international situation, it does seem to accept that certain actors (notably the US and PRC) conceive of the world in that way and the USSR must respond to those perceptions. What is more, the Kremlin points to the simultaneous pincers exerting pressure from the West and China as the major aspect of Soviet defence needs.[5] Within the triangular framework Moscow sees the USSR-US axis as pre-eminent, but relations with China are clearly the second most important aspect. The establishment of a Sino-American section in Moscow's Institute for the study of the USA and Canada signalled acceptance of tripolarity in the all important Soviet bureaucratic terms.[6] By the early 1970s Soviet academic institutions, but also the various ministries, began establishing special China sections that included analysis of the US factor. Contemporary Soviet scholars and decision makers repeatedly refer to the interaction of the two superpowers and China in what can only be classified as analysis of triangular politics.[7]

From Moscow's point of view the necessity to perceive at least certain elements of the strategic balance in tripolar terms is derived from two main motivations. The first relates to the PRC. According to the USSR '. . . China is still short of material resources to force its will on other countries. That is why it has been seeking allies. . . .'[8] and specifically an alliance with the US. What is more, the USSR is so strong that China cannot successfully challenge the USSR directly. Thus China's objectives are said to be born out of weakness even though it is manifested in an offensive manner.

A second and similar motivation is attributed to the US. The weakening of Washington's global position has led the US to seek alternative ways of defeating the USSR and therefore it seized upon China's anti-Sovietism as a way of shoring up its position.[9] Although there are certain variations in the Soviet view (to be discussed below) the fundamental view of the triangle appears to be that both the US and PRC are motivated by weakness and that the Chinese policy of anti-Sovietism is the underlying cause of triangular politics.

The historical roots of tripolar manoeuvres are traced well back into ancient Chinese history. From the time of *The Romance of the Three Kingdoms* to the 'ancient Chinese strategic precept' of 'suppressing barbarians with the help of barbarians' or 'sit on the top of a mountain and watch the tigers fight', the PRC is said to have ample experience in tripolar politics.[10] What is more, the Chinese Communists' were said to have learned triadic games as early as the 1940s.[11] The 'Dixie Mission' of Americans to Mao's forces in Yenan and the CPC's attempt to obtain arms is cited as proof of the Chinese Communists' longstanding efforts to play triangular politics and remove Soviet influence.

Moscow's view of China's strategic efforts to play triangular politics can be divided into three main aspects. The broadest plane is the political struggle which, as we have already seen, has deep historic roots. Even in the 1950s China was said to have sought to set 'spear-against-spear' and foment a US-USSR clash.[12] At that time it was an attempt to ally with the USSR against the US, but since the early 1970s it has been by way of an alliance with the US against the USSR. The objective is seen as the same: to benefit by a superpower clash that leaves the international scene wide open for Chinese domination.[13] As in the 1950s, this policy is dominated by an anti-détente position and an attempt to stir up international tension.

This policy of 'collusion' with the US is not confined to the political realm but it is here that it has received great publicity in the USSR. The epitome of collusion in this respect was surely the normalization of Sino-American relations in December 1978. Although the USSR asserted that it did not object to normalization *per se*, it did raise a hue and cry regarding the announcement because of what Moscow called the 'anti-Soviet nature' of the action.[14] China was said to have made an inordinate number of concessions to the US for the sake of its broader anti-Soviet goals. Anti-Sovietism is clearly the litmus test for Sino-American actions as far as the Soviet view of the strategic triangle is concerned.[15] Soviet prestige is also a key concern on this political level, for after the visit of Deng Xiaoping to Washington was announced, one Soviet official said, 'if you thought you could invite our general secretary to Washington before Teng, what kind of people do you take us for?'[16] Anything that challenged Moscow's sense of the primacy of the superpower axis and their own importance above any other state, was sure to be denounced.

The second aspect of Soviet concern regarding US-PRC ties is the economic sphere. In Moscow's view, economic policy explains both Chinese and American interests in anti-Sovietism. The PRC is said to require Western aid in its modernization drive and therefore seeks to collude with Washington. The US is seen as gaining new markets in China but more importantly, relieving itself of the sole burden of challenging the USSR. By tying the PRC to the West, Moscow feels that the US thereby hopes to prevent a normalization of Sino-Soviet relations.[17] The granting of most favoured nation status to China and not to the USSR is highly resented by Moscow and is seen as part of this anti-Sovietism on economic issues. China is said to repay this economic benefit with 'political services and military interests'.[18]

This raises the third and most important aspect of Soviet concern with US-PRC relations: the military sphere. It seems clear that the single most salient trip wire for Moscow's concerns about Sino-

American collusion is the question of arms sales by the West. For the USSR it is apparent that China desires the arms so as to modernize its defences and obtain great power status.[19] As G. Arbatov said in 1978, 'If your military relationship with China changes, we will have to reassess the situation'.[20] The Soviet view of the American role on this issue has changed as the US decision makers deliberated whether to sell arms directly to China, but it has always remained a crucial issue. The memory of US arms sales to Yugoslavia after the break with Stalin is a sensitive point for the USSR and a vivid historical lesson. By mid-1979, as the US moved more sharply towards direct arms sales to China, the Soviet level of concern increased even more rapidly.[21] The visit of US Defense Secretary Brown to China brought Moscow's expressions of displeasure on this issue to a new high pitch.[22] Depending on the audience at which the comment was directed, the USSR viewed the Brown visit as either signifying the US falling victim to a Chinese ruse to arm the PLA, or alternatively the PRC falling victim to an American ruse to use Chinese soldiers as 'cannon fodder' in the United States anti-Soviet war effort. The visit by Vice-President Mondale and his statements supporting 'mutual strategic interests' resulted in a new level of blame being attributed to the US for the state of superpower relations in the triangle.[23] In the wake of the deterioration of US-USSR ties after Afghanistan, the explanation blaming the US more than China seemed to predominate.[24] By September 1980 the accepted method of dealing with the problem of who was playing cards against whom was epitomized in Andrei Gromyko's UN speech in which he said, 'Setting aside the question of who is playing whose cards more, it must be emphasized that this game is a phenomenon dangerous to the cause of peace.'[25] Whatever the case, the USSR was deeply disturbed by the talk of arms sales, although partly placated by the limited scope of the actual Sino-American agreement on this issue.[26]

Another important aspect of the military sphere is the SALT process. There is repeated testimony of Moscow's concern to involve the PRC in the SALT discussions, if only so as to obtain an agreement with the US to contain the Chinese threat.[27] The USSR has also clearly stated that the course of SALT III will necessarily include a discussion of the Chinese factor and its effect on the strategic balance.[28] SALT II involved discussion of China at several stages and Washington's normalization of relations with the PRC delayed the closing stages of the negotiations. The USSR clearly indicated that 'stability and trust' in the SALT process was being undermined by US action in the triangle.[29]

The precise linkage of SALT to the China factor is difficult to ascertain as it is by no means clear whether the USSR perceives a 'China dividend' (military expenditure now freed for the China front) or an increasing problem as SALT limits the Soviet's ability to deal simultaneously with threats from the US and PRC. In the past the USSR has targeted some strategic forces at China and by the late 1960s there were 120 SS-11s deployed against the PRC.

But SS-11s are now counted in SALT ceilings and an ABM system that could have been effective against China was abjured in SALT I. The fact that SALT II did not limit Backfire bombers or theatre nuclear weapons deployment can be seen as part of the continuing Soviet need to deal with China, as can the Soviet desire for an MBFR agreement in Europe so as to free conventional forces for the China frontier.[30] Furthermore, in other arms control forums such as the Geneva Disarmament Committee, the newly active Chinese role has added a new string to Moscow's anti-China bow on these issues. Peking is now denounced for assuming the Western position on these issues, thereby stressing the US' leading role on arms control in the triangle.[31] What emerges from all this is that the superpower strategic balance in general, and the SALT process in particular, are already integrally concerned with the Chinese factor, and are likely to be increasingly so preoccupied in the future.

The Triangle in Asia

Having analysed the Soviet view of the nature of the strategic triangle, it would be useful to focus on the more specific aspects of triangular politics in various areas of the world. The Asian theatre is most often cited in Soviet commentary, no doubt because it is here that China is less limited by its paucity of military and economic power. It is also clear that Moscow's interest in the China factor in the Asian balance is concentrated on the Sino-Soviet border.

In as much as China's challenge to the USSR is perceived as a problem that will only increase in the future and in so far as the Soviet Union's Asian territories are seen as the key to the future growth of the Soviet Union,[32] the China factor looms large in the strategic balance. The extensive visit by Brezhnev to the Far East in 1978 was a graphic demonstration of the intensive Soviet interest in Asia. Although political and economic factors assume a certain importance in this area, the military factor and the Sino-Soviet frontier is pre-eminent. The threat of war on the border remains critical, as Soviet military writing in the 1970s shows an obvious concern with the planning for a lightning war on the Sino-Soviet frontier.[33] The build-up of Soviet forces on the border since the 1960s has been dramatic, accounting for 80 per cent of the total increase in Soviet military manpower between 1969 and 1978. There are 100,000 more Soviet troops on the USSR-PRC border than in East Europe. About a quarter of all Soviet military spending concerns the PRC and these costs have grown at twice the rate for the rest of the Soviet armed forces.[34] Following the invasion of Afghanistan this build-up process has continued especially by way of Soviet force modernization along the frontier.[35] According to some military observers, by 1980 the USSR had acquired the ability to fight a full-scale war on both the European and Pacific fronts,[36] an essential component to a tripolar military posture. One third of Soviet nuclear forces are reportedly targeted on China with up to another one third available from the 'swing' forces.[37] The repeated Soviet inability to improve relations with China despite numerous efforts, while Sino-American relations improve apace, only heightens Moscow's perception of collusion and a threat to its critical eastern frontier.[38]

The Soviet Union's concern with the threat posed by China's nuclear capability has apparently not increased to any significant degree since the late 1960s. This was apparent following the renewed Chinese nuclear weapons efforts of 1980, and pre-eminently the flight tests of an apparently solid-fuel powered ICBM. Moscow correctly assessed the test as a threat to the continental US rather than to Soviet targets already within reach and, in the light of continuing US arms aid to China, suggested with blatant *schadenfreude* that 'Chinese leaders seem to be playing the American card against America's security'.[39]

The USSR makes a direct connection between what it sees as 'intensifying anti-Sovietism' by China[40] including the worsening of Sino-Soviet relations, and the pattern of Sino-American collusion.[41] This point, as with many others already noted, makes the case that the USSR accepts the importance of triangular politics *de facto*, even if it denounces the ideological and conceptual basis for it. The Soviet Union argues that China seeks US aid to further its grievance in Sino-Soviet relations basically because the USSR is too strong,[42] but the continuing reinforcement of Soviet troops along the border indicates less than the stated sanguinity. The fear that Sino-American normalization would allow Chinese troops facing Taiwan to be moved to the Sino-Soviet border figures prominently in Soviet assessments of the current situation.[43] However, Soviet strength is constantly noted and the declaratory position, for example on Chinese nuclear capability, remains that the threat is to weaker Asian states but not to the USSR.[44]

The second most important Asian issue where triangular politics affects the USSR, is the role of Japan. Although the range of issues discussed in Soviet commentary on Japan is in many ways similar to that on the US in general, certain areas are emphasized more than others. The broad political sphere was of greater importance in the period prior to the Japanese decision to sign the anti-hegemony clause in the August 1978 Treaty of Peace and Friendship with China. At that time the USSR had struggled to prevent Tokyo from aligning with the West and China against the USSR in the triangle. Moscow's intransigence regarding the sensitive northern Japanese islands issue was probably the main problem.[45]

Once the Japanese signed the friendship pact economic issues emerged as the main concern for the USSR. The bogey of Japanese money and expertise allied to the Chinese masses was no doubt seen as a major threat to the Soviet Union's Asian position.[46] While the PRC and not Japan bore the brunt of the Kremlin's attacks, the general deterioration in Soviet-Japanese ties was evident. The potential for Japan to affect the military realm of the triangle was also discussed although apparently it did not raise the same sort of alarm bells as did direct US-Chinese arms deals.[47] The history of Japanese 'militarism' was often cited by Soviet commentators as potentially to be repeated and the exchange of visits by Japanese and Chinese military delegations was seen as moving part of the way down that road. Once again it seemed to be the potential for Japanese collusion in anti-Sovietism in the triangle which most upset the USSR, but this time the threat was seen as lying in Japanese militarism, and not the Chinese variety.

The third major Asian concern for the USSR in the great power triangle involves Vietnam in general and most recently and specifically the Sino-Vietnamese war. In the Soviet view, there has been Sino-American collusion regarding Vietnam extending well back into the 1960s. The Chinese were said to have hampered Hanoi's struggle against the US by taking an 'extreme' position while Moscow pursued a 'sensible' and less provocative policy.[48] A new variation on the collusion theme was stressed in the Soviet commentary on the 1979 Sino-Vietnamese war especially since it broke out after President Carter was told by Deng Xiaoping on his American visit that China would 'punish' Vietnam.[49] The Kremlin's judgement on the war was to a certain extent a changing one as the Soviet view of the precise extent of Sino-American collusion fluctuated. In the final analysis the Chinese 'defeat', the enhanced Soviet reputation for calm yet clear support and the increased Vietnamese dependence on Moscow all meant that the USSR was reasonably pleased with the outcome. Collusion had been rebuffed and fundamental Soviet concerns in Asia reinforced, including the concrete aspect of basing rights in Vietnam. However the Chinese were not seen to be chastened by this experience and thus the dangers of triangular collusion continue to loom large for Soviet policy in Asia.[50]

The Triangle in Europe

While triangular factors played an important role in Moscow's view of the pressures on 'socialist' Vietnam, the same factors apparently do not seem to be nearly as important for the 'socialist' states of East Europe. China on its own is regularly pilloried by the USSR for anti-Sovietism and undermining the socialist community, but rarely in the context of co-ordination with the West. Peking's major threat as seen from Moscow is in encouraging 'national isolation' and 'anti-socialist elements' in East Europe, but not until 1977 and China's renewed interest in the area did Moscow persistently raise the spectre of 'co-ordination' of Sino-American policy.[51] Hua Guofeng's visit to Rumania and Yugoslavia in 1978 was a clear validation for the USSR of this new trend and reinforced the view of China as the 'initiator' of this collusion.

Ideological factors are most regularly stressed by Soviet comment on this triangular aspect of the East European balance and this no doubt is linked to longstanding Soviet concerns regarding Western attempts to 'roll back' Moscow's influence in its sphere. However it is perhaps reasonable to speculate that the USSR is more concerned with the broader political aspects of the triangular configuration. In this respect the GDR is singled out as a particular problem. China is seen as espousing 'revanchist' policies and encouraging West German forces who refuse to accept the moves towards a political settlement of the German question.[52] Some of the other and more obvious candidates for Soviet concern on political problems, for example Rumania and Yugoslavia, do not seem to figure in open Soviet comment. However, not all basic fears need be discussed in public. On the more positive side for the USSR, Chinese problems with Albania are seen as improving the Soviet Union's relative political standing in East Europe. Finally, as regards the military component, it seems hardly to figure at all in Soviet calculations on triangular factors in East Europe.

The military aspect is however a primary focus of Soviet concern with respect to tripolarity in West Europe, and in fact this area has been the target of some of the most sophisticated calculations and analysis by the Kremlin on triangular politics. West European states have in recent years been an important focus of Soviet comment on tripolarity and this can be divided up both according to specific states and areas of interest.

In the sphere of political interests, China is seen as linking the 'forces of reaction' in Europe to its policy of anti-Sovietism. Both forces are 'trying to make a cat's paw of other peoples',[53] but China is more often singled out as the main initiator of anti-Sovietism. The PRC challenge takes place in Europe because it is such an important place in the East-West confrontation, and because it has seen an era of détente in recent years. China's anti-Sovietism is designed to exacerbate tension and confront the 'socialist community' by using anti-détente forces in Europe.[54] Encouragement of German 'revanchism' and opposition to détente in Europe are particularly worrisome to the USSR. Hua Guofeng's tour of West Europe in October-November 1979 raised these broad issues for Soviet policy and drew a revealing series of commentaries from the Kremlin. In general though, the policy of détente was said to have won out and China proved unable to manipulate tripolar factors.[55]

The sphere of economic interests is also said to be crucial as both the West and China seek material gains from this relationship. Although less overtly anti-Soviet and less concerned with triangular aspects, China's search for aid for modernization and the EEC desire for markets, are noted by the USSR as an important component of the China factor in West Europe. West Germany is the main focus of discussion on the economic plane, but since relatively little opprobium is attached to this level, Bonn is not criticized to any significant degree.[56] After all, even the USSR's trade with China has increased in recent years so economic issues are generally minimized.

This German model for 'proper' behaviour of Western states

towards China is most striking in the area which most concerns the Kremlin: the military sphere. Bonn's steadfast refusal to sell arms to China, as well as other broader political concerns, makes West Germany Moscow's favourite when it comes to tripolarity in Europe. The trip wire for Soviet military concerns in Europe was set by G. Arbatov in 1978.

> There are several possibilities. One — which I hope will not materialize — is for China to become some sort of military ally to the West, even an informal ally. Then the whole situation would look different to us. We would have to re-analyse our relationship with the West. If such an axis is built on an anti-Soviet basis, then there is no place for detente, even in a narrow sense. For instance, what sense would it make for us to agree to reduce armaments in Europe if armaments are simply to be channeled by the West to the Eastern front? . . . You cannot reconcile detente with attempts to make China some sort of military ally of the North Atlantic Treaty Organization. . . .[57]

Attempts to make China the 16th member of NATO apparently even include arms sales to China and such actions provoke immediate and harsh comment from the USSR.[58] If it is considered that an important reason for the USSR to engage in détente with the West is to be free to concentrate on the China problem, it is clear that European military dealings with Peking are likely to harm détente and not browbeat the USSR into concessions. The MBFR talks or proposals to limit tactical or theatre nuclear weapons in Europe are probably all in part attempts to settle one front so as to secure the other. These détente efforts would no doubt be viewed even more critically in Moscow if they were perceived as merely manoeuvres in an anti-Soviet policy.

The presence of Chinese diplomats at NATO manoeuvres, the exchange of military delegations and above all arms sales, are sharply denounced by the USSR. Moscow pays such close attention to these events that perhaps the most efficient way to discover a list of China-West Europe military discussions is via the Soviet press. If the West Germans stand out as the most favoured West European state in Soviet eyes, the UK is notably the least satisfactory.[59] Conservative rather than Labour governments are denounced and the Harrier jump-jet deal is the main issue. All these aspects came together in vivid fashion for the USSR in April 1978 when the Chief of the British Defence Staff, on a visit to China, asserted that Britain and the PRC had a common enemy in Moscow. Other European states lie somewhere in between Bonn and London with the French representing a prime example of the differentiations in the Soviet view. Paris's arms sales are denounced but the cool reaction to Hua's 1979 visit is praised.[60]

West Europe is important in tripolar politics not only for what the Europeans as US allies can do with China, but also for what pressure the allies can place on the US to support China in its anti-Soviet policy.[61] This linkage between Europe and the US is a key concept for the USSR in its perception of an anti-Soviet coalition. Thus the Kremlin has devised an intricate policy to meet this challenge. In some senses it is the area of greatest Soviet success, as the evolution of the German model stressing trade with China on a non-anti-Soviet basis is likely to be satisfactory to Moscow. Basic Soviet satisfaction with the course of the 1979 Hua visit and the cool reaction in West Europe to anti-détente statements illustrates Moscow's belief that Europe cannot risk an anti-Soviet policy especially along the lines of the Chinese model.[62] Triangular politics can be controlled and far from giving the West greater leverage against the Soviet Union, tripolarity in Europe has by and large meant that Moscow can stress the necessity for Europe-USSR ties and diffuse the impact of the anti-Soviet forces. While the great power triangle is clearly important for the USSR, at least in Europe it appears to be manageable. What is more, Europe-US linkage may perhaps aid the management of the triangle on the superpower strategic level. Card players in Washington can also have cards played against them.

The Triangle in the Non-aligned World

Perhaps the most striking aspect of the USSR's view of tripolarity in the non-aligned world is the overwhelming attempt to minimize the notion of collusion and Sino-American anti-Sovietism that so dominated Moscow's analysis of other areas of the world. The Soviet Union appears to be overwhelmingly concerned with the bilateral competition either with the US or China for influence among the non-aligned, but it is relatively rare for the Kremlin to express any great concern over US-PRC collusion in those areas.[63] The USSR notes 'identical or similar positions' or the 'joining of hands' between China and the US, but the comment consistently remains vague and the issue is by no means a major focus of criticism. The September 1979 Havana Conference of Non-aligned States is a prime example where the United States and especially China's anti-Sovietism was attacked, but rarely as a joint venture in the style of tripolar policies elsewhere in the world.[64]

To a certain extent this policy has been modified by recent events as conflicts in the non-aligned world have become increasingly salient. In the case of the unrest in Iran the US is castigated first and foremost but Chinese 'support' and 'approval' of US efforts including arms build-ups is denounced. Alleged co-operation between the Chinese 'special services' and the CIA and Savak was also noted, and PRC support of the US position on the embassy hostages has been cited.[65] Nevertheless this collusion is not seen as anti-Soviet and does not appear to involve triangular politics to any significant degree.

The only place where tripolar politics in the non-aligned world does seem to play an important role for Moscow is in the recent crisis in Afghanistan. Once again China is said to take a subsidiary role to the main challenge from the US, but this time the co-operation in 'anti-Socialist' policy is said to be concrete. Arms aid to 'local reactionaries' and consultation on 'parallel strategic interests' forms a prime focus of the Soviet attacks.[66] The US emerges as the main enemy but China is the 'henchman' of NATO countries. The main threat is seen as being to Asian states and not the USSR,[67] but given the heavy Soviet involvement in Afghanistan, it is most unlikely that the Soviet Union could ignore Sino-American co-operation in an anti-Soviet venture. The evolution of Pakistan as the focus of American and Chinese counter-moves to the Soviet invasion of Afghanistan and the flow of arms to Afghan rebels from Pakistan all add to the Kremlin's fear of anti-Soviet collusion and the pincers in the great power triangle. Perhaps a change is in the wind away from the USSR's previous relative unconcern with tripolar politics in the non-aligned world to a perception of greater triangularity as is the case in Asia and to a lesser extent in Europe. Although the vast differences in area and issues make it difficult to outline a specific pattern to Soviet concerns in the great power triangle, it is clear that the USSR is acutely attuned to the issue of tripolarity.

Tactics in the Triangle

The USSR clearly feels a need to respond to tripolarity in various strategic areas but what of the tactics used in these global relations? The most often noted tactic is 'playing the China card' or 'playing the American card', but what does this mean and how does the Soviet Union perceive these games?

There can be little doubt that the USSR is fully aware of the discussions about playing cards and is in even less doubt as regards the target against whom they are being played. In its broadest sense these card games are said to describe Chinese and American attempts to employ each other in their policy of anti-Sovietism.[68] The normalization of Sino-American relations and the machinations of Z. Brzezinski are seen as a prime example of such card playing but the tactic also extends to various other levels of relations and tripolarity in other areas of the world. As Brezhnev declared:

> The point is not at all the establishment of diplomatic relations. The point is that attempts are being made to encourage in every way and to stimulate with economic baits, and now, gradually, also with deliveries of modern weapons, material and military technology those who, while heading one of the biggest countries in the world, have openly declared their hostility to the cause of detente, disarmament and stability in the world. . . .[69]

But just how serious a process does the USSR see this card playing?

Although it is plain that the USSR takes such card playing very seriously, it does not seem to feel threatened by it. It should also be kept in mind that Moscow continues to sell military-related technology to China while criticizing the US for doing less.[70] The politics of the card playing theme cannot be overestimated. Nevertheless, the primary reason for the USSR not perceiving card playing, so far, as a military threat is because the open discussion in the West and especially the US about playing the China card, has revealed deep fissures regarding the question of whether and how to use China against the USSR.[71] The Soviet press has a keen eye for those divisions, for as one observer noted

> As for the United States' hopes that the nationalism of the Chinese leaders will work in America's interests, their naivety is self-evident. An ever greater number of sober-minded people in

the West, in the USA itself included, have come to realize that it is impossible to play the 'Chinese card' without running the risk of falling a victim to that dangerous game. They are aware that time-serving tactical advantages will be followed by a major strategic fiasco.[72]

The precise size of the 'greater number of sober-minded people' changes in the USSR according to different commentators, but the existence of a split in the West is almost always acknowledged. The same is not true of playing the American card and thus the 'sober-minded people' tend to be those who understand that Peking is willing to fight to the last Westerner and those who recognize the primacy of stability in East-West relations.[73] In a key *Izvestia* article, A. Bovin wrote,

> . . . On a strategic level the American leaders obviously understood that a worsening of Soviet-American relations would create difficulties and problems for the USA that could not be compensated for by an improvement of Chinese-American relations. . . .[74]

The policy spectrum for tripolar tactics as seen from Moscow spans from the extreme card playing of 'Chinese leaders and the enemies of détente' in the West, to the moderates such as West Germany. Trade with China is one thing in Moscow's view, but Brzezinski style card playing 'is a different story altogether'.[75] The spectrum also spans various areas including the broadly political and the more specific economic interests. For example, some 'business circles' in the US are said to be concerned about China's economic stability and solvency and do not wish to jeopardize Soviet trade by playing cards.[76] One important Soviet commentator noted that attempts to play the China card by witholding most favoured nation status from the USSR while granting it to China have 'brought nothing but losses to US firms'. He addressed US business circles in their own language — *Realpolitik* — when he added that card games

> . . . can only be contemplated by people who are new in politics and who are out of touch with political realities. The really important thing, the thing that really counts, are not some academic schemes dreamed up by ex-college people holding academic degrees, but the real balance of forces. This balance of strength

proves that China remains, despite its size, an underdeveloped country both economically and militarily. . . .[77]

Power is the essence and card games do not reflect the complexities of its manipulation.

The most important spectrum of views is on the military issue of arms sales. The best guide to Soviet views on card players is whether they desire to sell arms to China. These forces are said to be especially strong in Britain, Japan and now the US, while weakest in Germany and France.[78] The potential subtleties in the process, such as US approval of sales by allies but not direct arms deals, was appreciated by Moscow and treated with the relatively reduced concern that Washington intended to provoke.[79] Such intricacies in card games are equally well appreciated by all participants in the triangle and the utility of crude card games was obviously cast into doubt.

At times distinctions were also made between strategic and tactical card playing, or games in the short term or long term, but it is clear that the USSR's perception was complex and variable depending on the specific circumstances of tripolar tactics. Further indication of the sophisticated Soviet grasp of card games is the way in which their responses have changed over time as the discussion in the West over playing the China card has altered.[80] The Americans were seen as especially prone to 'vacillation' on the subject because the US 'carries within itself the opposing factors of the militant and more moderate tendencies'. The China card is said to be 'returning like a boomerang and is beginning to be played by one group against another in the internal political struggle inside America itself . . .'[81] This process was most apparent in the case of Sino-American normalization of relations followed by the Sino-Vietnamese war. Moscow watched American policy on card playing very closely, noting every nuance of policy pronouncements for signs of anti-Soviet card playing. The Kremlin repeatedly said it was waiting and watching to see the true nature of US policy as revealed in whether it attempted to play China off against the USSR.[82]

These issues returned to the fore following the invasion of Afghanistan when as a result of the deterioration in Soviet-American relations the US was generally more sharply criticized. In terms of tripolarity, the US was said to try to compensate for its weakened position by playing cards, e.g. the Brown visit to China. Once again the policy stressing the primacy of superpower ties came out when A. Bovin declared 'Washington could hardly manage to compensate for a worsening of Soviet-American relations by establishing "close ties" with China.'[83] The anti-American line in fact reached a new level as the stress on the PRC as mere 'cannon fodder' and 'kowtowing to US imperialism' evidently reflected the view that China's interests were subservient to those of the US.[84] Following Geng Biao's visit to the US in May 1980 and new non-lethal arms deals, Moscow found that the US was 'lifting one ban after another' and that much of the talk of not playing cards was disproven as some military co-operation 'has become a fact'.[85] Despite this new and harsher line, the Soviet Union remained relatively calm. As I. Alexsandrov noted, 'This is naturally not yet an open military alliance. However, this kind of contact between China and imperialism is creating a dangerous situation in the international arena.'[86] Thus in the Soviet view, card playing seemed to be more of a reflection of American (and to a lesser degree Chinese) intention rather than a real threat to the USSR. The complexity in using this card playing tactic was the major problem both for the US and China in its implementation, and for the USSR in the way it hindered what Moscow perceived to be the primary agenda of superpower ties.

The complexities of the process of card playing were well reflected in Soviet counter-tactics to such games. The most striking aspect of the USSR's reaction was its ambiguity.[87] One commentator said, 'Should the need arise, it [USSR] will take every step it deems necessary.' Another added,

> The Soviet Union has all the necessary means to ensure the vital interests of the State as well as the interests of the fraternal socialist countries. Naturally, our country will draw the necessary conclusions for its defence in the face of actions which create a threat to peace.

Just what these conclusions are is uncertain and this seems to be the impression the Soviet Union would like to encourage. On the one hand it urges that the general policy of détente be pursued but more specifically calls for its collective security plan, especially in Asia, to be implemented.[88] The USSR does not see that it is directly threatened itself, but believes that guarantees to others may be needed. As Bovin noted, '. . . The USSR has at its disposal everything it needs to guarantee its security efficiently. But the question of guarantees is much broader.'[89] On trade issues in card playing the USSR has taken a more personal view of the matter. For example, in an effort to prevent its being used as a 'means of political pressure' in December 1979, a meeting of a joint US-USSR commission on economic matters was cancelled by Moscow.[90]

Furthermore, on such crucial matters as SALT, the USSR rejects the notion that card playing can have any effect in forcing concessions, and seemingly just to prove that point the signing of SALT II was delayed in part to protest the tenor of Sino-American normalization in December 1979.[91] Attempts at linkage are met by more clear signals that such a policy will not work. Thus the USSR rejects card playing as an effective tactic and adopts a very amorphous reactive policy. In sum, card playing is little more than a version of linkage politics. This kind of tactic clearly has not been successful in the past in pressuring the USSR — e.g. 1972 summit diplomacy and ending the war in Vietnam. Arms sales to China in exchange for a withdrawal from Afghanistan are likely to suffer the same fate especially since the worsening of superpower relations is set against the background of improving US-PRC ties instead of mutually improving US-USSR and US-PRC relations in the previous administration. As one Soviet commentator noted with apparent longing for the Kissinger days of tripolarity,

> . . . Formerly, there was a general trend in Washington's foreign policy, unstable as it was, towards promoting its relations with China and the USSR at one, and the same time, whereas now, the influential US circles responsible for framing and implementing government policy, give priority to taking more vigorous steps to establish closer relations with China and simultaneously, to aggravate relations with the Soviet Union.[92]

The USSR apparently refuses to trade in negotiations except on a bilateral basis and policy that makes linkage public is even less likely to succeed.

There are other aspects of tactics in the triangle that can be discussed much more briefly, not because they are less important but because they receive little comment from the USSR. Firstly, the pattern of communications in tripolar politics is emerging as distinct from the bipolar era. The virtue of clear communication between all three members of the triad was appreciated and the USSR engaged in both bilateral and trilateral signalling. For example, in the 1960s the USSR had discussed China with Washington and this continued to be a feature of the 1970s, including the SALT process.[93] However, when the US engaged in the same kind of trilateral communication with China, the USSR blasted Washington for violating the unspoken rule of superpower negotiations.[94] Moscow's attempt to have only the benefits of tripolarity reinforced the need to engage in clearly differentiated signals as the amount of suspicion normally present in bilateral negotiations was vastly increased in a tripolar environment.

Secondly, the pattern of great power deterrence also developed triadic aspects. This meant that two powers rather than one issued deterrence commitments against the initiator, and the initiator of challenges to deterrence now had to consider two powers rather than one in its calculations. The resulting caution in the deterrence pattern was apparent in the escalation of the Vietnam War in the mid-1960s,[95] and was also present in the Sino-Vietnamese war of 1979.[96] Moscow's careful concern to deter both the US and PRC in that conflict was a model of tripolar deterrence. What is more, there evolved a tendency for one non-initiator power to incorporate the deterrence posture of the other non-initiator power in its own deterrence. The Soviet Union in particular used this formula, for example in the 1962 Sino-Indian war and the 1965 India-Pakistan conflict.[97] During the Sino-Vietnamese war the USSR was upset with the US in large measure because the US failed to deter the PRC and Moscow had to deter China on its own.[98] The USSR had come to accept this new aspect to tripolar deterrence and made its displeasure known when it did not emerge. In sum, it is clear that tripolarity in the Soviet view has fostered new tactics to cope with new problems, all in the context of a far more complex international environment. What is more this complexity is further compounded by some important factors in the realm of internal Soviet politics.

The Triangle and Soviet Policy Divergences

One of the main components in Moscow's refusal to accept card playing as an effective tactic was derived from its view that the West was not united on policy in the triangle. This lack of Western unity, coupled with already existing internal Soviet divisions, has also led to a series of policy divergences in Soviet policy on the triangle. These splits can be seen as further reason why linkage politics are unlikely to work. Just whom are they directed at and what is likely to be their reaction? This is a key issue and a qualification that must underlie the above discussion of the Soviet view of the triangle and its tactics. Clearly there is no uniform view in the Kremlin.

Broadly speaking the divergence of views in the USSR on triangular diplomacy can be seen as lying on a continuum. The argument of the moderates is essentially that the superpower détente process is appreciated in Washington and both superpowers accept the fundamental balance of power realities in the world. China is blamed for encouraging anti-détente forces and for having cards played in an anti-Soviet fashion.[99] On the radical end of the spectrum the essential argument is that the US is not committed to détente. Washington plays the China card as part of its global anti-Soviet policy and the PRC is largely a pawn in the American game.[100] A middle ground, along with various nuances, can be identified combining aspects of both policies. This centre ground shifts to a certain extent in response to specific events but essentially argues that although the anti-Soviet card playing circles in the US are important, the process of détente is overwhelmingly important even for US decision makers. Relations with the US should therefore be pursued, albeit cautiously.[101] The election speeches for the Supreme Soviet made in February 1979 offer a useful basis of comparison in order to highlight the policy divergences. Seven leaders' statements can be compared on three major issues:[102] Do they favour détente, do they see the Chinese problem as very serious, do they see US connivance with China as a serious problem? The cross cutting cleavages on these issues are numerous but four positions can be isolated. The moderates are those favouring détente with the West, perceiving the Chinese threat as a significant problem and minimizing the connivance of the West with China. Brezhnev and Kirilenko are the most clear-cut examples. The second view appears to be the idiosyncratic one of Foreign Minister Gromyko whose position is akin to the moderates except that he takes great exception to Sino-American connivance. Perhaps Gromyko stands out as one of those who believe that détente is important, but find the 'playing of cards' in the triangle a transgression of tripolar rules. The third group is firmly centrist viewing détente, the Chinese threat and US-PRC connivance with relatively equal concern. The military seems to fall into this category as epitomized by Ustinov, but it also covers such figures as Kosygin. The final group is somewhat more diverse, but united in their relative disbelief in the importance of détente. As led by Andropov, one strand does not see the Chinese threat as especially significant and is very concerned about the US manipulation of cards in the triangle. M. Suslov on the other hand sees the PRC threat as crucial and takes a far less alarmist view of US-PRC collusion. Thus the balance in the Soviet leadership is delicate, with a myriad of opinions represented. It is no wonder that the Kremlin's position on the triangle has shifted regularly, but not in a sudden fashion. The bewildering options and subtle developments in triangular politics apparently have bred caution and conservatism in the Soviet attitude.

When analysing an even larger number of speeches a year later, and following the invasion of Afghanistan, it was next to impossible to identify a significant divergence in policy on triangular issues.[103] Perhaps this was because the moderates were forced to trim their sails in the face of strong anti-American winds in Moscow after the Afghan invasion, but whatever the cause, the general conclusions seemed to be that the US was the prime anti-Soviet force, not China, and there was little talk of collusion. Bilateral relations, especially with the US, seemed to predominate. The moderate voices, such as they were, persisted, but were now arguing even more forcefully for the need for détente.[104] In this respect they shared a view with the centrist majority, i.e. that US-Soviet relations were paramount and that triangular issues were less important. It seems that in crisis, card playing and tripolar politics are less important in Moscow and therefore are less likely to be useful in pressuring the USSR.

One of the more significant conclusions to be drawn from this breakdown of the Soviet political spectrum is that it is difficult to formulate a linkage policy towards the USSR if there is a shifting policy in Moscow. Nevertheless, if the West does seek to encourage moderate forces, an important question would be: What kind of policy would be best suited to the task?[105] There seems to be a process of interaction between moderate and radical forces both in the US and USSR. The moderates in Moscow appear to be those who see the moderates in the West as dominant and basically believe in the big power 'realities' and the 'correlation of forces'. They are not swayed by short-term linkage games although a certain degree of Sino-American trade and normal relations are accepted. The moderates see the West as confused but a necessary 'partner' in détente. On the other hand, to engage in linkage games would be to play into the hands of the radical anti-détente forces; those who see the West as unreliable and struggling in a last ditch attempt to save itself by aligning with China. These radical forces are also more likely to be sympathetic to a potential Chinese argument that the real danger lies in the US and that there should be a return to a Sino-Soviet alignment against Washington. Thus, to the extent that the differences of opinion have an effect on the formulation of the Kremlin's policy in the triangle, the West must be particularly careful how it plays games in a tripolar world.

Trends in the Triangle

The Soviet Union clearly has an understanding of the triangle's operation and certain policy divergences in Moscow can be identified, but what of the overall judgement of tripolarity? Does Moscow feel that triangular strategy has been effective and how important is the China factor likely to be in the future?

At first glance the USSR clearly claims success in warding off triangular politics. The correlation of forces is such that the power of the USSR and 'its socialist allies' continues to grow and problems in Sino-Western ties continue to increase.[106] Events in Kampuchea, Angola, Ethiopia, Mozambique and Afghanistan are all cited as examples. China's internal weakness and Western self doubts about China are said to reinforce the positive trend for the USSR. The non-aligned refuse Chinese overtures and West European states by and large decline to enter into an anti-Soviet coalition.[107] Although factions in the USSR may disagree on the degree to which the triangle has been unsuccessful, the ideological notions of the forward march of history tend to mean that almost all pronouncements on the triangle are couched in optimistic language. In this vein the Chinese theory of 'three worlds', which is said to underlie Peking's approach to the triangle, is deemed to be not 'Marxist-Leninist' and 'has nothing in common with the actual alignment of class forces in the modern world'. 'It is only logical that this theory and the policy based on it are suffering one setback after another.'[108]

As already noted the ideologically based denunciations of tripolarity do not mean that the USSR does not accept its relevance for the present situation. While stressing the long-term inevitability of its view, the Kremlin is able to accept in the short term that some tripolar problems are real. The deterioration in relations with the US is said to be in part due to the Chinese tripolar tactics, and the inability to progress in Sino-Soviet relations is similarly attributed in part to US machinations in the triad.[109] At times these global problems are seen as 'particularly urgent' and the failure of previous

Soviet warnings are lamented. Conflicts around the globe, such as the Sino-Vietnamese war, are said to be in part caused by tripolar manoeuvres, so clearly the great power triangle is policy relevant for Moscow. As indicated above, the USSR's preferred reaction to these 'short-term' problems is to refuse to play tripolar games and proceed in a careful and cautious manner. Perhaps more than the US or PRC, the USSR has a grasp of the complexity of the great power triangle, for it certainly has accepted the importance of a Chinese factor in the strategic balance.[110]

What allows the USSR to be so optimistic in the long term and not in the short term is its views on likely international trends. As has already been pointed out, the US is seen as eventually recognizing that there is no reasonable alternative to détente. However, this is based on an assessment of the 'middle term' wherein the West wakes up to the dangers of arming China much like the allies in the Second World War woke up to the threat from Hitler. As Leonid Brezhnev declared,

> Plans to use the new stronger regime in Peking as a weapon in NATO's policies . . . [are] nothing more than cocksure naivety. It is enough to recall how the Munich policies ended for Western powers. Can it really be that the lessons of history are so soon forgotten?[111]

This analogy to the Second World War for the present international situation is also used in the USSR, but in a different way than in the West. Once the short-lived gains of the 'naive' and 'dangerous' in playing the China card are seen as not worth the candle, the long-term trend to détente will win out. Sino-American conflict of some sort is seen as inevitable by Moscow and thus the triangle will collapse.[112] One Soviet commentator has said, '. . . But those who regard politics as a card-game probably forget the rule that in no games of chance is there a system that guarantees a win . . .'[113] Because China plays its own game, Western Europe was reminded 'It should not be forgotten that the distance separating China from those countries is not so long in our nuclear age.'[114] Thus card games and linkage are not seen as effective policies, particularly in the long term.

Whether or not this is the true feeling of the Soviet leadership is difficult to ascertain. By minimizing the China factor perhaps the USSR seeks to deny the US leverage it might have in Sino-Soviet relations, but since the early 1960s this has seemed less likely. Soviet expressions to the US of deep concern and 'neuralgia' on the subject of China would seem to indicate that the USSR accepts the relevance of the tripolar system.[115] Even moderate voices in the USSR on the subject of China accept that at best Sino-Soviet relations would be similar to Yugoslav-Soviet ties.[116] Soviet troop deployments and efforts in SALT to include the China factor reinforce this point. What is perhaps more likely is that by assuming that all problems are temporary and will be solved by the 'correlation of forces' at some future date, the ideological problems are dealt with and the leaders are then able to debate the here and now in a more pragmatic fashion.[117] Present and future are then linked and the triangle becomes an acceptable concept so long as referred to obliquely. As one commentator noted in reference to the triangle, 'In the present conditions, given the present balance of forces, the future undoubtedly lies with the policy of detente . . .'[118] It is important to note that even the future may be tripolar if for some reason those who take upon themselves a 'truly historic responsibility' continue to play triangular games.[119] According to Henry Kissinger, Soviet Ambassador Dobrynin 'suggested that there was still time for the two superpowers to order events, but they might not have this power much longer.' Soviet soundings of the Americans on a surgical strike against China are a vivid case in point.[120] Thus at the present time the China factor must be continually assessed, especially since Chinese policy is seen as the main cause of tripolar problems.[121] As has already been demonstrated, in the Soviet view certain aspects of the international system, for example deterrence or politics in Asia, have taken on distinctly tripolar features. The balance of political, economic and military factors and the way they are used in relations with various states determines the specific way in which the USSR views the triangle in these areas. While making overall judgement on the Soviet perception of tripolarity next to impossible, it does not negate the importance of these concepts for Soviet policy. Similarly the existence of various policy differences in Moscow on the great power triangle makes it difficult to isolate a clear Soviet policy, but serves to emphasize the importance of the tripolar perspective in analysing USSR foreign policy.

In sum, the USSR has come to accept, at least for the present, the importance of the China factor in the strategic balance and a degree of tripolarity. It is clear however that the USSR responds differently to various types of tactics in the triangle. Attempts to pressure

Moscow by worsening superpower ties and improving US-PRC ties will not work, whereas the Kissinger tripolar policy of simultaneous improvement in US-USSR and US-PRC ties is somewhat more likely to be successful. The former is a negative policy while the latter is a positive manipulation of triangular forces. This cautious and incremental policy suits Moscow well and when manifest, for example in moderate West European policy in the triangle, the Kremlin rarely complains. As the US moves to the extreme policy of card playing, the gap with its allies is likely to open wider. Ironically, Moscow may then find it possible to play its own cards against Washington.

Notes

1. Gerald Segal, *The Great Power Triangle, 1961–1968*, London: Macmillan, 1982.

2. Henry Kissinger, *The White House Years*, London: Weidenfeld and Nicolson/Michael Joseph, 1979.

3. Michael Pillsbury, *Soviet Apprehensions About Sino-American Relations 1971–4*, P-5459, Santa Monica: Rand Corp, June 1975 and 'Future Sino-American Security Ties: The View From Tokyo, Moscow and Peking', *International Security*, Vol. 1, No. 4, Spring 1977. Morris Rothenberg, *Whither China: The View From the Kremlin*, Miami: Center for Advanced International Studies, 1978. Kenneth Lieberthal, *Sino-Soviet Conflict in the 1970's: Its Evolution and Implications for the Strategic Triangle*, R-2342-NA, Santa Monica: Rand Corp, July 1978.

4. N. Kapchenko, 'Beijing Policy: Calculation and Miscalculation', *International Affairs*, July 1979, and V. Kuzmin, 'China in Washington's Aggressive Policy', *International Affairs*, April 1980.

5. For example Tass, 9 May 1980 in *The Times*, 10 May 1980.

6. Rothenberg, *Whither China*, p. 254.

7. E. Stuart Kirby, *Russian Studies of China*, London: Macmillan, 1975, and Oded Eran, *The Mezhdunarorniki*, Ramat Gan, Israel: Turtledove Press, 1979.

8. 'Peking's Foreign Policy: Hegemonism and Alliance with Imperialism', *International Affairs*, March 1980, p. 47, and Y. Semyonov, 'Beijing's Policy Constitutes a Military Threat', *International Affairs*, April 1979. V. Petukhow, 'PRC-WA: A Threat to Peace and Security', *Far Eastern Affairs*, No.3, 1980.

9. I. Ivkov, 'USA: Playing the "Chinese Card" in Asia', *Far Eastern Affairs*, No. 2, 1979.

10. Ibid., and V. Krivtsov, 'The Maoist's Foreign Policy Strategy', *Far Eastern Affairs*, No. 3, 1978.

11. A. Titov, 'Peking and the American Lobby', *Far Eastern Affairs*, No. 4, 1978, and Kuzmin, 'China in Washington's Policy'.

12. Krivtsov, 'Maoist Foreign Policy'; V. Borisov, 'Peking: A Destructive Policy', *FEA*, No. 3, 1980.

13. Also F. Divov, 'A Policy of Provocation and War', *Far Eastern Affairs*, No. 2, 1978. G. Apalin, 'Peking: Militarism and War Mongering', *International Affairs*, April 1978. Also 'Peking, the West and Detente', *International Affairs*, Feb. 1979. A. Apalin, 'Peking: A Course Towards Provoking a World War', *Far Eastern Affairs*, No. 3, 1979, and Borisov, 'A Destructive Policy'.

14. Round Table, 'Some Aspects of Peking's Home and Foreign Policy', *Far*

Eastern Affairs, No. 2, 1979, and Kapchenko, 'Beijing Policy' and 'Peking's Foreign Policy'. Petukhov, 'PRC-USA'.

15. Ibid., and G. Arbatov, *Observer*, Nov. 12, 1978, and V. Timoshin, Tass comment, 6 Dec. 1978 in *BBC*/SWB/SU/B5998/A3/2. M. Georgiyev in *Pravda*, 19 Dec., No. 5999/A3/1.

16. *International Herald Tribune*, 28 Dec. 1978.

17. Apalin, 'Peking, the West and Detente' and 'Peking's Foreign Policy'. Also A. Bovin, *Izvestia*. Moscow Home Service, 13 Jan. 1979. *BBC*/SWB/SU/6017/A1/2.

18. Comment by V. Alenin, Radio Peace and Progress in English for Asia. 31 Jan. 1979. *BBC*/SWB/SU/6034/A3/2. Comment by I. Dmitryev, Moscow Radio in English, 15 Sept. 1979. No. 6221/A3/1. Comment by V. Yelyutin, Moscow in English for N. America, 7 Nov. 1979. No. 6268/A1/2.

19. Apalin, 'Peking, the West and Detente'.

20. *Time*, 6 Nov. 1978, p. 43.

21. For example, V. Kozyakov, Comment, Radio Moscow in English for N. America, 11 May 1979. *BBC*/SWB/SU/6115/A3/2.

22. For example, Mitin Comment Radio Moscow in standard Chinese 4 Oct. 1979. *BBC*/SWB/SU/6239/A3/1 and N. Nitkin, *Pravda*, 15 Jan. 1980. *Current Digest of the Soviet Press*, Vol. 32, No. 2, 13 Feb. 1980, p. 8.

23. Petukhov, 'PRC-USA'. See also the visit of Geng Biao to the US in May 1980, especially I. Alexsandrov, 27 May 1980. *BBC*/SWB/SU/6430/A3/1–3. Also Tass, 30 May in No. 6434/A3/4 and comment by Y. Kornilov in Tass in Russian, 5 June 1980 in No. 6439/A3/1.

24. Kuzmin, 'China in Washington's Policy'. Krasnaya Zvezda article reported by Tass, 13 Jan. 1980, *BBC*/SWB/SU/6319/A3/1.

25. On 23 September 1980, *Soviet News*, 30 Sept. 1980. See also V. Borisov, 'Peking: A Destructive Policy', *Far Eastern Affairs*, No. 3, 1980.

26. Comments on the visit of Zhang Wenyin to the US. V. Fedorov, Radio Peace and Progress in English for Asia. 18 March 1980, and V. Shragin, Radio Moscow 19 March, both in *BBC*/SWB/SU/6377/A3/1–2.

27. Kissinger, *White House Years*, for example p. 183. Also John Newhouse, *Cold Dawn*, New York: Harper and Row, 1973.

28. V. Pavlov and A. Karenin, 'SALT-2-Its Content and Importance', *International Affairs*, Nov. 1979; Apalin, 'Peking: Militarism', and S. Losev, comment Radio Moscow in English for N. America, 7 Feb. 1979 in *BBC*/SWB/SU/6038/A3/3.

29. Strobe Talbott, *Endgame*, New York: Harper and Row, 1979, and see 13 May 1980, Krasnaya Zvezda. *BBC*/SWB/SU/6422/A1/2.

30. Edward Warner III, 'Soviet Strategic Force Posture: Some Alternative Explanations', Frank Horton (ed.), *Comparative Defense Policy*, Baltimore: Johns Hopkins Press, 1974 and William Garner, 'SALT II: China's Advice and Dissent', *Asian Survey*, Vol. 19, No. 12.

31. See for example V. Baburov, 'Disarmament: Peking Obstruction', *New Times*, No. 39, 1980, and Borisov, 'A Destructive Policy'.

32. Robert North, 'The Soviet Far East: New Centre of Attention in the USSR', *Pacific Affairs*, Vol. 51, No. 2, summer 1978. Drew Middleton, *The Duel of the Giants* New York: Charles Scribner's Sons, 1978. Victor Louis, *The Coming Decline of the Chinese Empire*, New York: Times Books, 1979.

33. Lilita Dzirkals, *Lightening War in Manchuria: Soviet Military Analysis of the 1945 Far East Campaign*, P-5589, Santa Monica: The Rand Corp., Jan. 1976, and John Despres, Lilita Dzirkals, Barton Whaley, *Timely Lessons of History: The Manchurian Model for Soviet Strategy*, R-1825-NA, Santa Monica: Rand Corp., July 1976.

34. Testimony to the Subcommittee on Priorities and Economy in Government of

the Joint Economic Committee. 95th Congress 2nd Session, June 26, July 14, 1978. 'Allocation of Resources in the Soviet Union and China—1978'.

35. NATO sources cited in the *International Herald Tribune*, 23 May 1980.
36. NATO sources cited in the *International Herald Tribune*, 26 May 1980.
37. US State Department officials cited in the *Observer*, 1 June 1980.
38. Lieberthal, *Sino-Soviet Conflict in the 1970's*.
39. Comment by N. Kozakov, Radio Moscow in English for N. America, 16 May 1980. *BBC*/SWB/SU/6423/A3/2, and from 'USA: Economics Politics and Ideology' on Tass 11 Aug. 1980, in No. 6496/A3/3.
40. Commentary on Radio Peace and Progress in Chinese, 15 Oct. 1980, in *BBC*/SWB/SU/6571/A3/1.
41. Kapchenko, 'Beijing Policy', and Divov, 'A Policy of Provocation'.
42. V. Semyonov, 'Peking's Policy Constitutes a Military Threat', *International Affairs*, April 1979.
43. Ivkov, 'USA: Playing the Chinese Card', and Apalin, 'Peking: Militarism'.
44. For example comment by N. Fedorov, Radio Peace and Progress in English for Asia, 19 Dec. 1979, *BBC*/SWB/SU/6304/A3/1.
45. Pillsbury, 'Future Sino-American Security Ties', and Donald Zagoria, 'The Soviet Quandary in Asia', *Foreign Affairs*, Vol. 56, No. 2, Jan. 1978. Also, 'Peking's Foreign Policy', Divov, 'A Policy of Provocation', Apalin, 'Peking, the West and Detente,' and Ivkov, 'USA: Playing the Chinese Card'.
46. Soviet sources in Ibid.
47. Apalin, 'Peking the West and Detente', and Divov, 'A Policy of Provocation'.
48. Ivkov, 'USA: Playing the Chinese Card', and Segal, *The Great Power Triangle*, Report of 2 Sept. *Pravda* article by Ustinov. *Soviet News*, 9 Sept. 1980, p. 275.
49. On the war and Soviet comment see, for example, 'The Lessons of Peking's Adventure in Vietnam', *Far Eastern Affairs*, No. 3, 1979, and Tass, 5 March 1979 in *Soviet News*, No. 5963, 13 March 1979, and Y. Zhukov, *Pravda*, 5 March 1979, in *CDSP*, Vol. 31, No. 9, p. 9. Also on the war see Gerald Segal, 'China and the Great Power Triangle', *The China Quarterly*, No. 83, Sept. 1980. Harlan Jencks, 'China's Punitive War on Vietnam, A Military Assessment', *Asian Survey*, Vol. 19, No. 8, Aug. 1979.
50. N. Kapchenko, 'The Threat to Peace From Peking's Hegemonistic Policy', *International Affairs*, Feb. 1980.
51. Divov, 'A Policy of Provocation' and 'Peking's Foreign Policy'.
52. Divov, 'A Policy of Provocation'.
53. Ibid. and especially S. Yurkov, 'China and Western Europe', *Far Eastern Affairs*, No. 4, 1979.
54. Apalin, 'Peking, the West and Detente'.
55. Yurkov, 'China and Western Europe' and reports of Soviet comment in October 1979 in *BBC*/SWB/SU/6252/A3/1, No. 6258/A3/2, No. 6259/A3/1.
56. Yurkov, 'China and Western Europe', and Apalin, 'Peking, the West and Detente'. See also the EEC and China in *Soviet News*, 24 June 1980.
57. Interview with Jonathan Power, *Observer*, 12 Nov. 1978.
58. This issue appears in all previous comments on West Europe listed above as well as Kapchenko, 'The Threat to Peace', V. Matveyev, in *Izvestia*. Tass 8 Jan. 1979 in *BBC*/SWB/SU/6021/A1/1, also No. 6158/A3/1−2 and 6219/A3/1, and comment by V. Chalin, Radio Peace and Progress in English for Asia, 18 Dec. 1979, in No. 6302/As/3-4. Petukhov 'PRC-USA'.
59. Based on Yurkov, 'China and Western Europe', and especially A. Larin, 'Britain in China's Foreign Policy', *Far Eastern Affairs*, No. 3, 1979.
60. Yurkov, 'China and Western Europe', and Apalin, 'Peking, the West and Detente'.

61. Larin, 'Britain in China's Foreign Policy'.

62. On the Hua visit see, for example, V. Shragin comment on Moscow world service, 6 Nov. 1979, in *BBC*/SWB/SU/6266/A3/1, and A. Bovin in *Izvestia*, 10 Nov. 1979 in No. 6270/A3/1–3, and Yurkov, 'China and Western Europe'.

63. S. Yurkov, 'China's Shadow Over South Asia and the Middle East', *Far Eastern Affairs*, No. 3, 1979. Yu. Ryakin and V. Stepanov, 'The Nonaligned Movement and Peking's Intrigues', *Far Eastern Affairs*, No. 1, 1980. Y. Semyonov, 'Peking and the National Liberation Movement', *International Affairs*, January 1980. V. Krivtsov, 'China's Anti-Socialist Policy Vis-a-Vis Developing States', *Far Eastern Affairs*, No. 3, 1980.

64. Especially Ryakin and Stepanov, 'The Nonaligned Movement', and for a vague non-committal Soviet view on collusion see 'China connives with USA in the Militarization of Indian Ocean', *Soviet News*, 2 September 1980, p. 271. On the Gulf and other arenas also in the vague vein see Moscow in Arabic, 29 May 1980, in *BBC*/SWB/SU/A4/2, and Radio Peace and Progress in English for Asia, 28 April 1980, in No. 6411/A3/2, where it was said that 'almost everywhere co-ordinate their action'.

65. N. Nitkin, *Pravda*, 15 Jan. 1980, in *CDSP*, Vol. 32, No. 2, 13 Feb. 1980, p. 8, and comment by N. Gradov on Radio Peace and Progress in English for Asia in *BBC*/SWB/SU/6287/A3/6–7. Also Tass in Russian for abroad, 28 April 1980, in No. 6411/A4/2.

66. Ibid. and Tass in Russian for abroad, 27 June 1979, in *BBC*/SWB/SU/6154/A3/1 and A. Petrov in *Pravda*, 31 Dec. 1979, in No. 6038/A3/1–4, and Petukhov, 'PRC-USA' and Radio Moscow home service, 20 May 1980, in No. 6426/C/3–4 and also No. 6418/C/2–3.

67. Tass in Russian from Peking, 2 Jan. 1980. *BBC*/SWB/SU/6310/C/8 and comment by A. Bokhonko, Tass, 4 Jan. 1980, in No. 6313/A3/1 and N. Fedorov in *Izvestia*, 13 Feb. 1980, in No. 6346/A3/1.

68. For example Ivkov, 'USA: Playing the Chinese Card', Kuzmin, 'China in Washington's Policy', and Kapchenko, 'Beijing Policy'.

69. Kapchenko, 'The Threat to Peace'.

70. For example the 1979 Soviet sale of helicopters to China. *Observer*, 1 June 1980.

71. Note 68 and Y. Shalygin, comment on Radio Moscow, 18 Dec. 1978, in *BBC*/SWB/SU/5998/A3/2.

72. Ivkov, 'USA: Playing the Chinese Card', p. 86.

73. Semyonov, 'Beijing's Policy'. See also the favourable comment on Secretary Vance's moderate line, Radio Moscow in English for N. America, 7 June 1980, *BBC*/SWB/SU/6441/A3/2.

74. Moscow Home Service, 13 Jan. 1979, in *BBC*/SWB/SU/6017/A1/2. See also Moscow radio in standard Chinese for China, 2 Feb. 1979, in No. 6035/A3/1–5.

75. Also Divov, 'A Policy of Provocation', Krivtsov, 'The Maoists Foreign Policy', and Kapchenko, 'The Threat to Peace', and Y. Yelyutin, comment. Moscow in English for North America, *BBC*/SWB/SU/6268/A1/2.

76. For example 'Peking's Foreign Policy'.

77. V. Zorin, 'Moscow Viewpoint', Moscow in English for N. America, 12 May 1979, in *BBC*/SWB/SU/6117/A3/1–2.

78. See 'The Triangle in Europe' section in this chapter and Apalin, 'Peking, the West and Detente', and Larin, 'Britain in China's Foreign Policy'.

79. Apalin, 'Peking, the West and Detente'.

80. Generally see 'A New Stage', p. 37.

81. S. Kondrashov, *Izvestia*, Tass, 7 Feb. 1979, in *BBC*/SWB/SU/6038/A3/3–4.

82. For example, *Pravda* 'rejoinder', M. Georgiyev, Tass in Russian, 19 Dec. 1978, in *BBC*/SWB/SU/5999/A3/1. A. Bovin, *Izvestia*, Moscow Home Service, 13 Jan. 1980, No. 6017/A1/2. Petukhov, 'PRC-USA'.

83. *Izvestia*, Tass, 7 Jan. 1980, in *BBC*/SWB/SU/6314/A3/1.

84. Comment by Lovrov, Moscow in Standard Chinese, 12 Jan. 1980, in *BBC*/SWB/SU/6319/A3/3 and *Pravda* article, Tass, 14 Jan. 1980, in No. 6322/A3/1. Comment by I. Dmitriyev, Moscow in English for N. America, 11 Feb. 1980, No. 6344/A3/3.

85. Tass comment by V. Nashedchenko, 20 May 1980, in *BBC*/SWB/SU/6426/A3/1. Tass, 30 May 1980, in No. 6434/A3/4, and Tass comment by Y. Kornilov, 5 June 1980, in No. 6439/A3/1.

86. Radio Moscow, 27 May 1980, *BBC*/SWB/SU/6430/A3/1–3.

87. Kapchenko, 'Beijing's Policy' and 'The Threat to Peace', and comment by N. Timoshin in Russian for Abroad, 5 Jan. 1979, *BBC*/SWB/SU/6010/A1/1, and V. Matveyev in *Izvestia*, Tass, 8 Jan. 1979, in No. 6021/A1/a.

88. Ivkov, 'USA: Playing the Chinese Card'.

89. A. Bovin in *Izvestia*, Moscow Home Service, 13 Jan. 1979, in *BBC*/SWB/SU/6017/A1/2.

90. Y. Yelyutin, comment Radio Moscow in English for N. America, 7 Nov. 1979, in *BBC*/SWB/SU/6268/A1/2.

91. See *Pravda* article, 6 Jan. 1979, broadcast in English on Radio Moscow World Service which linked SALT to normalization but in Russian for abroad on 7 Jan. it did not. *BBC*/SWB/SU/6010/A1/1–2. Also on linkage see Talbott, *Endgame*.

92. Kuzmin, 'China in Washington's Policy', p. 28.

93. Segal, *The Great Power Triangle*, and Kissinger, *The White House Years*, pp. 171–3, 184, 187, 524, 548–9, 554–5, 712, 725, 731, 735, 763–8. Talbott, *Endgame*.

94. Kuzmin, 'China in Washington's Policy'.

95. Segal, *The Great Power Triangle*.

96. I. Alexsandrov, *Pravda*, 10 Feb. 1979, in *BBC*/SWB/SU/6040/A3/1. Soviet government statement, Feb. 18, 1979, No. 6046/A3/1, and I. Alexsandrov in *Pravda*, Feb. 28 1979. *Soviet News*, No. 5962, March 6 1979, pp. 70–1.

97. Segal, *The Great Power Triangle*.

98. Soviet comments on the US turning a blind eye to the Chinese attack are frequent. See for example statements in note 49 and S. Kulik, Tass political observer, 22 Feb. 1979, in *BBC*/SWB/SU/6051/A3/1 A. Petrov, comment Moscow Home Service, 26 Feb. 1979, in No. 6053/a/3, and 'Moscow Mailbag', 11 March 1979, in No. 6065/A1/2–3.

99. For example V. Zorin, 20 Dec. 1978, *BBC*/SWB/SU/6000/A3/1–2. V. Pozner, 13 Jan. 1979, Radio Moscow, in No. 6018/A1/4–5. Mitin comment, 9 Feb. 1979, Radio Moscow in Chinese, in No. 6040/A3/2–3. A. Bovin, *Izvestia*, 19 Feb. 1979, in No. 6050/A3/2.

100. For example S. Losev, 19 Dec. 1978, in *BBC*/SWB/SU/6000/A3/1. V. Bolshakov in *Pravda*, 24 Dec. 1978, in *CDSP*, Vol. 30, No. 51, p. 3. Glebov, comment, 19 Feb. 1979, Radio Peace and Progress, *BBC*/SWB/SU/6050/A3/102.

101. Brezhnev letter in *International Herald Tribune*, 22 Dec. 1978, and *Time* magazine, in *BBC*/SWB/SU/6018/C2/1–3. *Pravda*, 4 Feb. 1979, in No. 6035/A3/1–2. A. Petrov, in *Pravda*, 19 Feb. 1979, in No. 6048/A3/1–2. Krasnaya Zvezda reported in Radio Peace and Progress, 21 Feb. 1979, in No. 6050/A3/3.

102. All references to this data is based on the following. Although it was considered that the dates of the speeches could account for the differences, no such trend is apparent. It should be noted that the differences are relative and all the positions can be seen as lying on a continuum where some disagreements are ones of degree. Y. Andropov, 22 Feb., *Soviet News*, No. 5961, 27 Feb. 1979, p. 64. D. Ustinov, 23 Feb. Ibid., p. 57, and also I.G. Pavlovsky, the commander of land forces, on 22 Feb., both in *BBC*/SWB/SU/6052/C/2–4. A. Gromyko, 26 Feb., *Soviet News*, No. 5962, 6 March 1979, pp. 74–5. A. Kirilenko, 27 Feb., in *BBC*/SWB/SU/6055/C/203. M. Suslov, 28 Feb., No. 6056/C/1–2, A. Kosygin, 1 March, *Soviet News*, No. 5962,

p. 72. L. Brezhnev, 2 March, Ibid., pp. 65–7.

103. Twenty-two Soviet leaders' election speeches from 30 Jan. to 22 Feb. 1980 were analysed as reported in issues of *BBC*/SWB/SU covering this period.

104. Moderate views of G. Arbatov in *Pravda*, 3 March 1980, *BBC*/SWB/SU/6361/C/1, and V. Falin on Moscow World Service discussion programme, 2 March 1980, p. C/4. For the centrist military view see Krasnaya Zvezda, Tass, 4 March 1980, in No. 6362/C/3.

105. More generally on this issue see Morton Schwartz, *Soviet Perceptions of the United States*, Berkeley: University of California Press, 1978.

106. 'Peking's Foreign Policy' and Apalin, 'Peking, the West and Detente', Ivkov, 'USA: Playing the Chinese Card', Kuzmin, 'China in Washington's Policy'.

107. Ryakin and Stepanov, 'The Nonaligned Movement', Yurkov, 'China and Western Europe' and S. Kondrashov, in *Izvestia*, Tass, 7 Feb. 1979, in *BBC*/SWB/SU/6038/A3/4.

108. Kapchenko, 'The Threat to Peace', p. 72.

109. Kapchenko, 'Peking's Policy' and 'Peking's Foreign Policy', and V. Timoshin, comment in Russian for abroad, 5 Jan. 1979, in *BBC*/SWB/SU/6010/A1/1.

110. N. Shishlin comment, Radio Moscow in English for N. America, 8 Jan. 1979, *BBC*/SWB/SU/6021/A1/3, and Kuzmin, 'China in Washington's Policy'.

111. *Pravda*, 16 Jan. 1979, quoted in Ivkov, 'USA: Playing the Chinese Card'.

112. Generally, Titov, 'Peking and the American Lobby', Apalin, 'Peking, the West and Detente', and V. Falin on Moscow World Service discussion programme, 2 March 1980, *BBC*/SWB/SU/6361/C/4, and Krivtsov, 'The Maoists Foreign Policy', and Kapchenko, 'Peking's Policy'.

113. A. Petrov, Moscow Home Service, 26 Feb. 1979, *BBC*/SWB/SU/6053/A3/3.

114. V. Gorcharov, Tass in Russian, 8 Sept. 1979, *BBC*/SWB/SU/6219/A3/1. See also Kapchenko, 'Peking's Policy'.

115. Dobrynin to Kissinger, 20 Jan. 1970. Kissinger, *The White House Years*, p. 524.

116. *Observer*, 20 April 1980, on Soviet academics' views of China.

117. This is not to suggest that ideology is merely a long-term consideration and of no value in the short term. Essentially there is no ideologically preferable course considering the choice of better Soviet-American or Sino-Soviet relations. In as much as ideology is therefore reduced to a minimal guide in these matters, it therefore does not pose the problem of one policy being ideologically superior.

118. N. Shishlin, Moscow Home Service, 18 Dec. 1978, *BBC*/SWB/SU/5999/A3/1.

119. Ibid. and V. Timoshin, comment Radio Moscow in Russian for abroad, 5 Jan. 1979, *BBC*/SWB/SU/6010/A1/1.

120. Kissinger, *The White House Years*, p. 173, and August 1969 meeting, pp. 183–4.

121. See 'Strategic Aspects' section in this chapter and Ibid. p. 172, when Dobrynin told Kissinger that China was everybody's problem. Also Kapchenko, 'Beijing's Policy'.

4 THE UNITED STATES AND THE GREAT POWER TRIANGLE

Banning Garrett

The strategic relationship between the United States, the Soviet Union and China has formed the context for US policy analysis and decision making toward the People's Republic of China since the early 1970s. Bilateral issues between Peking and Washington, including Taiwan, have been important but ultimately secondary concerns. Virtually all key US policy makers have viewed Sino-American relations through the lens of the strategic triangle.

There has been an evolution of US China policy in the triangle over three administrations. The Nixon administration, by responding to Chinese feelers for *rapprochement*, made the triangular relationship operative with both China and the Soviet Union seeking to improve their ties with Washington in the 1971–3 period. The Ford administration, while continuing the Nixon administration's publicly defined policy of 'evenhandedness' toward China and the Soviet Union, began a secret debate over 'tilting' toward China in the triangular relationship. This debate centred on the notion of establishing 'military ties' with China — moves ranging from initial steps such as exchanging military attachés, allowing Western European arms sales, or selling advanced US technology with military applications to the Chinese. Other possible steps were alliance-like defence relations with China, including military training, joint contingency planning and manoeuvres, joint production of intelligence, and co-ordinated strategic action against the Soviet Union on a global scale, as well as direct sales of lethal arms to China. The first cautious moves in this direction were made in 1975–6, although evenhandedness was maintained as the official policy. The Ford administration bequeathed to the Carter administration in January 1977 a bitter struggle over this idea — which came to be known as 'playing the China card'. After initially rejecting it, Carter decided to play the China card in May 1978. Over the following year and a half, a series of key decisions were made leading to the development of an overt Sino-American military relationship in 1980.

The US-Chinese defence relationship inherited by the Reagan

administration in 1981 represented neither a long-term strategy nor a consensus among policy makers. Policy struggles over how far to go in developing US-Chinese military ties had continued in the Carter administration until the end. Each new move in that direction was bitterly contested by officials who wanted to maintain an ostensibly 'evenhanded' policy. Nevertheless, the President made specific policy decisions that moved the US step by step closer to China. Despite the appearance of seesaw battles between Carter administration officials on the China issue, the opponents of 'tilting' toward China won only temporary victories which amounted to slowing the development of such ties, not to a reversal in direction of US policy.

Decisions to move forward in military ties were made in the context of crises or chronic worsening in US-Soviet relations and of Chinese pressure to improve Sino-American ties. Triangular interactions influenced the balance of power between factions in the administration, often by undermining the opponents of military ties with China whose argument that such ties would be too provocative toward Moscow, lost currency as the Soviets increasingly became seen as aggressive and engaged in a threatening military build-up.

The result of this process of triangular interactions and bureaucratic politics was a series of discreet moves toward military ties with China — decisions, for example, to sell China advanced computers with military applications, to allow Western European arms sales to China, to send the Secretary of Defense to Peking, and to permit transfer of non-lethal US military equipment to the Chinese. According to participants in many of the key meetings at which these decisions were made, no long-term policy or strategy implications of the particular move were discussed, much less agreed to. Only the issue at hand, such as whether or not to send the Secretary of Defense to China, was decided, with proponents hoping to push the policy forward another step the next time, and opponents trying to minimize the damage of the decision and hoping to halt forward movement at that point.

This process led to the emergence of the Sino-American military relationship and then its strengthening as US-Soviet relations worsened. Proponents of military ties with China pushed for moves in that direction continuously, gaining presidential approval for specific steps in response to crises in US-Soviet relations and the President's search for measures to punish and pressure Moscow (as well as in response to Chinese pressure for forward movement in

Sino-American relations). One consequence of this process is that there have been no 'carrots' for Moscow: the US had only the stick of another step toward China with which to threaten the Soviets.

The process of decision making in the US and the nature of triangular interactions is of course very complex and variegated over time. The above outline of the process is an attempt to identify some patterns in these phenomena in order to answer the questions of how and why the US and China developed a military/strategic relationship in the late 1970s, and what exactly has been US policy in the triangle.

Origins of US Triangular Policy

For both the United States and China, strategic concerns about the Soviet Union were at the heart of the 1971–2 *rapprochement*. For President Richard Nixon and his National Security Adviser Henry Kissinger, these strategic motivations included:

(1) Gaining Chinese support for the scaling-down of the US defence posture in Asia, while benefiting from the strategic implications of the Sino-Soviet split that eliminated the need to plan for simultaneous wars against China and the Soviet Union.

(2) Capitalizing on the Sino-Soviet split to gain diplomatic leverage over both the Soviet Union and China.

(3) Heading off a possible Soviet attack on China leading to a Sino-Soviet war — which could become global or which could lead to Soviet domination of China.

(4) Heading off a Sino-Soviet *rapprochement*, which would again raise the prospect of co-ordinated Chinese and Soviet strategy against the US.

In the 1960s, US policy makers had justified US military involvement in Vietnam as necessary to contain China. US forces in Asia and the Pacific had been deployed to meet this objective since the Korean War. The American global military posture presumed a monolithic Soviet and Chinese threat and ostensibly was based on '$2\frac{1}{2}$war' strategy that envisioned fighting major wars simultaneously in Asia against China and in Europe against the Soviet Union — and at the same time meeting a 'minor' contingency elsewhere, such as the Middle East. Kissinger notes in his memoirs that the United States never had sufficient forces to implement such a policy, and that if war broke out simultaneously against the Soviet Union and China, it would therefore be likely to become nuclear. Soon after the Nixon administration came to power in 1969, Kissinger ordered a review of the $2\frac{1}{2}$ war strategy and successfully recommended a scaling down of US military posture to a $1\frac{1}{2}$-war strategy, with the emphasis clearly on planning for a war in Europe against the Soviet Union.[1]

Kissinger has said that in publicly announcing this change in strategy in February 1970, and by reflecting it in US military planning, Washington had sent a signal to Peking: 'We would no longer treat a conflict with the USSR as automatically involving the People's Republic. We would treat our two adversaries on the basis of their actions toward us, not their ideology; we publicly acknowledged their differences and the unlikelihood of their cooperation.'[2]

Nixon and Kissinger hoped that Sino-American reconciliation would elicit Chinese support for stability in Asia while the United States was reducing its force levels in the region. According to Kissinger, they were given such assurances by Chinese leaders in 1972.[3] The Sino-American *rapprochement*, including the shift in US military posture, allowed the Chinese, who had been preparing for a possible two-front war against the United States (and Taiwan) in the south and southeast, and against the Soviet Union in the north and northwest, gradually to focus their military planning primarily on the Soviets. The Soviet Union — which had been building up its military forces in the Far East since 1965 — now faced the prospect of potential US support to China in the event of a Sino-Soviet war, or of a two-front war against China and NATO.

These strategic military factors were part of the perceived benefit for Washington of the global realignment that occurred in 1969–71. Of more immediate concern to Nixon and Kissinger than these strategic factors, however, was capitalizing on the Sino-Soviet split and China's overtures to the US to gain diplomatic leverage over the Soviet Union on SALT, Vietnam and other issues. The Soviets, fearful of potential Sino-American collusion against them, sought to improve relations with the US in competition with Peking. Nixon's dramatic summitry of 1972 consolidated this new situation: within four months, the American President formally established the 'new relationship' with China and détente with the Soviet Union. The Shanghai Communiqué, signed by the President at the end of his February visit to China, set forth the principles of the new

US-Chinese relationship, including a declaration indicating US opposition to any effort by the Soviet Union to dominate China.[4] Nixon then went to Moscow in May where he signed the first US-Soviet strategic arms limitation agreement (SALT I) and the principles for conduct of US-Soviet relations, thus laying the cornerstone for the structure of détente.[5]

Another factor in Nixon and Kissinger's triangular policy was concern to prevent Soviet domination of the People's Republic. Kissinger writes:

> From the beginning Nixon and I were convinced — alone among senior policymakers — that the United States could not accept a Soviet military assault on China. We had held this view before there was contact of any sort; we imposed contingency planning on a reluctant bureaucracy as early as the summer of 1969. Obviously, this reflected no agreement between Peking and Washington. . . . It was based on a sober geopolitical assessment. If Moscow succeeded in humiliating Peking and reducing it to impotence, the whole weight of the Soviet military effort could be thrown against the West. Such a demonstration of Soviet ruthlessness and American impotence (or indifference — the result would be the same) would encourage accommodation to other Soviet demands from Japan to Western Europe, not to speak of the many smaller countries on the Soviet periphery.[6]

During the India-Pakistan War of December 1971 — six months after Kissinger's secret trip to Peking — Nixon and Kissinger apparently were prepared to risk war with the Soviet Union if Moscow attacked China.[7] That contingency did not arise, however, and there is no evidence that US communication with Chinese leaders about Washington's willingness to risk war on China's behalf in that crisis went beyond the strategic signalling of sending a carrier task force to the Bay of Bengal.[8]

Origins of 'Military Ties'

Although it is possible that Chinese leaders personally approached Kissinger about obtaining US arms, he never indicated that such probes had taken place to anyone who revealed the probes to the rest of the government, and no positive response was made to any possible Chinese overtures in the 1971–3 period for arms or other military ties. Kissinger asserted in October 1976, near the end of his tenure in government: 'We have never had any defense discussions with China. We have never had any request for the sale of arms to China. We have never had any discussions with China about the sale of arms.'[9]

Even if Kissinger's statement is accurate that government officials had not held defence discussions with Chinese leaders, such discussions were held on a semi- or quasi-official level beginning in mid-1973 and helped stimulate exploration of the idea of a Sino-American military relationship during the last part of the Nixon administration and throughout the Ford administration.[10] Regular monthly discussions, memoranda of which were distributed within the intelligence community, were held between Michael Pillsbury, then a RAND consultant, and three People's Liberation Army (PLA) attachés to the UN (two generals and an admiral). As a result of these discussions, Pillsbury suggested the idea of military ties with China in a short memo in the fall of 1973. The memo sparked sufficient interest that the Pentagon asked him to expand on his ideas. Pillsbury circulated a detailed study of the issue in March 1974 which was entitled 'L-32' (its RAND designation). According to several sources, L-32 catalogued Chinese probes for Western military technology and other defence ties and outlined Soviet reaction to the possibility of military ties between the US and China. A version of the study, published in September 1975 in *Foreign Policy* under the title 'US-Chinese Military Ties?', suggested a wide range of possible US initiatives to encourage such ties.[11] L-32, in fact, appears to have added up to a plan and rationale for developing a far-reaching defence relationship with China — including virtually all the elements established through the end of the Carter administration. The Pillsbury study remains highly classified, however, and its contents can only be presumed based on the later published version and confirmation by well-informed sources.

In the published version of the study, Pillsbury cited the precedent of US military aid to Yugoslavia in the early 1950s after Tito's break with Stalin and argued that Sino-American military ties could have the following advantages for the United States:

(1) Provide a 'payoff' to Chinese leaders for their opening to the United States, which had been stagnating in the previous year and

thus bolster those in the Chinese leadership fighting to defend that policy. A US military assistance and arms sales programme to China would, in particular, give the PLA a major stake — defence technology — in preserving the Sino-American *rapprochement*.

(2) Help prevent a Sino-Soviet *rapprochement* by maintaining suspicion and tension between Peking and Moscow as well as by tying Chinese leaders to the policy of tilting toward the US.

(3) Indicate a direct US interest in China's security and give Moscow reason to fear American aid to China in the event of a new Sino-Soviet military conflict. Even *discussion* of possible US military ties with China creates uncertainty in Moscow that requires the Soviets to plan for the possibility of wartime US military assistance to the Chinese.

(4) Improve China's nuclear deterrent capability by providing military-related technology such as computers to control over-the-horizon radar and satellite cameras for photo reconnaissance of Soviet military installations. This would increase Peking's early warning capability, thus decreasing the danger to China of a Soviet surprise attack in a crisis, and the danger to the Soviets of a premature launch of Chinese missiles out of fear of Soviet preemption. This could reduce the risk of a Sino-Soviet nuclear war and insure a more stable Sino-Soviet nuclear balance without significantly increasing the Chinese nuclear threat to the US.

(5) Improve China's conventional military capability and deterrent to Soviet conventional attack through the transfer of certain advanced defensive weapons and military technology. The study argued that an improvement in Chinese military capabilities, especially if deployed near the Sino-Soviet border, could lead the Soviets to deploy an even larger percentage of their ground, naval and air forces in the Far East, thus reducing pressure on NATO in the West.

Pillsbury's plan for military ties with China sparked an intense secret debate among several small circles of government officials. Kissinger and Nixon were indeed looking to the US *rapprochement* with China to counterbalance and pressure the Soviet Union for diplomatic gains. But in 1974, a proposal to establish actual defence ties with China seemed, if not preposterous, at least unrealistic to some of the officials within the US government who were aware of the idea. China experts in the intelligence community were especially sceptical that the Chinese wanted any such relationship; they argued that the Chinese would never abandon self-reliance and seek defence equipment or military relations with the West. They also were convinced that the key issue in Sino-American relations was Taiwan — not defence ties, or, by implication, Chinese security *vis-à-vis* the Soviet Union.

At the Pentagon, which was preoccupied with Vietnam and other issues, some among the small number of officials who were aware of the Pillsbury proposal, were unreceptive in principle to the notion of a defence relationship with the Chinese — especially uniformed military officers at 'J-5', the planning staff of the Joint Chiefs of Staff. In the first place, China was a Communist country. Secondly, the Chinese might go back to an alliance with the Soviets at any time. Thirdly, China had been a US military adversary in Korea, the Taiwan Straits crisis, and even peripherally in Vietnam. And finally, China was still backing North Vietnam in 1974 (although the US had withdrawn its forces from Indochina by then). This history seemed to many officials to provide little basis for Sino-US trust and co-operation in such a sensitive area as national security.

But L-32 hit a responsive chord with key officials in the Office of the Secretary of Defense (OSD). The arguments and implications of the Pillsbury study intersected with a growing intra-governmental struggle over the build-up of Soviet military strength and a perceived shift in the balance of power, especially in the strategic nuclear balance. There were increasing divisions within the administration over alleged Soviet SALT I violations; estimates of Soviet military capabilities, spending and intentions; and the overall policy of détente. To those officials concerned with the US-Soviet global balance of power — such as Secretary of Defense James Schlesinger — the notion of establishing US military ties with China to bolster the US strategic position was intriguing.

In the spring of 1974, a secret study was begun for Schlesinger that incorporated some of the ideas and information of L-32. The study, which was directed by Morton Abramowitz, Deputy Assistant Secretary of Defense for East Asian and Pacific Affairs, was presented as a briefing to Schlesinger in late December 1974 and to key NSC and State Department officials, including Kissinger deputy Winston Lord, in early 1975.[12] Schlesinger's later advocacy of strengthening China as a counterbalance to Soviet power through developing Sino-American defence ties apparently dates to this briefing. But Schlesinger apparently felt at the time — four months before the fall of Saigon — that neither the public nor the Congress was yet ready for a military relationship with 'Communist China'.

By mid-1975, and probably earlier, Kissinger was aware of the ideas of L-32. Although Kissinger may have been probed directly by Chinese leaders for military ties two years earlier, he had done nothing about it. Now it was coming back to him on a different track — both from low-level probes and through Pillsbury's study being circulated to key national security officials, including his rival, James Schlesinger. At this point Kissinger apparently became attracted to the idea of military ties with China, although for very different reasons and far more reluctantly than Schlesinger.

Both officials viewed China in a triangular context. However — judging from their statements and interviews during this period and from interviews by the author with former officials and others knowledgeable about their thinking — the two men saw China's role in the strategic triangle in very different ways, based primarily on their conflicting views on US-Soviet relations.

For Kissinger, détente was aimed at 'strategic enmeshment' of the Soviet Union in a web of relations with the US and the West which could be used to constrain the extension of Soviet influence at a time when Moscow's global power, especially its military power, was growing and US power seemed to be peaking in relative terms. Détente was supposed to be a system of carrots as well as sticks to induce acceptable Soviet behaviour by linking issues in bilateral relations and global politics. SALT was to be the political as well as the arms control foundation of détente. Although strong US military power, including 'essential equivalence' of strategic forces, was said to be a prerequisite for carrying out this strategy, it was fundamentally a diplomatic approach to the problem of coping with Soviet power.

Kissinger's approach toward China was in large part a function of this policy toward the Soviet Union. Kissinger (and Nixon) sought to gain leverage over Moscow by manipulating Soviet anxiety about possible Sino-American collusion against them. Any gestures toward military ties with China, therefore, had to be calculated in this context: the aim would be to gain new leverage over the Soviet Union without provoking the Soviets and undermining the whole détente relationship.

For Schlesinger, coping with Soviet power was more a military than a diplomatic problem. In his view, détente had not slowed the build-up of Soviet strategic and conventional military power, nor had it altered long-term hegemonistic goals of Soviet leaders. The shift in the global military balance resulting first from the Sino-Soviet split and then from China's tilt toward the US, had become an increasingly important factor in efforts to maintain or improve the US military position *vis-à-vis* the Soviet Union, especially in Asia. As a strategic ally, China offered great potential to tie down a substantial portion of Soviet military capabilities and resources, and greatly to complicate Soviet defence planning for both conventional and nuclear war with the West. The Soviets would have to plan for the possibility of a two-front war, and thus could not expect to shift resources from the east to west in the event of a war in Europe. They also would have to target Chinese nuclear weapons as well as US, British and French nuclear forces. Military ties with China would offer a means of improving Chinese deterrence to Soviet attack and increasing the expense and complexity of Soviet defence planning. This was particularly significant in an era of decreasing US military spending in the aftermath of the Vietnam War. From Schlesinger's more military point of view, the preservation of détente had less significance than did the maintenance of a favourable balance of military power.

These conflicting strategic views and the role of military ties with China have formed the basic parameters of the debate within the US government since 1975.

First Moves toward Military Ties with China

The first serious consideration of military ties with China by top US officials came in the fall of 1975 in the context of worsening US-Soviet relations and increasing domestic pressure on the President to take strong action against Moscow — a pattern frequently repeated over the following five years.

By late 1975, both US-Soviet and US-Chinese relations were deteriorating and policy and power struggles within the Ford administration were intensifying. Kissinger was facing strong opposition to his détente policies, especially from Schlesinger and from vocal members of Congress. Efforts to finalize the SALT II agreement based on the Vladivostok formula were stalled. Kissinger's strategy of 'strategic enmeshment' had been seriously crippled by the December 1974 Jackson-Vanik amendment, which had tied improved US-Soviet trade relations to Soviet emigration policies, leading Moscow to abrogate the US-Soviet trade agreement signed in 1972.

Kissinger was at odds with Moscow over the Middle East, and was especially pressed by the growing confrontation in Angola. He also was under attack for the Helsinki agreement, signed in July 1975 by President Ford, and for his failure to criticize the Soviets directly on the issue of human rights. Although Kissinger was trying to defend and repair his faltering détente policy, he apparently was becoming increasingly disenchanted with the Soviet view of détente.[13]

The Chinese, meanwhile, were accusing Kissinger of 'appeasement' of the Soviet Union and indicating that US weakness *vis-à-vis* Moscow raised serious doubts about the reliability and usefulness of the US as a strategic counter to the Soviets. Kissinger had failed to follow through on the Shanghai Communiqué and normalize relations with Peking, and he had not responded to the secret Chinese probes for military ties through the Pillsbury channel. He was under strong pressure to do something to move US-Chinese relations forward, yet the up-coming presidential election and the conservative challenge to Ford from Ronald Reagan ruled out the option of severing diplomatic and defence ties with Taiwan to normalize relations with Peking.[14]

In this context, 'administration officials' — almost certainly Kissinger or Lord — expressed concern in an interview with the *New York Times* that the slippage in Sino-American relations had weakened US leverage over the Soviet Union.[15] The 'officials' said that in their view, Soviet fear of US-Chinese collusion against them had greatly diminished and that the Soviet concern over Sino-American ties which had moderated Moscow's behaviour in the early seventies no longer was a factor restraining Soviet 'adventurism' in Portugal and Angola. Under this logic, a move toward military ties with China — if not handled in a way that would backfire in Soviet-American relations — could serve to improve Sino-American ties and therefore potential US leverage over the Soviet Union. It could make the Soviets nervous that there might be more aid to China in the future and provide useful leverage for the SALT II talks to be resumed in early 1976 as well as on other issues. Finally, a gesture toward military ties with China would allow Ford to give the Chinese something of significance at a time when he was unwilling to compromise on Taiwan.[16]

Kissinger and Ford made that gesture in December 1975, during a trip to Peking, approving the British sale to China of Rolls-Royce Spey jet engines — used in the British version of the F-4 Phantom fighter-bomber — and a Spey factory, a deal which had been under discussion since 1972.[17]

The death of Chairman Mao Zedong on 9 September 1976, and the arrest of the Gang of Four on 6 October, provided the occasion for a second US gesture. Kissinger was sufficiently concerned that the unsettled political situation in Peking could yet turn against US interests — through changes in Chinese foreign policy or exploitation of a power struggle by the Soviets — that he decided to make another major move toward military ties with China. On 12 October the National Security Council, at Kissinger's urging, approved the sale to China of two advanced Control Data Cyber 72 computers with military applications. (The Chinese request to buy the computers had been around for more than a year.) A former Kissinger aide involved in the decision said in an interview with the author that it 'was one of the most concrete actions on the military ties question. It was considered in light of its impact on the Soviet Union and the PRC.'

Kissinger made one more important move in the security realm before the end of the Ford administration. At a news conference on 15 October, he said that 'the territorial integrity and sovereignty of China is very important to the world equilibrium and we would consider it a grave matter if this were threatened by an outside power.' Nine days later, Kissinger went even further in linking US and Chinese security, and adding that the United States 'would take an extremely dim view of a military attack or even military pressure on China'.

Carter Inherits the Debate

Kissinger's moves toward China in the security realm were highly significant but they did not constitute an overall US policy. When Jimmy Carter assumed the presidency in January 1977, he had already indicated that improving US-Soviet relations would be of paramount concern for his administration, while Sino-American relations were far down the list of foreign policy priorities. Secretary of State Cyrus Vance had indicated that he would not let US relations with China interfere with SALT and other outstanding issues between Washington and Moscow.

But shortly after Carter took power, the 'China card' was pushed to the front of the presidential options deck. Carter's outspoken human rights policy and his SALT 'reductions proposal' quickly led to a serious strain in US-Soviet relations. In response, the administration considered playing the China card to pressure the Soviets to be more forthcoming. But the idea — strongly backed by National Security Adviser Zbigniew Brzezinski — was rejected in June on the basis that it was potentially too provocative and might lead the Soviets to reconsider their entire policy of détente. The issue was addressed in an interagency study — Presidential Review Memorandum (PRM) 24 — which was leaked to the *New York Times* in June.[18] PRM 24 concluded that

> since the desire to head off Chinese-Western collaboration was a major impetus to the present [Soviet] leadership's policy of detente, there is presumably a point at which the present Soviet leadership or its successors would conclude that this policy is not achieving the desired objective. Despite the difficulties for other Soviet objectives, Moscow would then be compelled to make a fundamental reassessment of its policies toward the US . . . At some undefined point, Soviet perceptions of the threat of US-Chinese military collaboration would stiffen Soviet positions on even the major issues of US-Soviet relations such as SALT, especially if initial Soviet efforts to reverse the trend failed. The Soviets might also increase tensions with China.

The decision to accept the recommendations of PRM 24 and thus reject playing the China card at that time was based not on a consensus (the conclusions of PRM 24 represented primarily the views of the State Department Soviet and China experts, while the NSC, the OSD and CIA analysts reportedly were in favour of military ties with China), but rather on the dominance of Vance and other pro-détente officials within the administration at that time. During the summer and fall of 1977, Vance had presidential support in his efforts to focus on improving overall US-Soviet relations and to finalize SALT II. In this period, the administration also concluded a voluminous study of the global balance of power, PRM 10, which argued that US and Soviet military power were roughly equal, while long-term economic, political and diplomatic factors favoured the United States. Vance and other pro-détente officials argued on the basis of this assessment that the Soviets' weaknesses and US strengths provided a basis for Soviet interest in accommodation with

Washington (Brzezinski and others, however, viewed the conclusions of PRM 10 as arguing for exploitation of Moscow's vulnerabilities to diminish Soviet power).

Vance's strategic assessment and his desire to deal with Sino-American relations as primarily a bilateral matter brought a negative reaction from Chinese leaders, who conveyed their disapproval to the Secretary of State when he visited Peking in August. The Chinese condemned Vance's strategic view as 'appeasement' of Moscow. US-Soviet relations, on the other hand, further improved following Vance's return from China and after another negotiating round, President Carter suggested that a new SALT agreement was only weeks away.

While the issue of military ties with China had been placed on the back burner at the presidential level during the last half of 1977, it was still the subject of intense debate and political struggle at lower levels of the government, as revealed in a series of interviews with administration officials and others involved conducted by the author during this period. Those opposed to the idea consistently made the following points:

(1) The Chinese are not interested in and cannot afford significant arms purchases and other military ties with the West, especially the United States, nor do they want any form of military alliance with the US against the Soviet Union. They may seek to purchase some high-technology items and a few weapons that they can try to duplicate, but they will not abandon self-reliance.

(2) US military contacts with China, such as exchange of military attachés or the visit to Peking of the US Secretary of Defense, could dangerously exacerbate Sino-Soviet tensions, and could even provoke the Soviets to launch a pre-emptive strike against the Chinese.

(3) US-Soviet relations could be seriously damaged by military assistance to China. Instead of pressuring the Soviets to be more compliant in negotiations with the US, including SALT, and be more restrained in their international behaviour, they could be provoked into a hardline reaction (this view generally reflecting the conclusions of PRM 24).

(4) US military contacts with China are not needed to 'pay off' to the pro-US group in Peking and thus head off a Sino-Soviet *rapprochement* because such a development is extremely unlikely. In any case, a limited détente between the Soviet Union and China, if it

were to occur, would not be harmful to US interests, because it would reduce international tensions and lessen the chances of a Sino-Soviet war.

The proponents of US military ties with China generally took the opposite point of view on these issues. They argued:

(1) The Chinese, or at least pro-US leaders in Peking, do want to develop significant military ties with the US, including an informal quasi-alliance against the Soviet Union. While financial and political constraints prevent China from ever buying massive amounts of Western arms, the Chinese want to buy key items of military technology and some Western arms, and to develop farreaching security relations with the US as a deterrent to Soviet attack.

(2) Although the Soviets would be upset by a Western military relationship with China, there is little they could do about it. US assistance to China could help stabilize the Sino-Soviet military balance rather than increase chances for war; an unprovoked Soviet attack on China would lead to an extremely damaging international reaction against the Soviet Union while offering little hope for long-term success.

(3) Although the Soviets might threaten a harsh reaction to US-Chinese military ties, they *ultimately* would be more cautious and more co-operative with the US, because their strategic position would be weakened and they would try to head off even worse collusion against them by improving relations with Washington.

(4) At least a limited Sino-Soviet *rapprochement* has been and continues to be a serious possibility and could undermine the US global strategic position *vis-à-vis* Moscow. Although a limited détente between the Soviet Union and China would not at first necessarily be contrary to US interests, such a warming of relations could ultimately go much further toward an effective Sino-Soviet alliance against the West, even while some Sino-Soviet ideological differences remained.

These characterizations of views do not consistently fit all opponents and proponents in that period, of course. Many of those who in general opposed military ties, for example, might nevertheless favour some careful military technology transfers to China to bolster its deterrent while trying to maintain evenhandedness toward the Soviets. And some who favoured extensive military ties with

China might distinguish between various possible moves to avoid the most provocative options, such as selling advanced fighters or even nuclear-capable missiles to the Chinese, with the aim of minimizing Soviet reaction.

The objectives offered by those seeking to develop military ties with China also varied, following the lines of the Kissinger-Schlesinger differences. For some, the primary goal was to improve the US strategic military position *vis-à-vis* Moscow. Others saw military ties as part of a diplomatic strategy aimed at punishing the Soviets or at tightening the encirclement of the Soviet Union to weaken its overall political and economic as well as military position. Still others saw military ties as offering a graduated series of steps to pressure Moscow while still leaving an opening for the Soviets to influence the pace of the Sino-American defence relationship by moderating their own behaviour.

Carter Plays the China Card

The 'China card' was played in the context of worsening US-Soviet relations and a presidential search for options to pressure/punish the Soviets.

By late winter of 1978, President Carter was under mounting domestic pressure to take a tough position in the SALT talks and in response to Soviet and Cuban military intervention in Ethiopia. Brzezinski strongly urged that the US make a show of military force in the region of the Horn of Africa and that the administration link progress in the SALT talks to Moscow's behaviour in Ethiopia. After an intense struggle within the administration, Carter rejected Brzezinski's approach on linkage and the Horn and instead adopted Vance's view that SALT should be isolated from the overall deterioration of US-Soviet relations.

But, ironically, once Vance and the State Department convinced the President to rule out linkage and direct confrontation with the Soviets in Africa, the China card became a more attractive option to pressure Moscow. Carter decided to send Brzezinski to Peking in May where the National Security Adviser was to lay the foundation for a strategic relationship with China.

Brzezinski and his staff made certain that the Soviets and others were aware of the strategic nature of his talks in Peking by leaking to the press that the sale to China of US dual-purpose, military-related technology and Western arms had been discussed, and that Chinese leaders had been given a detailed briefing on the SALT negotiations during his 21–3 May visit. In addition, Brzezinski and his aides also later revealed that they had briefed the Chinese on the NSC's strategic view, which contrasted sharply with Vance's. They stressed that Soviet weaknesses and long-term US advantages should be exploited to extract greater concessions from the Soviet Union and to contain its influence, even at the expense of possible deterioration in US-Soviet relations. This view was far more acceptable to the Chinese, and it indicated a greater American willingness to pursue a potentially provocative informal alliance with Peking against Moscow. As was later revealed, both sides had agreed that their common strategic views set the basis for overcoming the six-year deadlock on normalization of relations. Although hard bargaining remained to reach final agreement on the terms of normalization, less than seven months later, 15 December 1978, the two sides announced they would establish full diplomatic ties on 1 January 1979.

The normalization announcement served to undermine what was expected to be a final round of SALT talks held on 22–3 December in Geneva. Soviet Foreign Minister Gromyko, according to State Department sources, spent much of the session lecturing Secretary Vance on the 'China threat' and the talks reached an impasse as the Soviets waited to see the outcome of the visit of Vice-Premier Deng Xiaoping to Washington in early 1979 — a visit also announced on 15 December. Vance apparently had not been consulted on the timing of the normalization announcement and was appalled at its implications for SALT.

Normalization and the visit of Deng to the US were victories for those seeking to move strategic ties with China forward. But the Chinese invasion of Vietnam less than two weeks after Deng left the United States delayed further steps in that direction.[19] The US refrained from all-out support for China, and after reassuring the Soviets of a commitment to SALT during the invasion, went ahead with talks to finalize the strategic arms agreement in the spring, culminating in the Carter-Brezhnev summit in Vienna. The June 1979 summit was limited to signing the SALT II agreement, however, and US-Soviet relations failed to improve significantly.

The forces within the Carter administration pushing for a Sino-American military relationship succeeded in taking major steps in that direction in the late summer and fall of 1979. This began with a visit to Peking by Vice President Walter Mondale in late August. Mondale broadened the security guarantee offered by Kissinger in 1976, stating on nationwide Chinese television that 'any nation which seeks to weaken or isolate you in world affairs assumes a stance counter to American interests'. He also said that the US was committed to joining with China to 'advance our many parallel strategic and bilateral interests' and that 'both our political interests are served by your growing strength in all fields, for it helps deter others who might seek to impose themselves on you'. These key statements were not in the State Department approved version of Mondale's speech, but were added later by the NSC staff. Also apparently without prior approval of Vance or the State Department, Mondale raised the subject with Chinese leaders of visit to Peking by Secretary of Defense Harold Brown.

By the time Mondale returned to Washington, the US and the Soviet Union were on a new collision course over US intelligence leaks of an alleged Soviet 'combat brigade' in Cuba. While President Carter's public response on 1 October focused on stepped up surveillance activity and naval operations in the Caribbean aimed at Cuba, Carter quietly approved a number of measures to step up pressure on the Soviet Union. These included moves indicating the US would begin further to restrict the flow of high technology to the Soviet Union — and that the administration would move toward overt military ties with China. On the same day that Carter announced measures against Cuba — Chinese national day — the White House leaked to the press that Brown would visit China. Although the administration continued to insist publicly that the US would not sell arms to China, officials pointedly said this did not rule out providing military training and technical assistance to the Chinese.[20] It was also reported in the press that the administration was considering widening contacts with Peking in the security and intelligence fields.[21]

In addition, the administration leaked a secret Pentagon study, 'Consolidated Guidance Number 8: Asia During a Worldwide Conventional War', which said that in view of China's 'pivotal role' in the global balance of power, it would be to the US benefit 'to encourage Chinese actions that would heighten Soviet security concerns. Such encouragement could include arms transfers or the employment of US forces in joint operations.'[22] 'CG-8' recommended possible US military assistance to China to increase the likelihood of Chinese participation in a global war, including provision of advanced technology and intelligence data, sale of advanced arms, Chinese production of American weapons and joint military exercises. Vance responded to the leak of CG-8 by emphatically denying that the administration had changed its policy, insisting 'we are not going to sell arms to the Chinese'.[23] State Department officials tried to downplay the significance of Brown's upcoming trip to China by likening it to his short and contentious meeting with the Soviet defence minister at the Vienna Summit in June.[24] Privately, however, State Department officials interviewed by the author in November and early December said that the 'China tilters' had won the battle for military ties with China and predicted that US-Soviet relations would continue to worsen and that the US would move closer toward an alliance with China, including sales of military-related technology and possibly even US arms.

The Soviet invasion of Afghanistan in late December sent US relations with Moscow into a tailspin and sharply weakened the position of those in the State Department who had hoped to limit the substance of Brown's upcoming trip to China to prevent further damage to détente. A 'senior official' — probably Brzezinski — told the *New York Times* on the eve of Brown's departure for China in early January that the Soviet invasion had given Brown's mission a 'new dimension,' and asserted that 'the Soviets have forced us and the Chinese into a posture in which we both see the world in the same way'.[25] The official added that closer security ties with Peking were viewed by many officials as a principal way the United States could respond to Soviet actions in Afghanistan. Brown apparently received two new instructions in response to the Afghanistan invasion: to be highly public in his anti-Soviet rhetoric, and to discuss with Chinese leaders the sale of non-lethal military equipment to China on a case-by-case basis.

The administration retained its ban on arms sales to China, however, and Secretary of State Vance sought to minimize the impact of Brown's trip on US-Soviet relations. The Secretary of State, who obviously did not share the 'senior official's' view that the US now saw the world the same way as the Chinese did, said shortly after Brown returned from China that 'there may be a degree of parallelism on steps that should be taken in connection with Afghanistan, but that does not mean that there is any military alliance or such relationship between the United States and China.'[26] The Pentagon undercut Vance a week later by announcing the decision to sell non-lethal military equipment to China and revealing that the decision had been made just before Brown departed for Peking.[27]

This sequence suggests that once again, the Carter administration had failed to forge a new consensus on developing a military relationship with China and a new strategic posture *vis-à-vis* Moscow in which that relationship was to be an integral part. Rather, the NSC pushed through key decisions as US-Soviet relations deteriorated and the President faced strong domestic pressure to punish Moscow. The key moves during Mondale's trip were apparently unilateral actions by the NSC. As US-Soviet relations reached a new crisis over the 'combat brigade' in Cuba in September and the Soviet invasion of Afghanistan in late December, the position of the 'China tilters' was further strengthened.

There is an important distinction between decisions that can be made unilaterally at the White House and those which require participation of the larger national security bureaucracy, especially the State Department. The President, at the urging of the National Security Adviser, for example, could decide to send the Secretary of Defense to China and present that decision as a *fait accompli* to the Secretary of State. But implementation of the decision required a new set of decisions which involved participation of more officials regarding Brown's instructions and who was to accompany him. At this point in the process, those seeking to 'limit the damage' of the Brown visit could try to minimize the content of his trip by restricting the content of the discussions in China and signalling in advance that the US would not drop its arms sales ban. Those seeking to maximize the impact of Brown's trip could fight for the opposite positions, including a push to drop the ban on arms sales prior to the trip. In this case, the Soviet invasion of Afghanistan strengthened the position of the latter group, resulting in a new compromise position of allowing sales of non-lethal military equipment to the Chinese, and in raising Brown's rhetorical profile while he was in China. When the Reagan administration took power in January 1981, the momentum in Sino-American military relations had led to a broad range of military and intelligence contacts and exchanges with deepening US involvement in China's defence and defence equipment production problems. President Ronald Reagan and Secretary of State Alexander Haig both indicated they viewed China in a strategic context similar to the Schlesinger view of 1975, and that they would resist right-wing pressure to upgrade ties with Taiwan and distance the US from the 'Communist Chinese'.[28] The first moves of the administration confirmed a basic continuity with

Carter administration policy on military ties with China and on US-Taiwan relations.

Conclusion

By the end of the Ford administration, the logic had been set for the process of bureaucratic politics and decision making in the US on the one hand, and the interaction of the three great powers on the other, that would propel the Carter administration toward developing a military relationship with China:

(1) The terms of the strategic debate had been articulated and represented in the Kissinger/Schlesinger dispute over détente and the role of the China factor in US posture toward Moscow. Despite their differences, and the differences between senior officials in the Carter administration over China policy, the strategic triangle has formed the basic framework for policy: the question has been how, not whether, the Sino-American relationship should be used to improve the US position *vis-à-vis* Moscow, and since 1975, the focus of that debate has been on developing 'military ties' with China. Only at lower levels of the government, especially among China and Soviet specialists, was there a strong emphasis on 'de-linking' Sino-American and Soviet-American relations.

(2) No overall policy toward the triangle and the issue of military ties with Peking was adopted by the Ford administration, despite several key decisions with broad policy implications. In effect, the President made a specific decision in each case: he allowed the British to sell military jet engines and Control Data to sell advanced computers to the Chinese. Both of these were decisions with recognized implications for Sino-American security ties, yet no new policy was developed. In the Carter administration, the President again made very specific decisions without agreement on broader policy issues, despite the recognized profound implications for US-Soviet relations of moves toward China. Carter decided to allow the Western Europeans to sell arms to China; to allow the Chinese to buy certain items of advanced US technology with military applications that would not be sold to the Soviets; to send the National Security Adviser to China to develop strategic ties with Peking; to send the Secretary of Defense to China to develop an overt military relationship with the Chinese; and to allow the sale of non-lethal

military equipment to China. In each case, only the specific issue was decided, not the larger policy concerns of where US policy was going with China, and how Sino-American military ties fit into US-Soviet policy and US strategy for coping with the expansion of Soviet power. Often the key decision was made in the White House without consultation with the Secretary of State and his staff, and in other cases, the objections coming from the State Department were simply overruled. In any case, there was no agreement within the administration on the larger policy issues, and participants in the process told the author that the policy fights were limited to discussion of only the immediate options and not the broader implications.

This is not to say that key presidential advisers did not have their own strategies in mind. Just as Kissinger and Schlesinger, for example, had larger strategic ideas behind their support for specific options toward China, so did Brzezinski and Vance. Furthermore, despite the lack of a formally agreed upon policy toward the triangle and the role of military ties with China in that policy, the discrete moves in that direction added up to a clear policy direction: a web of ties and a powerful momentum were created that would be difficult to untangle or reverse without profound negative implications for Sino-American and Sino-Soviet relations as well as for bureaucratic interests in the United States.

(3) The intermeshing of the issue of military ties with China with US policy toward, and relations with, the Soviet Union began in the Ford administration and continued to define the context of the struggle over China policy. Crises in US-Soviet relations brought the issue of the 'China card' to the level of presidential decision making, with a set of specific options for moves toward China. A pattern of triangular interaction was established which would tend to compel the US toward closer military ties with China as US relations with Moscow deteriorated. The US would consider strengthening ties with China to pressure the Soviets in response to tensions with Moscow. When the US and the Soviet Union were making progress in SALT and other US-Soviet negotiations, the Chinese would charge the US with appeasement and cool their relations with Washington to pressure the US for improvement of relations. When the US moved toward improved relations with China on a strategic, anti-Soviet basis, the Soviets would express increasing anxiety about US-Chinese collusion against them and warn that détente itself could be undermined by Sino-American military ties. And the Soviets and

the Chinese would each hint at possible Sino-Soviet détente to pressure the United States.

(4) These developments in turn would influence the balance of power of competing factions in Washington. As relations worsened with the Soviet Union, the faction favouring stronger anti-Soviet measures, including strategic ties with China, would gain the upper hand in the Washington power struggle, leading to specific decisions that moved the US closer and closer to China. By late 1979, this complex dynamic had produced a Sino-American military relationship in the context of near Cold War tensions between the US and the Soviet Union. And the process would appear to be irreversible: in a ratchet-like manner, the defence relationship would advance with the opponents simply delaying, but not preventing, the next move toward China.

Yet, as this framework suggests, the Soviets have influenced US policy toward China. Crises in US-Soviet relations, such as those produced by Soviet actions in Angola, Ethiopia and Afghanistan, have pushed options for military ties with China to the top of the list for presidential consideration and have often undermined the position of the opponents of such moves. Improvements in US-Soviet relations have strengthened the position of those seeking to keep the 'China card' in reserve or, after it was played, to slow the pace of development of military relations with the Chinese.[29]

While the Soviets have failed generally to recognize the effect of their behaviour on US policy, the United States has also failed to examine seriously the impact of playing the China card on Soviet policy and actions. The 1977 interagency study PRM 24, which concluded that military ties with China could be counterproductive, was never followed up by another study, either to challenge its conclusions before the China card was initially played in spring 1978, or after the US began forging a strategic relationship with China to assess its effect on Moscow. Such an assessment, which would likely find that the impact on the Soviets had been counterproductive in the terms predicted by the opponents of military ties with China,[30] would seem crucial to setting future policy, especially in calculating how the US hopes to affect Soviet behaviour beyond complicating the Soviets' strategic planning environment.

To place the current triangular configuration in a long-run perspective, it should be noted that the United States could again change alliances. The opening to Peking in 1971–2 indicated that the United

States was playing balance of power politics with the Chinese and Soviets. Although prior to that period, US policy makers had felt constrained by domestic politics from capitalizing on Sino-Soviet differences (going back to the 1940s[31]), Washington nevertheless had set a precedent for developing ties with Communist states to counterbalance Soviet power by its military aid programme to Yugoslavia in the early 1950s. The notion of 'containment' as articulated by George Kennan always included exploiting tensions between the Soviet Union and other Communist states.[32] A State Department Policy Planning Staff document prepared under Kennan and approved by President Truman in December 1949, for example, called for fostering 'a heretical drifting-away process on the part of the satellite states' that might eventually result in the formation of 'two opposing blocs in the Communist world' which could 'provide us with an opportunity to operate on the basis of a balance in the Communist world, and to foster the tendencies toward accommodation with the West implicit in such a state of affairs.'[33] Kennan himself not only welcomed Tito's break with Stalin in the summer of 1948, but also cited China as a country where Titoist tendencies might emerge.[34]

A *realpolitik*, balance of power approach to triangular relations has been a policy current in the US since the late 1940s, although US policy makers have often been blind to such possibilities or unable to seize them because of domestic politics. In the broadest sense, the triangular policies since the early 1970s have been consistent with a Grand Strategy of the United States since the Second World War of seeking to prevent the domination of Eurasia — especially the industrial heartland of Europe, but also the rich potential of Asia — by any one power. The US sided with the Soviet Union in the Second World War to prevent Nazi Germany from achieving such hegemony, and later Washington formed NATO to contain Soviet power and consolidate an American foothold in Europe. From this perspective, it seems consistent for the US to side with China against Moscow to contain growing Soviet power. But it also suggests that the US might shift alliances again in the future. If, in the unlikely event the US-aided Chinese become economically and militarily powerful and threaten US interests ten or twenty years from now — as the Soviets constantly warn — then the United States would likely seek to counterbalance Chinese power, perhaps by colluding with the Soviet Union.[35]

Notes

1. Henry Kissinger, *The White House Years*, Boston: Little, Brown, 1979, p. 222. Kissinger notes that the shift from a $2\frac{1}{2}$ war to a $1\frac{1}{2}$ war strategy was publicly announced in Nixon's first *Foreign Policy Report to the Congress*, 18 February 1970. According to the *New York Times*, 9 October 1979, Nixon endorsed a secret 'swing strategy', which had actually been the basis of US planning since the mid-1950s and which reflected the inability of the US to achieve a $2\frac{1}{2}$ war capability. According to *The Times*, in the event of a war in Europe, US plans call for shifting forces from Asia and the Pacific to Western Europe — even if a war might break out in Asia as well. *The Times* reported that NATO governments were informed of this secret strategy, but not US allies in Europe, including Japan.

2. Ibid., p. 222.

3. Ibid., p. 1062. Kissinger says that Chinese Communist Party Chairman Mao Zedong, in his conversations with Nixon during the President's February 1972 visit, gave assurances that China would not intervene militarily in Indochina and that China posed no threat to South Korea and Japan. Kissinger also says that Mao made clear that the Soviet Union was his principal security concern.

4. See Robert Sutter, *China-Watch: Toward Sino-American Reconciliation*, Baltimore: Johns Hopkins University Press, 1978, p. 3, pp. 109—12.

5. See John Newhouse, *Cold Dawn: The Story of SALT*, New York: Holt, Rinehart and Winston, 1973, p. 100, pp. 168—9, on the China factor in détente and the SALT negotiations.

6. Kissinger, *White House Years*, p. 764. Knowledgeable sources have told the author that the contingency planning in 1969 did not include active US assistance to the People's Republic but simply what steps the US might take elsewhere.

7. Ibid., p. 910.

8. Ibid., p. 910.

9. Press conference, Harvard University, Cambridge, Massachusetts, 15 October 1976 (transcript).

10. For details of this period and the historical account that follows through 1981, see my forthcoming *The 'China Card' and its Origins: U.S. Bureaucratic Politics and the Strategic Triangle*, to be published by the Institute of International Studies, University of California, Berkeley. See also Banning Garrett, 'The Origins of the Strategic Relationship Between China and the United States', testimony before the Subcommittee on Asian and Pacific Affairs, Committee on Foreign Affairs, House of Representatives, 26 August 1980, in *The United States and the People's Republic of China: Issues for the 1980s*, published by the Committee in 1980.

11. Several sources said that L-32 was similar to but not exactly identical with Pillsbury's article in *Foreign Policy*, although that there are sections of L-32 which were not drawn on for the article which would be 'explosive' if they were revealed. The Department of the Air Force, in a letter to the author, 5 February 1980, confirmed the existence of L-32 but refused to declassify the document under the Freedom of Information Act. The Air Force similarly confirmed the existence of Pillsbury's memorandums of conversation with the PLA officers, but refused to declassify them.

12. A censored version of the 'Abramowitz study', as it was called, was obtained by the author in February 1980 through an FOI request. For a detailed discussion of the document, see my *China Card*. Pillsbury worked on the study along with another RAND analyst and several analysts in the Pentagon.

13. See Robert Legvold, 'Containment Without Confrontation', *Foreign Policy*, No. 40, Fall 1980.

14. According to several sources, by Fall 1975, Schlesinger was pushing hard for a positive response to Chinese probes for military ties. Although he did not publicly express his views on China policy while he was in the administration, in an April 1976

interview he said that, depending on the circumstances surrounding military aid to China, he 'would not reject it out of hand'. He termed China a 'quasi-ally', while describing US-Soviet relations as 'very close' to the cold war status of the 1950s. (Interview on CBS's 'Face the Nation', 11 April 1976.)

15. 'Washington Senses Loss of Leverage Against Soviets', Leslie Gelb, *New York Times*, 30 November 1975. Peter Osnos, writing from Moscow for the *Washington Post*, 7 December 1975, concluded that the Soviets 'apparently believe that relations between China and the United States are essentially stalled,' and consequently seem relatively unconcerned about possible Sino-American collusion against them.

16. By this time the Pillsbury article had been published and had created international interest. Both Kissinger and Schlesinger had encouraged publication of the article, according to several sources. Pillsbury predicted that defence relations with China would be considered in the context of US-Soviet relations: 'If detente seems to be deteriorating, then the temptation to experiment with some of these initiatives would increase. A President more hostile to the Soviet Union and detente than Ford might be particularly attracted to the idea, risky as it is, of forging a close US-Chinese bond in the Pacific, perhaps embracing Japan, as a new form of anti-Soviet containment.'

17. The role of the US in 'acquiescing' to the British deal was not revealed until four months later in leak to Gelb of the *New York Times*, 25 April 1976. Gelb reported, and other sources have confirmed to the author, that Kissinger agreed to allow the British to bypass COCOM (the NATO minus Iceland plus Japan co-ordinating committee for control of strategic exports to Communist countries) to facilitate the sale. Gelb also linked Kissinger's decision to his reassurances to the Chinese that the US had a vital concern in maintaining the Sino-Soviet balance of power. The leak to Gelb was itself intended to be a gesture toward the pro-US elements of the Chinese leadership during the power struggle following the Tien An Men riots of 5 April 1976 and to provide pressure on Moscow in response to Angola and other sources of US-Soviet tension.

18. *New York Times*, 24 June 1977.

19. For a detailed account of this period, see Banning Garrett, 'The Strategic Triangle and the Indochina Crisis', in *The Third Indochina Conflict*, David Elliott (ed.), Boulder, Colorado: Westview Press, forthcoming.

20. *Washington Post*, 2 October 1979.

21. Henry Brandon, *Washington Star*, 7 October 1979.

22. 'Study Urges U.S. Aid to Chinese Military', by Richard Burt and 'Louder than Words', by columnist William Safire, both in the *New York Times*, 4 October 1979.

23. *New York Times*, 5 October 1979. The Soviets were not convinced. See report on *Pravda* commentary in *The Times*, 6 October 1979.

24. *Washington Post*, 2 October 1979; *Boston Globe*, 3 October 1979.

25. *New York Times*, 3 January 1980.

26. Interview with the *New York Times*, 16 January 1980.

27. *New York Times*, *Los Angeles Times*, 25 January 1980.

28. At a press conference reported by the *Los Angeles Times*, 29 May 1981, Ronald Reagan said arms sales to China would be a 'natural development'. Alexander Haig, who stressed the strategic importance of China to the US both before and after he was appointed Secretary of State in the Reagan administration, had, according to informed sources, met frequently with Chinese military officials while he was NATO commander. His first contacts with the Chinese apparently were in 1975.

29. In a major policy speech on 4 June 1980, Assistant Secretary of State Richard Holbrooke suggested that the US and China were friends, not allies, but that future aggressive behaviour by the Soviet Union could lead the US and China to forge an alliance and to engage in joint military planning, and that the US might also drop its

ban on sales of arms to China in such circumstances. This was the first time a linkage between Soviet behaviour and US-China policy had been publicly articulated by the United States. But the statement did not represent a long-term policy or an administration consensus on a strategy toward the triangle. Rather, as the author of the speech told me, it was an 'observation' about the impact of potential Soviet behaviour on US policy.

30. Based on a study of Soviet perceptions of China and Sino-American military ties by the author (which included extensive interviews with Soviet Sinologists and strategic experts in Moscow in February 1981 as a guest of the Institute of US and Canadian Studies), it seems that 'playing the China card' had a profound impact on Soviet actions and overall assessments of the strategic environment after May 1978. On the one hand, it further complicated the Soviets' problem of two-front war planning, and on the other, led to more aggressive and rigid behaviour *vis-à-vis* the United States.

31. See Gerald Segal, 'China and the Great Power Triangle', *China Quarterly*, September 1980, on Chinese appeals to the US in the late 1940s.

32. See John Lewis Gaddis, 'Containment: A Reassessment', *Foreign Affairs*, July 1977, Vol. 55, No. 4.

33. Quoted by Gaddis, Ibid.

34. Ibid.

35. For an analysis of the collusion – anti-collusion dynamics of the triangular relationship, see Banning Garrett, 'China Policy and the Strategic Triangle', in *Eagle Entangled: U.S. Foreign Policy in a Complex World*, Kenneth Oye, Donald Rothchild and Robert Lieber (eds.), New York: Longman, 1979, pp. 250–7.

Part Two
The Great Power Triangle in Europe

5 THE TRIANGLE IN WESTERN EUROPE

Lawrence Freedman

The notion of a Sino-Soviet-American 'triangle' has only slight
meaning for policy makers in Western Europe. In the continent
where the concept of a balance of power was invented there are no
problems with the idea of making the most of divisions among
potential adversaries for strategic gains. Arguably the principle
behind the use of the 'China card' was most vividly expressed by
Winston Churchill, except in this case he was talking about joining
forces with the Soviet Union against Nazi Germany, when he spoke
in 1940 of how: 'If Hitler invaded Hell I would make at least a
favourable reference to the Devil in the House of Commons!' Nor
would Europeans deny the importance of the 'China factor' in the
foreign policies of the Soviet Union and the United States. The problem comes with promoting to the centre of international affairs a
set of relationships that assigns excessive importance to China while
excluding Western Europe altogether.

Apart from the sheer size of its population and its ownership of a
small nuclear arsenal, China does not rank high on any of the main
indicators of international power.[1] Such influence as it does have is
largely concentrated within Asia. The days when China appeared as
the natural leader of an increasingly radical Third World have now
passed. If China matters at all on the international scene it is largely
because the two superpowers continue to act as if it does matter.
Western Europeans have long been puzzled and concerned at the
obsessive attitudes that both the United States and Soviet Union
have, at different times, shown over China, which has only served to
exaggerate China's potential for either mischief-making or strategic
support.

The obsession with China has resulted in a large part because of
the erratic course it has steered over the past 30 years. During this
same time Western Europe has worked within a remarkably stable
framework of allies and adversaries. The greater movement, and
the alarms this has set off within the superpowers, has given China the
appearance of being more important to the pattern of international

relations than the staid Europeans, but the surface appearance bears little relation to the underlying realities. A European shift in allegiances of the sort that has become quite regular in China's foreign policy would completely and irreversibly transform international politics.

China also tends to propound its theories of the moment with an unqualified certainty that belies its own propensity to change course. Furthermore, China's approach often involves encouraging others to take a firmer stand against a common enemy, be it the Soviet Union against the United States or the United States against the Soviet Union, without itself contributing much to the common effort. At times the Chinese are more European than the Europeans, urging a degree of unity and common purpose that remains beyond the dreams of the most committed supporter of the Treaty of Rome.[2] All this leads to a marked contrast between China's erratic earnestness and Europe's fervourless consistency.

China's seemingly greater freedom of international manoeuvre is believed to be one of the benefits of a largely self-sufficient economic system. It is able to provide most of its own food, fuel and raw materials, and has only a small portion of its GNP devoted to trade. This means that a break with some erstwhile partner does not have many awkward repercussions in domestic economic management, while the same is patently not true for Western Europeans who are far more dependent on trade and imports of key resources.

One of the interesting questions for the future is whether China's growing reliance on international markets will in itself force it to settle down with a stable foreign policy. For the moment China probably remains sufficiently marginal to the international economy to enjoy more strategic flexibility than the Europeans. If anything it is able to use the promise of new markets for manufactured goods and a welcome new source of oil and some vital non-fuel minerals, which so attract the hard-pressed economies of the West, as an instrument of its foreign policy.

So China's international power may be largely negative, a capacity to disrupt political expectations and disappoint commercial hopes, rather than a more positive capacity to fund new economic ventures, support clients, organize regional groupings, project military power, and so on. However, even this negative power requires an ability to continue to offer economic carrots or the political stick of *rapprochement* with the Soviet Union. If, as I will argue may be the case, the commercial prospects are a mirage and the political options are by no means as varied as many assume, then China's relevance for West Europeans may be limited.

Furthermore, if it started to develop positive rather than negative power, then the attitudes of Europeans could quickly move from one of limited interest and amity to a cool suspicion. China's revolutionary zeal has been calmed by circumstances: economic failure and international isolation. There is natural concern that success in remedying these problems, combined with an ideological revival, could lead to a renewal of the radical challenge that China once presented to the international system. Thus the Soviet Union warns in its propaganda of how Western aid to China may backfire and a threat will emerge to the 'Southern Flank of Capitalism'.

There are also concerns in Western Europe lest China, even if politically tame, discovers the secret of the rapid industrial success of the highly productive Asian economies, which have already had dramatic consequences for the rest of the less-competitive industrial world. China is obviously impressed with the industrial prowess of Japan and the 'four tigers' — South Korea, Taiwan, Singapore and Hong Kong. European industrialists, thinking ahead, cannot but wonder about the prospect of similar industrial growth in the largest country of them all, noting the role of imports of Western technology as a possible fertilizer.

Thus whereas China only really has value to Western Europe if its current modernization programme is successful, there could soon be anxieties if this programme looked like being too successful.

In practice China is unlikely to develop as fast or as impressively as its neighbours because of the drag imposed by its vast population, its minimal technological base and its unsuitable political structure. In turn this means that militarily it will remain relatively weak. The most likely policy debates in the commercial sphere will be over whether dealings with China will eventually be profitable and advantageous despite the current frustrations, and over whether concessions and favours in this sphere will bring dividends in the political sphere. In the political sphere the issue is whether China has much to contribute beyond adding to the pressure on the Soviet Union and whether encouraging this pressure could turn out to be counterproductive.

The European instinct has therefore been to limit the China factor in its own political relations with the Soviet Union, while accepting the military benefits of the Sino-Soviet split. What has been uncertain is whether these benefits might be lost without an active policy by Europe, or whether they will accrue because of the extent of Sino-Soviet hostility irrespective of European policy being active or passive.

For Western Europeans, policies towards China have to be judged in terms of their effects on the relationship with the Soviet Union. This relationship is expressed in terms of the twin objectives of détente and defence. China is generally considered to aid Europe's defence by drawing a substantial amount of the Soviet Union's military attention and effort away from its Western to its Eastern flank. However, in terms of détente, China is a more disruptive influence as it makes it difficult for the West to have friendly relations with it without appearing to be engaged in an anti-Soviet conspiracy. The question for Europe (and for the West in general) is whether it is possible to secure the strategic dividend from Sino-Soviet hostility without putting excessive strain on relations with the Soviet Union.

Out of Alliance

As the Sino-Soviet split developed during the 1950s it was by no means universally viewed in the West as a major boon. There was a common perception of China as a maverick power, while the Soviet Union was maturing with its new international strength and responsibilities. At least up to the 1968 invasion of Czeckoslovakia it was assumed that the Soviet Union was moderating both its domestic and external policies and therefore did not constitute as great a danger as before. Meanwhile China under Mao was resisting this 'revisionism' (which in the West seemed to be a synonym for common sense), offering instead the spectre of an uncontrollable radical force with nuclear weapons as well as vast and fanatical manpower at its disposal.

It was also possible to take seriously Maoist concepts of the under-developed nations being turned against the industrialized nations, including members of Comecon, in an uprising fuelled by resentment at the exploitation of the world's rural poor. This implied a common cause with the Soviet Union against this Third World threat and confirmed that China was the most hostile and disruptive of the Communist countries. There was some regret that the Russians had failed to keep their erstwhile ally under control.

The socialist camp as a whole was left looking less impressive, and the reduction in the absolute strength available to Soviet leaders could be welcomed. However, if anything there was sympathy with the Russians as they were berated by the Chinese for their revisionism, lack of revolutionary zeal and unwillingness to risk a nuclear confrontation. The Soviet response to these charges and its attempt to moderate China showed up the Kremlin to the West in its most favourable light. It was China, for example in the public polemics of 1963 that drew out of the Soviet leaders the admission that the 'atom bomb does not obey the class principle', the denial of the inevitability of war and the warnings on the folly of adventurism.[3]

The perception of China as an international menace was evidently influential in the United States, which reoriented its grand strategy to cope with a Communist threat that now appeared most likely to manifest itself as guerrilla groups and liberation movements in the Third World, and in 1967 could even justify expenditure on an anti-ballistic missile system by reference to some imminent Chinese nuclear threat against American cities (which has still to materialize).[4]

Though the reactions were more modest, the concern was by no means absent in Western Europe. If nothing else, the association of Maoism with the most unruly elements in the ultra-left and student movements of the late 1960s ensured a degree of hostility to China. Britain, in particular, still had substantial interests in the Far East. It had to worry about Chinese-backed insurgencies, for example in Malaya, and riots in Hong Kong. It also suffered from the excesses of the Cultural Revolution in having its embassy in Peking burned down. Another indication of the seriousness with which the Chinese 'threat' was viewed in Britain was the apparent willingness of the Labour Government in 1964–5 to toy with the idea of offering India a nuclear umbrella against a Chinese threat.[5]

Only General de Gaulle among European leaders saw any real merit in China's assertiveness, for in the opposition to superpower political hegemony and nuclear monopoly, China was playing the same role within the socialist bloc that France was attempting to play in NATO. They joined in opposition to the Partial Test Ban Treaty of 1963 and then to the negotiation of the Nuclear Non-Proliferation Treaty, which they saw, with some justice, as designed to keep them both out of the nuclear business. Together they developed as nuclear powers during the 1960s, despite international condemnation. Together they seemed to be the harbingers of a new era of international politics more fluid than in the past, with individual powers enjoying a greater freedom of manoeuvre than permitted in a system dominated by the superpowers. It was therefore not surprising that France became the first Western power to exchange ambassadors with China in 1964.

There were differences in their approach, which became very important over time. France never quite severed its links with the United States. China broke completely with the Soviet Union. To China in the 1960s, moving away from a liaison with one super-power did not require some form of *rapprochement* with the other. The sentiment was essentially 'a plague on both your houses'. To France, demonstrating its autonomy from American direction meant establishing an independent relationship with the Soviet Union.

When the two began to break away from their respective alliances they were obvious kindred spirits. The impression was of former great powers, still smarting from the humiliations of the past, attempting to regain their self-respect by escaping from a stultifying dependence on a superpower.

But France was acting out of a sense of a national destiny as an independent actor in international affairs. The Gaullist vision was not so much of a shattered alliance but of a much looser set of relations within Europe cutting across the East-West divide, incidentally allowing powers such as France a more active and prominent role.

Ostensibly China had a much more revolutionary vision of a whole order overturned, in which imperialist states could no longer pick on the weak and underdeveloped. Yet in practice it was reacting against a particular alliance. It soon became preoccupied with resisting a specific imperialist power, rather than imperialism in general, and started to look favourably on anyone who might help.

All France could achieve was a loosening of alliance ties and a contribution to the easing of East-West relations. It elevated this in its rhetoric to a dispensation from the full responsibilities of alliance membership and some special understanding with the Eastern bloc. By the late 1970s this approach was in complete contrast to that of China whose argument with the Soviet Union had now led it to favour strong alliances against an habitual aggressor. Instead of France and China moving in parallel lines within their respective camps, they began to differ on how to approach a dominant feature in both their strategic maps — the Soviet Union. China broke out of its bloc to the point where it could challenge the West to match it in its anti-Sovietism.

The Common Enemy

It is this anti-Sovietism which has made talk of a tacit alliance between the West and China at all plausible. It has been argued that the two sides in their distrust of the Soviet Union share a basic organising principle in their foreign policy — to put it crudely 'a common enemy'.[6]

To those professionally concerned with planning the Western defences the coincidence of interest with China was obvious. In the early 1970s, once the basic directions of Chinese policy had become clear, it was possible in NATO circles to hear ironic little jokes about China being the sixteenth member of the Alliance. It seemed self-evident that it was better to have an enemy preoccupied with another flank than one who could concentrate all his attention on you. As always, in practice, matters were not quite so straightforward.

The prospect of serious military benefits first became noticeable in the late 1960s, as the Soviet Union began to fortify its Eastern defences. The depth of Sino-Soviet hostility became clear in March 1969 when fighting broke out around the Amur and Ussuri Rivers. The Western media began to pay attention to the border dispute and soon speculation was rife of an imminent war between the two Communist giants, with the possibility being mooted of a Soviet preemptive strike before China's limited nuclear capability was operational.[7]

The talk of war subsided but there could be no doubt of the bitterness between the two. Analysis of the fighting and the military positions of the two sides made clear how few non-nuclear options were available to the Soviet Union in that area. Its conventional forces were exposed, with enormous distances from stocks and reserves and the command centre, lines of communication vulnerable to Chinese attack (including the Trans-Siberian Railway so close to the border) and few established military facilities. The Russians had begun to take China seriously as a military problem in late 1967, and in 1968 there were the first moves to create an effective military presence. After the clashes of 1969 these moves were expedited.

There was a tangible reduction in the nuclear threat facing Western Europe as a quarter of the SS-4 and SS-5 medium-range ballistic missiles were moved from the Western to the Eastern Military Districts. Over the next few years the Soviet Union constructed a whole military infrastructure, with airfields, roads, railspurs, barracks, stores and all the other paraphernalia necessary to support a large garrison for an extended period. Work even began to construct an alternative to the Trans-Siberian Railway, this time well away from the border with China. New divisions were formed or brought in from Central Asia. Soon the Chinese were complaining of a million Soviet troops massing on their borders in some 40 divisions. While the reality was not quite so formidable (perhaps half a million men), for many of the divisions were maintained at lower states of combat readiness without a full complement of men and equipment, it was nonetheless impressive. Soon about a fifth of the Soviet military effort was devoted to China.[8]

During this period there were few changes in either the quality or the quantity of the Soviet forces facing Western Europe. There were increases in Soviet forces strengths, but these were mainly with the newly-established divisions in Czechoslovakia, consolidating the 'fraternal assistance' of August 1968. Thus Europe experienced no great sense of relief of a potential adversary decisively switching its attention from one flank to another. Some new military projects not directly related to China may have been cancelled or deferred, but in general the 'China threat' appears to have been used to justify additions to the Soviet defence budget rather than the redirection of resources already allocated. Furthermore, the steady improvement of Soviet military technology continued, and new equipment was available for use on either flank.

The ambiguity of the strategic message contained in the Soviet military response to China can be illustrated by the movement of SS-4 and SS-5 missiles to the east. At the time these missiles did not have the notoriety that they have since acquired. Generally within NATO they were seen as relics of an earlier period when the Soviet Union had lacked a credible nuclear capability against North America and had to make do with threatening Western Europe. It was presumed that intercontinental missiles had rendered SS-4s and SS-5s virtually redundant, so that no great sacrifice was being made by moving them east.

Since then the attitude in NATO to such long-range theatre nuclear forces (to use the new nomenclature) has changed. A key factor in effecting this change was the SS-20 intermediate-range missile which became operational in 1976. This missile is in all aspects — mobility, range, accuracy, multiple warheads and speed of launch — superior to the SS-4s and SS-5s it replaces. Its introduction was taken in Europe to indicate that the Soviet Union was still interested in posing a theatre nuclear threat, despite the fact that it could now adequately target its main adversary, the United States, and despite the previous assumption that it would wish to spare the main prize of any aggression, Western Europe, from nuclear bombardment if at all possible.

There is no reason to believe that a longstanding Soviet interest in targeting American bases in Europe as well as watching over actual and potential European nuclear powers, would not have provided sufficient justification in itself for a new missile, but there is circumstantial evidence that the need for something suitable for use against China was a crucial stimulus, and may well have influenced decisions on performance characteristics. Certainly its basing reflects more of a China bias than the SS-4s and SS-5s (all of which now appear to have been removed from the east). One third of the SS-20s are in the west, one-third in the east and one-third in swing sites in the middle of the country from where they are able to reach both Western Europe and China.[9]

Thus the Soviet Union's build-up in the east has not led to any marked decline in its forces ranged against NATO. The result has been a net increase in Soviet capabilities, so that a Sino-Soviet *rapprochement* or even a decline in the Soviet perception of the 'China threat' could result in these extra forces being turned against NATO.

It would need a real squeeze on the Soviet defence budget before the Kremlin would have to face hard choices between the competing demands of its western and eastern flanks. At the moment, NATO represents by far the most serious military threat, though the Kremlin may well fear and distrust Chinese intentions far more over the long term. As Chinese military capabilities have not continued to improve at the rate of the early 1970s and remain far less impressive than was once expected, it is quite likely that the Soviet General Staff would find it easier to relax its guard in the east.[10]

When, after the flight and death of Lin Biao in 1971, the Chinese began to trim military expenditure it was conveniently discovered that the real Soviet threat was against the industrial states of Europe, which offered a rich prize and whose conquest would be a manageable military operation. The growing Soviet presence on China's borders, previously described in lurid terms and in tones of great anxiety, was now seen more as a crude attempt at political intimidation, essentially a 'feint to the East' while expansionist plans were being worked out against Western Europe.[11]

Similarly, the doctrine of the inevitability of war, picked upon by Soviet propagandists as evidence of China's basic irresponsibility, was about a coming East-West clash. The Russians have argued that this reveals China's true aim, of provoking a destructive nuclear war between the established powers, after which it would pick up the pieces and dominate the world. The Chinese say that their limited role in these ćataclysmic scenarios is no more than an honest reflection of their limited power and resources. They offer an aggressor a small prize which given the size of the country and its population, could only be gained at enormous effort.

The simple canons of Chinese doctrine have proved to be remarkably flexible and disingenuously self-serving. They remain equivocal on how much the base characteristics of the Soviet policy actually put China at risk. Chinese behaviour suggests reasonable confidence that the Russians will not pounce on them, but sufficient concern that they might to encourage attention to the nation's defences and outside sources of political, and possibly military, support. What is clear is that the Chinese do not see themselves as mounting an increasing threat to the Soviet Union nor as drawing fire away from NATO.

It is an objective of China in discussions with the Soviet Union to argue for Soviet forces to be moved well away from the border. This is a precondition for any *rapprochement*. The Soviet response has thus far not extended much beyond an offer of limited withdrawals from Mongolia. From Moscow's perspective there remains a 'China threat', both because the Chinese are believed capable of some utterly reckless action and because key Soviet interests are vulnerable to assault in the mines and oil wells of the Asian part of the Soviet Union which are becoming increasingly vital to the economic health of the country. Prudent military planning will require a defensive barrier in the east, however qualitatively inferior the Chinese forces.

For this reason, Western Europe probably need not fear a real Sino-Soviet *rapprochement* and a sudden glut of raw military power in the Warsaw Pact as spare capacity is diverted from the east. This does not mean that the Soviet General Staff could not justify bringing over some forces from the Chinese border to consolidate its position in Europe if East-West relations took another turn for the worse. In addition, it is likely that NATO has now already received such military relief as it is going to receive from the Sino-Soviet conflict.

Alternative Roads to Socialism

In the political sphere the benefits to the West from the Sino-Soviet dispute have also been limited and qualified by a number of costs. The intensity of the Sino-Soviet dispute can always be cited as evidence that the Russians have problems in their foreign policy as substantial as those facing the West. However, it is not axiomatic that troubles for the East benefit the West. Arguably if China made the Soviet leaders nervous and jumpy then they would be less easy to deal with than if they were relaxed. Another source of possible concern in the late 1960s was the Soviet fear that the Maoists were capable of dividing the Communist world, in which case there might be a temptation to provoke some European crisis to hold the Warsaw Pact in line. There were some indications in 1969 that the support of European Communist parties was being sought for any action that might be deemed necessary against China; the Soviet Union was ready to be awkward with the West over Berlin (then the subject of sensitive negotiations) as a unifying agent. If the forces of international socialism were engaged in some struggle with those of imperialism, albeit at a low level, then the Chinese would be shown up as disruptive, providing sustenance to the imperialists by attempting to split the Communist movement. Alternatively, the Communist factions might compete to demonstrate their revolutionary credentials, in a 'prolier than thou' drive, stoking up national liberation movements in various parts of the Third World. In these ways, the Sino-Soviet split could lead to increased international tension, with adverse consequences for the West.

In practice the dispute did not have this sort of negative effect, especially as it moved out of the realm of progressive ideology and into the realm of old-fashioned power politics. The Chinese challenge to the Soviet Union in the 1960s had been of an alternative pole within international Communism, able to attract adherents away from Moscow by an uncompromising revolutionary commitment, a greater sensitivity to the problems and aspirations of the Third World, and a charismatic leader being offered as the main fount of Marxist wisdom. By contrast Soviet Communism appeared

116 The China Factor

dull and uninspired, hopelessly compromised by a craving for international respectability and domination by a bureaucratic elite.

The Chinese appeal was to those considered in Moscow to be ultra-left adventurists. These were largely to be found in splinter movements of Third World Communist parties, who had rejected the 'peaceful road to socialism'. Within Western Europe these splinter movements could also be found, usually close to the universities, but Maoism was by no means the only alternative to Communist orthodoxy in the left-wing market-place. Other goods were on offer, such as Trotskyism and Anarchism. In Britain, for example, Maoists made little headway against the Trotskyists in the student movement. In Italy they were more successful. The established Communist parties' strategies were based on winning power through elections and joint action with other 'progressive forces'. Ultra-leftism was still considered an 'infantile disorder' with which association would be politically disastrous. The refusal to be tempted to compete in militancy with the Maoists and their ilk was most clearly demonstrated in the 'May Events' in France in 1968 when the Communist Party acted with considerable caution.

Support in the West for China was no more soundly based than the latest intellectual fashion among the young bourgeoisie, with competition from more indigenous forms of romantic leftism, while that in the Third World was limited and often dissipated in heroic but futile applications of an activist philosophy of armed struggle. Moreover, the Chinese themselves reacted against the extremes of the Cultural Revolution. The move towards a more orderly domestic policy was eventually reflected in foreign policy. However, the basic change was in the seriousness of China's strategic position at the end of the 1960s, as the danger grew of Soviet hostility gaining a military expression. In facing this danger China found itself virtually friendless.

Within the Communist world, excepting tiny Albania, China had no friends. The effective challenge against Soviet leadership had been mounted from the right, not the left. Within Europe, the example of Yugoslavia was more influential than that of China. Of course, these were precisely the 'revisionists' that had been reviled for so long in Chinese propaganda. It was easier for the Chinese to concoct some tactical understanding with the imperialists than to explain the doctrinal shift that permitted ties with revisionists and Eurocommunists, as this constituted a major admission of ideological failure. It probably needed the demise of Mao himself before it was possible to follow the political logic of contacting other Communist parties that were not inclined to follow the Moscow line. In September 1977 Marshal Tito of Yugoslavia was warmly received in Peking, followed in May 1978 by President Ceausescu of Romania.[12] It was not until late 1978 that the role of the most independent of Western European Communist parties, particularly those of Italy and Spain, was re-examined. These parties had been assumed to be basically subservient to Moscow, but the Chinese were convinced by evidence to the contrary (such as denunciations of the invasion of Afghanistan) that they were genuinely independent. In April 1980 Berlinguer of the Italian Communist Party toured China, establishing the link. Not long before this, in an act of intellectual honesty, Peking stopped condemning Moscow for being 'revisionist'. Thus having failed to strengthen its position *vis-à-vis* the Soviet Union by an outflanking movement on the left, it attempted to outflank on the right.

In the West there was relief that the Soviet Union had refused to respond to the Chinese challenge in the 1960s by moving leftward. In the 1970s the interest was in whether the West could benefit by a competition between the two to establish co-operative relations with the West.

Divergence in Détente

The Soviet Union had a head start in this competition. Despite the invasion of Czeckoslovakia, there were agreements on Berlin, the start of serious progress in arms control, indications of a desire in the East to gain access to Western credits and technology, and a desire in the West to benefit from this new commercial opening. This, combined with a general desire to escape from the tensions of continual East-West confrontation, led to the establishment of détente.

One (among many) incentive for the Soviet Union to sort out its relations with the West was its growing difficulties with China. President Nixon and Henry Kissinger were well aware of this and used it to some effect in the diplomacy surrounding the strategic arms limitation talks and the attempt to find some form of honourable withdrawal from Vietnam. In Europe, however, the 'China factor' was of only slight relevance in the moves towards détente — such as West Germany's *Ostpolitik* and the 1975 Helsinki Conference on Security and Cooperation in Europe.

The role of China ought not to be exaggerated in discussing the problems that have overtaken détente since the mid-1970s. Any developing contact with Western Europe, particularly in the military sphere, was a potentially disruptive influence, but before this could be felt, East-West relations had already deteriorated of their own accord.

Throughout the 1970s China harped on the unreformed aggressiveness of the Soviet Union. This sounded a discordant note in the first half of the decade, but by the second half there were opportunities for it to say 'I told you so'. However, the main reasons for the decline in the Soviet image had little to do with China: the lack of progress in 'human rights' in the East; the build-up in Warsaw Pact forces; the various Soviet adventures in the Third World. Only in the last of these can a major Chinese dimension be discerned.

Until well on into the 1970s, the Western European instinct was to note the Chinese anti-Sovietism with a wry amusement, of the sort that longstanding Catholics reserve for recent converts. There was certainly no intention of imitating this: it was a phase they had recently passed through.

The West had suffered through a single-minded anti-communism (directed against the Chinese as much as the Russians). This was a common explanation of the trauma of the Vietnam War. A fixation on the Soviet 'threat' was considered responsible for a number of policy failures. Succour had been given to corrupt and tyrannical regimes whose only redeeming feature was that they were anti-communist. Other large issues, such as questions of development in the Third World, had been ignored. When China started in the 1970s to evaluate all internationl actors according to their attitudes towards the Soviet Union, it was suggested in Europe that the same mistake was being repeated. By way of mitigation it was noted that China still lacked diplomatic experience and had yet to appreciate all the nuances of international life and the problems of dealing with countries who do not share the same concerns and perceptions. In addition, its general lack of political and economic entanglements meant that it was not subject to the same number and variety of cross-cutting pressures as other major powers. This was not simply a matter of policy in Africa and the Middle East, but was also relevant to the central question of policy towards the Soviet Union itself.

To some extent it was the Soviet Union that forced the issue — initially successfully — as it began to use the character of a nation's contact with China as a means of testing its commitment to détente. Thus France, which saw itself as a pace-setter in détente, did not take kindly to being lectured by China on its folly as it sought to protect its 'special understanding' with the Soviet Union. West Germany, which soon developed substantial political and economic interests in détente, was also wary of jeopardising these by upsetting the Kremlin. By contrast, Britain had less to lose from East-West tension and could be more tolerant of China. Yet it still followed other Western Europeans in attempting to explain to Peking, as had once a frustrated and irritated Soviet Union, the limits to militancy and the necessity for compromise.

The China Market

During the 1970s European strictures on this score became increasingly less confident. Détente came to be presented in terms of hard bargains on a specific set of limited understandings, concerned with such matters as the status of Berlin, arms control, East-West trade, and so on, and less as steady progress towards a general set of understandings on proper forms of international behaviour and rules for the management of conflicts. The Soviet Union resisted being 'civilized' in terms of repression at home or adventures abroad.

At the same time, the Chinese managed to rectify their own image left over from the Cultural Revolution, though there were still some lapses into obscurantism as with the 'Anti-Confucius' campaign. Increasingly confidence grew that there were still some forces of rationality and order at work in China, and that these forces were pushing the country in a basic direction acceptable to the West.

After the death of Mao and the disgrace of the Gang of Four, the country appeared to be moving in a direction that was generally appealing to liberal democracies. Chinese socialism began to lose its image of fanaticism and xenophobia. Its style became less solemn and prurient, more open and honest. In some ways this 'westernization' was no more than a reaction against the excesses of the past, and so contained its own dangers: hostility to foreigners and foreign things could give way to imitation; rejection of reliance on technology rather than people could give way to an infatuation with gadgets and all things modern. As Western fascination with the 'New China' peaked in late 1978 and early 1979, the coincident convulsions in Iran, taking that country in the opposite direction, warned of the social and political fragility of countries pushing modernizaion programmes too hard and too fast.

Nevertheless, the combination of an anti-Soviet foreign policy with a concomitant improvement in relations with the West, a more liberal domestic policy (even if this did remain a matter of degree) and, most exciting of all, a development policy that would depend on imports of Western capital goods and technology, did wonders for China's 'image'.

If China's plans were to be believed then in the last couple of decades of the twentieth century, it was going to require enormous capital expenditure on goods that only the West could supply.[13] The surge in commercial contacts in 1978, with delegations moving backwards and forwards, offering and inspecting the fruits of modern industry from televisions to tanks, created a virtual euphoria among Western businessmen who began to contemplate a market of one billion with an apparently insatiable appetite. There were sufficient contracts signed, or at least hinted at, during 1978 to sustain the excitement.

It did not take long for the Chinese to be exposed as, by necessity, often no more than industrial voyeurs. By the middle of 1979 it had become clear that the leadership in Peking was having second thoughts on the pace and character of its industrial development programme, and in 1980 the frustration began to show among Western industrialists who had spent long hours and large sums of money attempting to negotiate contracts and had little to show for this effort.[14]

The limited reward was always likely, given the self-evident impediments to rapid growth in China: the large population putting a strain on the agricultural sector and necessitating huge imports of grain; the wretched state of education and science after years of neglect; the lack of basic managerial skills; the underdevelopment of the industrial infrastructure.[15] Once it became clear that the Chinese were unwilling to go too far into debt then hopes for some new trade bonanza faded, giving way for more modest but realistic expectations.

Even when there was still some hope of a bonanza, the Europeans were frustrated by the recognition of the favoured position of Japan in cornering some of the most lucrative markets. At least until 1978 there was an advantage over the United States, but after 'normalization' its competitive advantages could be exploited to the full. So long as the potential commercial benefits were believed to be large, Western countries fell over themselves in an effort to attract China's custom — the provision of subsidized export credits was one obvious example.[16] Much of this has been done without much thought for the general consequences in international trade — in putting strain on agreements for credit facilities or in making way in special trade pacts with China for yet another large textile producer. The evident favouritism shown China in such matters as grain sales, Most Favoured Nation status and membership of the IMF has probably annoyed the Kremlin as much as any putative arms sales.

Arms Sales

Here we come to the one lever available to the Europeans that the Americans and the Japanese seemed to be denying themselves — the willingness to sell arms. It was an advantage that in the American case lasted only until 1980 and in Japan's case was always qualified, as it was happily selling knowhow, for example in electronics, with clear military applications.

The American approach to arms sales with the Soviet Union has been largely political. The Americans had played the 'China card' slightly in the early days of détente, but it had been assumed, even as late as 1978, that they could not push it too far so long as they had a political stake in good, working relations with the Soviet Union. Such a stake came with the continuing effort to conclude the SALT negotiations. That the danger was real can be seen in the delay in the signing of SALT following the 'normalization' of Sino-American relations in December 1978.

This meant that once the balance in the political equation began to move, as happened most dramatically following the December 1979 Soviet invasion of Afghanistan, the attitude to arms sales could change equally dramatically. In 1980, so difficult was it to find effective punitive measures to mark irritation with Soviet behaviour, that the evident dislike of the Kremlin for any links between China and the West became a positive incentive to effect such links. In this way the Soviet Union created the 'China card' and during 1980 the United States played this card, not so much to exercise leverage over the Soviet Union, always a forlorn hope, but as a form of political retribution.

It had been assumed, up to this point, that the Western Europeans would find it easier to develop strategic relations with China, because their hands were not tied, just as it has been easier for them to develop relations with the Arabs because they were less committed to Israel. The Western Europeans were already much further advanced in terms of formal political relations with China, having long since considered Taiwan's position and the Kuomintang's claim for dominion over the whole country, anachronistic.[17] Furthermore, there was a sense in which a reasonably close US-Soviet relationship, which governed the general East-West relationship, allowed the West Europeans a limited freedom of manoeuvre.

In 1980, the deterioration in East-West relations was much more noticeable outside of Europe than within it. This meant that inhibitions upon upsetting the Soviet Union by improving relations with China were stripped away far more quickly in the United States than in Western Europe. Indeed the Europeans, in particular the West Germans, became anxious lest all the benefits of the past decade be lost, so they were unwilling to put extra strain on détente.

However, the main reason why the West Europeans moved less fast in 1980 was that negotiations begun earlier had already got bogged down. The Europeans had always tended to view arms sales in commercial rather than political terms. When a number of arms deals between China and European countries seemed to be coming to fruition, the Soviet Union objected vigorously. This froze the German interest, but Britain and France persevered. Nevertheless, they tried to deny the political content and camouflage any strategic message by insisting that prospective sales would not be directed against any 'third parties' and that only 'defensive' capabilities would be transferred, with a firm restriction on 'offensive' weapons. In fact, rather than present possible arms contracts to China as acts seeping with strategic significance, they instead tended to present them as a major political concession, given the flak both from the Soviet Union and the European left, for which they expected to be able to extract a financial price.[18]

The British case is instructive for in many ways it seemed to be in the best position to provide equipment to China. It had less to lose in relations with the Soviet Union and most to gain (because of the special status of Hong Kong) in improving relations with China. There was a precedent, in the sale of Spey engines by Rolls-Royce in 1975, and China had shown a clear interest in the Harrier vertical-take-off aircraft. The British government acted as if it was doing China a favour by even considering the sale of Harrier, because of the political costs in relations with the Kremlin, and therefore required a *quid pro quo* in civilian commerce. The position was that the relationship should not be dominated by arms sales, but should extend to all political and economic spheres.

Were it not for the invasion of Vietnam by China in early 1979, which seemed an inappropriate moment to be transferring military equipment to China, the deal might have been concluded. After that the opportunity passed. Though the new Conservative government in Britain indicated it was putting no conditions on the deal, it was hard to make it commercially attractive: the Chinese complained Britain was asking for too high a price, while British Aerospace were unhappy that China seemed interested only in technology and not in finished aircraft.

There have been a few small contracts signed, for example for communication equipment, and more deals may be reached in the coming years. The point is that limits to these deals have turned out to be less the assessments in Western capitals as to the possible political risks in terms of relations with the East, but more the limits to China's ability to fund and absorb major transfers of modern military technology. The pressing industrial and agricultural problems faced by China have left little spare for military modernization, and the substantial short-term costs associated with the 1979 war with Vietnam appear to have used up some funds that might otherwise have been spent on equipment.[19]

The sheer scale of China's military problem faces its planners with a depressing predicament. There are so many huge gaps in their defences to fill that it is not surprising that they are being tentative in deciding on which gaps to start filling and in what manner and to what extent they can afford to fill them. As in other forms of trade, Western salesmen have been left frustrated by the prudent refusal of China's leaders to put their society and economy under the strain of too-rapid growth.

Conclusion

The inescapable conclusion of this analysis for Western European – China relations is that neither in the strategic nor economic sense does China have much to offer Western Europe and that it is not able to pay for much of what Western Europe can offer China. This does not mean that perfectly amicable and mutually beneficial relations cannot continue to develop. If China provides few great benefits, it poses few threats. The probable limits to its future economic performance mean that it is unlikely to become a 'super-Japan', dominating any international market to which it devotes some effort, or to fulfil its potential for international disruption. A low-key relationship would suit Western Europe best. It has lost the taste for grand strategic games, especially when they are of high risk for limited and uncertain gains. Moreover, China may be coming to the end of the heroic phase in its foreign policy and strategy, and is coming to recognize that some of its more grandiose plans and strategic games are inadequate and inappropriate for current circumstances. The most useful role for Europe is to encourage this trend towards realism.

Notes

1. For a recent attempt to assess China's position on a variety of indicators see John Franklin Cooper, *China's Global Role*, Stanford, California: Hoover Institution Press, 1980. Cooper concludes: 'We should not expect China to act consistently as a major power — even most of the time — or play a role generally beyond that of the second-ranking powers. We certainly should not anticipate, hope, or fear that China will seriously alter the course or nature of world politics'.

2. For example in encouraging the reunification of Germany.

3. See Alice Langley Hsieh, 'The Sino-Soviet Nuclear Dialogue 1963', in Raymond L. Garthoff (ed.), *Sino-Soviet Military Relations*, New York: Praeger, 1966.

4. The extent to which President Johnson, for one, could take the Chinese nuclear threat seriously is discussed in Morton Halperin 'The Decision to Deploy the ABM', *World Politics*, XXV, October 1972. China tested its first intercontinental missile in early 1980 but it has yet to develop an operational capability.

5. The February 1965 *Defence White Paper* observed: 'The Chinese nuclear explosion casts a new shadow over the future making it more difficult to forecast the trend of political development in an area where we have Commonwealth and Treaty responsibilities to assist our friends'. Andrew Pierre, *Nuclear Politics: The British Experience with an Independent Strategic Force 1939–1970*, London: Oxford University Press, 1972, p. 286.

6. On a trip to Peking in April 1978, the British Chief of Defence Staff, Air Marshal Sir Neil Cameron, observed that Britain and China shared 'an enemy at our door whose capital is Moscow'. Prime Minister James Callaghan described these views as being 'unscripted and impromptu'. *Far Eastern Economic Review*, May 1978.

7. See, for example, series of articles in the London *Times*, 2 February to 6 February 1970, by Neville Maxwell, David Bonavia, Leonard Beaton and Richard Harris under the general title 'The Next War?'

8. A US Defense Intelligence Agency analyst suggested in 1979 that: 'We estimate that between 10 and 15 per cent of Soviet spending on operating and investment is allocated to their Far Eastern front'. Hearings before the Subcommittee on Priorities and Economy in Government of the Joint Economic Committee, *Allocation of*

Resources in the Soviet Union and China — 1979, Washington, DC: US GPO, 1980, p. 78.

9. Lawrence Freedman, 'The Dilemma of Theatre Nuclear Arms Control', *Survival*, XXIII:1, January/February 1981, pp. 5, 9.

10. Lawrence Freedman, 'Economic and Technological Factors in the Sino-Soviet Dispute', in Douglas Stuart and William Tow (eds.), *China, The Soviet Union and the West: Strategic and Political Dimensions for the 1980s*, Colorado: Westview, 1981.

11. Neville Maxwell in *The Times*, 13 June 1974, described this Chinese attitude as a 'riddle' given the extensive war preparations on both sides of the Sino-Soviet border.

12. See Chapter 6 by Edwina Moreton.

13. The 1978 plans are fully discussed in Joint Economic Committee, *Chinese Economy Post-Mao*, Washington, DC: US GPO, 1978.

14. 'The art of the enterprising British businessman lies in identifying products in a relatively narrow band of technical developments where the manufacturing "lead" is far enough advanced so that the Chinese cannot do it themselves, but not so far ahead that it is an idle luxury'. John Gittings, *Guardian* 29 April 1980.

15. Central Intelligence Agency, National Foreign Assessment Centre, *China: In Pursuit of Economic Modernization*, December 1978.

16. For example West German Economic Minister Otto Lambsdorff complained that Germany's inability to offer comparable subsidized export credits to those of other countries put it at a trade disadvantage, *International Herald Tribune*, 12 August 1980. However, a British trade minister, Cecil Parkinson, has grumbled that a British problem in trade with China is that other governments may be in a better position to use their aid programme to back up their businessmen than Britain can, *The Times*, 21 March 1980.

17. However, Holland has created a crisis in relations with the PRC over its willingness to sell submarines to Taiwan. This case is instructive in revealing the limits to China's leverage over even a small West European country.

18. The arms sales issue is discussed in Lawrence Freedman, *The West and the Modernization of China*, London: Royal Institute of International Affairs, May 1979.

19. See Central Intelligence Agency, National Foreign Assessment Centre, *Chinese Defense Spending, 1965–1979*, July 1980.

6   THE TRIANGLE IN EASTERN EUROPE

Edwina Moreton

To play cards with effect, whether in games of chance or inter-national diplomacy, requires at a minimum that the players be able to hold their cards reasonably close to their chest; and in the case of minor players, that they at least be able to throw in the occasional wild card to alter their luck. But for the East Europeans, when it comes to international politics, the partners, the hand and the grand strategy have traditionally been selected by Moscow.

For the East European members of the Warsaw Pact 'limited sovereignty' in domestic politics, meaning the obligatory retention of the basic structures of the Soviet model of socialism, has always been matched by similar restrictions on the conduct of foreign policy. Although the ultimate sanction to impose ideological and political discipline on Eastern Europe in both domestic and foreign policy remains Soviet military and economic power, in practice the pre-ssures on the East European regimes in their dealings with the outside world have always been more complex. This has been particularly true of relations between the East European states and the Soviet Union's two major rivals, China and the United States.

The Primacy of Party over State Relations

The primary reason for this limited sovereignty in the foreign policy sphere has been the Soviet Union's enduring stake in Eastern Europe. The region's acknowledged role as physical security buffer along the Soviet Union's western borders has been enhanced, rather than diminished, over time as the Soviet Union has made the post-war transition from diplomatic isolation, to become a regional superpower and then a global superpower. At each stage the import-ance of Eastern Europe to Soviet foreign policy has grown, both symbolically and ideologically.

It was in the late 1940s that Stalin first pulled his iron curtain across Europe to block out Western influence from Eastern Europe.

Since then Soviet emphasis on public discipline among its allies, together with the practical limits placed on the East European states by virtue of their membership in the Warsaw Pact and the CMEA, have largely prevented them from taking any major initiatives in foreign affairs.

In the early years foreign policy had in any case been the effective monopoly of the four major powers in Europe. Later the 'threat' from the West — and in particular from a resurgent West Germany — was sufficient to cement a large degree of alliance solidarity in support of primarily Soviet foreign policy objectives. To the Soviet Union at the time the 'threat' from this quarter was less that of a rearmed West Germany as such, than of a West Germany acting as the spearhead of American power and influence on the European mainland. Still, the threat was clearly felt and, from a Soviet perspective at least, played a major part in determining the early hostile relationship between East and West.

To the East Europeans, and particularly those states with a vested interest in resolving the German problem, West Germany did pose a credible political threat. As the only state in Europe actively working to change the political and territorial *status quo*, West Germany posed a direct challenge to East Germany (whose existence it ignored), to Poland (whose borders it refused to recognize) and to a lesser degree to Czechoslovakia. Until West Germany was prepared to modify this 'revanchist' stance, any attempt by the West to expand political relations with Eastern Europe was destined to run into a Soviet veto. Thus Western strategies towards Eastern Europe, from 'roll-back' in the 1950s to peaceful engagement and bridge-building in the 1960s, met with a consistent rebuff as being detrimental to Soviet — and Warsaw Pact — security interests.

But the Soviet stake in Eastern Europe was enhanced still further by the repercussions of the Sino-Soviet dispute. In a very practical sense, hostilities along the Sino-Soviet border in the 1960s reinforced the Soviet Union's need for security in the west. (And more recently instability in Iran and Afghanistan along the Soviet Union's southern flank has added to this recurrent Soviet preoccupation.) But perhaps more important in the longer term, the growing attraction in the 1970s of the Chinese and Eurocommunist models of development at the expense of the Soviet path has meant that Eastern Europe is now the only region where the Soviet model has taken root, however inadequately. In a very real sense, therefore, Eastern Europe provides not only the physical basis, but also the ideological justification for the Soviet Union's claim to superpower status, both towards the West and the rest of the developing and Communist world. And as the most recent Soviet response to the Polish crisis has demonstrated, Leonid Brezhnev is no more inclined than was Stalin or Krushchev to relax the Soviet Union's political and ideological grip on this strategically vital alliance.

That is not to suggest that the East European regimes have otherwise remained the quiescent satellites Stalin probably had in mind. Some 35 years after being installed in power in the 'baggage train' of the Red Army, all these regimes have evolved their own separate identities. The image of a monolithic Soviet empire in Eastern Europe always did lack credibility — and probably most of all in Moscow. But the notion of a polycentric order in Eastern Europe, with individual states engaged in the pursuit of wholly independent policies, is also equally absurd.

In fact, although the history of Soviet-East European relations has been turbulent, in the past where Communist Party regimes themselves have rebelled, as in Poland in 1956 and Czechoslovakia in 1968, they have done so primarily in support of domestic autonomy and the right to pursue their own paths to socialism. Whatever the propaganda justification used to defend Soviet actions — as, for example, the accusation in 1968 that Czechoslovakia was being subverted by Western influence — foreign policy has seldom been a crucial issue. It has generally been the Soviet response to such domestic upheaval which has turned these challenges to political and economic orthodoxy into security issues for the entire bloc. Even the call for withdrawal from the Warsaw Pact in Hungary in 1956 was — at government level at least — more a practical response to premature use of Soviet tanks than the unfolding of any premeditated grand strategy of realignment. Although throughout the Polish crisis of 1980 and 1981 all the protagonists were obliged to keep an eye firmly fixed on Moscow, they did so precisely to stave off unwanted fraternal interference in a crisis with primarily domestic roots.

Yet, although clearly hemmed in by the constraints of alliance with the Soviet Union, there is a second factor which limits the autonomy of the East European regimes: in the past they have not only had to defend themselves against the unwanted attentions of their eastern neighbour, but also against domestic challenges to regime security. As the series of upheavals in Eastern Europe over the past three decades suggests, it is this domestic challenge which has proved most potent and which therefore will continue to be a primary preoccupation for Eastern Europe's ruling Communist parties.

Although they may have their differences with each other and with Moscow, both individually and collectively, all the East European regimes now in power in Eastern Europe share some common concerns. Ultimately all claim to derive their legitimacy and authority to govern from their membership in the alliance of socialist states. Thus, none is likely to kick too hard at the ideological traces. All share a common commitment to the Warsaw alliance — however loosely they might wish to define it.

Given these dual constraints of ideology and geography, neither the West — nor indeed China — could ever offer any of the East European states a credible alternative to alliance with the Soviet Union, and none has ever been sought. This 'single alternative' of alliance with the Soviet Union has meant that the emergence of the great power triangle, which sent ripples across the surface of world politics in the 1970s, left Eastern Europe largely untouched. Undeniably all the East European states have maintained some contacts with both the Soviet Union's major rivals, despite chilly winds blowing from Moscow against American 'imperialism' or Chinese 'splittism'. But such state-to-state contacts arising out of trade and the occasional cultural exchange have offered the East Europeans little scope to exercise political leverage in whatever direction. When the chips are down, the higher interests of their political and ideological alliance with Moscow remain paramount.

Unequal Enemies and Reluctant Friends

Indeed from an East European point of view there is a good case to be made that the emergence of a triangular balance in world politics has had an almost exclusively negative impact. By generating new options and greater flexibility at the superpower level, the new three-cornered configuration has possibly reduced rather than enhanced the scope for East European action.

None of these states has really held an intrinsic interest for either of the Soviet Union's main rivals. Great power interest in Eastern Europe, such as it is, has in the past derived largely from the Soviet stake in the area, and hence the opportunity to signal policy changes to the Soviet Union through this East European back-channel. In the past individual East European regimes have been courted by both the United States and China in the interests of 'higher' politics; but they have also been neglected at crucial times for the same reason.

Nor does there seem to have been any real expectation on the part of any of the East European regimes, with the possible exception of Romania, that the emergence of a tripolar world would materially affect their relations with the Soviet Union. The Romanians have tried hardest to stretch the limits of Soviet tolerance and to engage in active diplomacy across bipolar, even tripolar, lines. But even they have found themselves less manipulating than manipulated by the major powers. In short, when it comes to international politics in general, the East Europeans have no cards of their own to play.

And even as only reluctant allies of the Soviet Union, the East Europeans would have found the cards stacked against them. From an East European vantage point the great power triangle seems decidedly unbalanced. Soviet relations with China and the United States have at times seemed equally bad; they have never yet been equally good. For the period of the 'cold war' in Europe the main enemy was always Western 'imperialism'. The United States had less leverage in Eastern Europe than some of the West Europeans, notably France. But even there, political relations had to be channelled through Moscow. And well before any real thaw set in sufficiently to change the shape of East-West relations, the Chinese were being vilified by Moscow as 'splittists' and worse. By the time the depth and bitterness of the Sino-Soviet dispute could be detected by the outside world, China's active involvement in the affairs of Eastern Europe was almost at an end.

In the early years the Communist Party of China (CPC) had enjoyed considerable prestige in the Soviet bloc. The Communist victory in China in 1949 had added some 600 million souls and a hefty chunk of the world's surface area to the socialist camp. And unlike the East European regimes — with the arguable exception of Czechoslovakia — Mao and the Chinese Communists had come to power by their own efforts. The natural authority this conferred on the Chinese leaders within the socialist camp was later enhanced following the revelations of Krushchev's secret speech to the 20th CPSU Congress in 1956. Although Krushchev had been careful to attack only what he claimed were the personal crimes of Stalin and to avoid any criticism of the political edifice Stalin built, some of the mud hurled at the old dictator was bound to stick to the men he had personally placed in power in Eastern Europe.

Indeed, the only period of direct Chinese involvement in East European politics came from 1956 to 1958, as the process of de-Stalinization got underway and domestic upheaval in Eastern Europe confronted the Soviet leadership with its first major political test of the post-Stalin era. But although China seems to have offered its services as mediator in the Polish and Hungarian events of 1956, and although both the East Europeans and the Soviet leadership appear to have looked to the CPC as a natural arbiter,[1] in the end no one seemed happy with the result.

It soon became clear that a common ideological language could not mask the important political differences within the socialist camp. Aside from small dissident elements within the individual East European Communist parties, it soon became evident that the East European regimes themselves were more fascinated at the time by the independent form rather than the content of Chinese policies. The Chinese great leap forward and the development of the commune system in agriculture were exciting new developments but had little practical significance for the more highly developed and industrialized states of Eastern Europe. (Only the Bulgarians flirted with the idea of a great leap forward, but then only briefly.) And although the hundred flowers campaign in China briefly awakened hopes within all the East European parties as well as the CPC itself that the rules of party discipline might now be relaxed to tolerate more discussion and debate, these hopes were soon dashed everywhere. Even Krushchev's pressure on some of the East European parties to speed up de-Stalinization and in some cases rehabilitate past victims of the purges fell victim itself to the challenge to Krushchev's position within the CPSU from the 'anti-party group' in 1957. The need for self-defence at home forced Krushchev to draw in his horns in Eastern Europe.

Despite the years of turbulence in Soviet-East European relations in the 1950s, the desire to pursue an autonomous foreign policy was not a central issue. Only the more independent-minded Poles might have hoped to gain CPC support for a loosening of the constricting bonds within the Warsaw Pact. Mao and Zhou Enlai on their travels to the Soviet Union and Eastern Europe at the time seemed to be arguing a similar point.[2] But in this hope, too, the Poles were to be disappointed. China was interested in a realignment of the strictly hierarchical relationships imposed on the bloc by Stalin, but not primarily to encourage the Poles — or for that matter the Hungarians — in their pursuit of autonomy from Moscow. On the contrary, after 1956 China seemed bent instead on re-establishing the by now somewhat tarnished authority of the CPSU as the leader of the socialist camp.[3]

But if the Poles were disappointed, so was the Soviet Union. The Chinese were clearly unimpressed by Krushchev's rather optimistic vision of a 'socialist commonwealth' with the Soviet Union as its natural leader. The CPC wanted to 'reconstruct a center',[4] but on Chinese terms and with active CPC participation. Chinese calls to the other members of the socialist camp to resist 'hegemony' already boded ill for the future. At the latest by the Moscow conference of Communist parties in November 1960 it was clear that the Chinese efforts to re-establish unity within the camp reflected a lack of confidence in Krushchev's personal leadership and not any political or ideological fealty to Moscow.[5]

Thus, although the CPC took an active interest in East European affairs in the 1950s, its involvement and influence even then was not what it first seemed. The opportunity for Chinese action was created by temporary indecision on the part of the Soviet leadership in the face of a political and economic challenge which had entirely domestic roots in Eastern Europe. And beyond common membership in the socialist camp, even at this stage the Chinese and the East European Communist parties shared few interests.[6] Not surprisingly, therefore, the rapidly worsening Sino-Soviet dispute in the late 1950s and early 1960s found the East Europeans with few real options.

Unlike the Communist parties beyond Moscow's immediate grasp, the East Europeans could neither declare 'neutrality' in the Sino-Soviet dispute nor alternate their support at will and to their own advantage between the two combatants. What is more, with the exception of the Albanians, all the East Europeans sided with the Soviet Union on the key ideological issues in dispute, including the Romanians who have always been most reluctant to toe Moscow's policy line. Chinese attacks on Soviet 'revisionism' must also have sent chills up spines in Eastern Europe, where the need for security, the avoidance of nuclear war and the pursuit of domestic political and economic stability were all felt particularly strongly.

Thus all the East European regimes had to choose sides immediately and only tiny and obstinate Albania chose to side with China (a move which had more to do with suspicions of Soviet and Yugoslav motives towards Albania than any deep-seated friendship with the CPC). Yet all, with the exception of Albania, tried initially to paper over the growing cracks, either in the interests of the unity and prestige of the world Communist movement (East Germany, Hungary, Czechoslovakia) or in the hope that by avoiding a final rift some limited room for manoeuvre could be preserved with Moscow (Poland perhaps, and Romania). However, once the split became final even these limited options narrowed and by the mid-1960s the seriousness of the Sino-Soviet dispute meant that its divisive impact on the Warsaw alliance was largely 'consummated'.[7]

As the argument picked up steam, Chinese attacks on Soviet 'imperialism' and attempts to use the theory of the 'three worlds' to discredit the Soviet Union ideologically, lump it with the United States as simply another oppressor and project the CPC as the new vanguard of the world revolution, merely enhanced the value and importance of Eastern Europe to the Soviet Union as an ideological buffer. But by this time, in a very practical sense Eastern Europe held little priority for a China preparing to withdraw into the splendid and turbulent isolation of the Cultural Revolution. Chinese forays into East European politics for the rest of the 1960s and early 1970s were effectively limited to anti-Soviet mischief-making. And although trade continued at a reduced level, for the East Europeans, as for the rest of the industrialized world, the Chinese market never lived up to its earlier promise.

By 1969, as the prospects for détente in East-West relations improved and Sino-Soviet relations sank to an all-time low with armed clashes on the Ussuri river in March, China officially displaced West Germany as enemy number one in the demonology of the Soviet camp. From a Soviet point of view the timing was suspiciously convenient: the Soviet leadership could now point to the threat from China, instead of West Germany, to maintain discipline within the Warsaw Pact. And their intention to do precisely that was signalled clearly in June 1969 at the international meeting of Communist and workers' parties in Moscow. Soviet party leader Brezhnev termed China — not the United States or West Germany — the greatest threat to world peace and accused the CPC of preparing for war against the Soviet Union. But if the Soviet leaders were hoping to substitute China for West Germany as the cement of alliance unity in Eastern Europe, they were to be disappointed. The Warsaw alliance had also changed since the Cold War days of the 1950s and lingering disquiet in Eastern Europe over the possible repercussions of the Sino-Soviet dispute meant that Brezhnev's call for what amounted to a 'holy war' on Peking in the world

Communist movement registered only a mixed response from Eastern Europe.

And despite the otherwise propitious timing of Brezhnev's call to ideological arms, the assumption of some Western observers at the time, that the threat from China would now force the Soviet Union to seek political accommodation on its western flanks and therefore increase the room for manoeuvre in Eastern Europe, proved false. Soviet policy towards Europe remains too important to become merely a reflection of Soviet policy towards China (and vice versa). And Soviet security in Europe is too vital to be entrusted to the good offices of the ideological enemy — no matter how de-lionized he may have become.

The message was largely overlooked at the time, but as the Soviet invasion of Czechoslovakia a year earlier in August 1968 had shown, the Soviet Union was prepared to contemplate a new political relationship with Western Europe and the United States, but with its grip on Eastern Europe if anything tightened rather than loosened. The premise underlying Western involvement in the unfolding process of détente — that by entangling the Soviet Union in a web of political and economic agreements, the West could among other things hope to influence Soviet foreign policy actions — was at best a shakey one. In the case of Eastern Europe it was likely to prove false. There was and is nothing the West could realistically offer the Soviet Union to compensate for a loss of Soviet control over Eastern Europe — nothing, that is, that would not undermine the security of Western Europe.

Nor could the prospect of greater access to Western trade and technology offset Soviet concern about ideological security. Both the East Europeans and the Soviets had shown clear interest in improving East-West trade throughout the 1960s. But then the level of trade had been depressed for political reasons on both sides. Western governments placed restrictions on goods which could be exported to 'hostile' states. And although West Germany set up trade missions in several East European countries in the early 1960s, its continued refusal formally to recognize post-war boundaries in Europe prolonged the effects of political constraints on relations at all levels from the Eastern side. Admittedly some East European regimes were less ready than others to allow the politics of the German problem to hamper an expansion of contacts with the West. (In 1967 Romania broke ranks and established full diplomatic relations with West Germany.) But it took a settlement of outstanding political issues and West German acceptance of post-war 'realities' to give East-West trade a hefty political shove.

In sum, throughout the 1950s and 1960s the great power triangle, such as it then was, could have only limited impact on Eastern Europe. Until the late 1960s and early 1970s the United States' role as the major ally of West Germany prevented any wider role in Eastern Europe. Effectively relations with Eastern Europe had to be conducted through Moscow. Likewise, once the Sino-Soviet split had occurred, China's impact on Eastern Europe appeared to decrease rapidly. By the middle of the 1960s the onset of the Cultural Revolution had reduced still further any interest China might still have had in the affairs of the Soviet camp.

By the early 1970s China had emerged from its self-imposed isolation. This coincided with a conscious effort to relax tension in Europe and expand East-West relations. By the early 1970s, then, there seemed at least the prospect that the Soviet Union's changing relationship with its two main adversaries would help loosen the mould for the East Europeans too. The Soviet Union's 'opening to the west' in both trade and political contacts seemed to offer scope for a more relaxed and interdependent relationship between Eastern and Western Europe. Soviet disquiet at China's *rapprochement* with the United States was obvious, and for sound strategic reasons. However, if the East Europeans were hoping for some major change as a result, this latest shake of the great power kaleidoscope has probably left them disappointed.

The Perils of Friendship: Romania and East Germany

The finer ambiguities in Eastern Europe's relations with both the West and China can best be illustrated by looking more closely at two members of the Warsaw alliance, each with a very different relationship to Moscow: Romania and East Germany. Although the Romanian Communist Party (RCP) remains fundamentally loyal to the socialist camp and the world Communist movement, Romania's foreign policy has been a consistent irritant to Moscow, belying all attempts to draw a mask of unity across the inevitable domestic disagreements within the alliance. In particular, Romania is thought to have worked hardest to use the Sino-Soviet split to its own advantage. East Germany, on the other hand, has traditionally been seen as the Soviet Union's most loyal ally in the Eastern bloc, even at times as Moscow's extended arm in Eastern Europe. Yet the East Germans, like the Romanians, have felt the uncomfortable side-effects of great power rivalries as they have sought to defend 'national' interests within the Soviet orbit.

The Romanian case is particularly striking. What started as a difference in policy perspective on nominally economic issues has tended to sour relations across the board. As early as the mid-1950s Romania first caused friction within the alliance by its attempts to avoid becoming the market garden and raw materials supplier to the more developed CMEA economies. And there is at least circumstantial evidence to suggest that from the earliest stages in 1956 Romania successfully used the bargaining chip of its support for Moscow in the emerging Sino-Soviet dispute to head off unwelcome Soviet political and economic pressure and in particular to induce Krushchev in 1958 to water down his proposals for the supranational integration of the CMEA.[8] Romania also took advantage of Krushchev's new mood of reconciliation following the revelations of the secret speech in 1956 to obtain withdrawal of Soviet troops from Romanian territory. And later the RCP sought to bolster its national autonomy still further by mediating directly in the Sino-Soviet dispute — although probably less in the expectation that it could be resolved than in the hope that the rift could be somehow contained within the world Communist movement. Thus, although the RCP, like the other parties of Eastern Europe, supported the Soviet Union on all major issues in dispute, it saw China in the late 1950s as a potential ally in defending its own desires for greater flexibility in the management of bloc affairs.

For good reason, therefore, Romania has always been seen as the state with the most to gain — and the most to lose — from the ups and downs of Sino-Soviet relations. Yet it was clear at the time — and has remained so since — that economic considerations and the need to defend national autonomy and national priorities provided the original catalyst to Romania's pursuit of an independent foreign policy. When its attempts to mediate between China and the Soviet Union had clearly failed, the RCP was left out on a limb in Eastern Europe. And it was in part in an attempt to fend off any renewed Soviet pressure to toe the policy line that the RCP first set out its own coherent foreign policy framework, emphasizing both national autonomy and party sovereignty. The Romanian leadership then sought to apply these principles consistently in its own self-defence.[9]

Romania's purpose was not, and still is not, to abrogate its alliance with the socialist community or the Eastern bloc. Rather the RCP set out to create sufficient space within the Soviet-led alliance of Warsaw Pact states for each individual country to be able to consider national priorities and rational alternatives to an increasingly outmoded alliance structure. Romania's goal was to redefine the principle of unity to allow for a co-operative, in place of a coercive alliance. Consequently during the 1960s and 1970s the RCP has worked hard to prevent both a return to the Cold War division of world politics along bipolar lines (which would stiffen Soviet resolve to increase bloc discipline) and a narrow definition of the socialist bloc (which, by excluding China, would reimpose a single — Soviet — source of ideological orthodoxy).

Inevitably this maverick approach to foreign policy has led Romania along some precarious pathways. In 1967 Romania not only became the first East European state to establish diplomatic relations with West Germany, it also opposed Soviet policy in the Middle East following the June 1967 war by refusing to break off diplomatic relations with Israel. The rationale behind both moves was essentially similar: to prevent the division of regions and issues along bipolar, superpower lines. The same principles have been followed within the Communist movement: in 1968 Romania refused to participate in the Warsaw Pact intervention in Czechoslovakia, not out of sympathy with the Prague reformers, but in support of the principle of national and party autonomy in Eastern Europe. Romania has since adopted a similar position with respect to the present Polish crisis. And at the same time the RCP has consistently and so far successfully resisted Soviet attempts to excommunicate China from membership in the world Communist movement.

In order to reinforce this trend away from bipolar world politics and a narrow definition of ideologically acceptable allies, the Romanians have also developed strong links, economic and political, with the capitalist West, the non-aligned movement and the states of the developing world. In particular the success of Romania's efforts to diversify foreign economic ties outside the CMEA is shown by the fact that unlike its partners in Eastern Europe, Romania is now a member of GATT, the IMF, the Group of 77 and has developed a close and preferential trading relationship with the EEC.

While Romania's basic strategy — to establish as many bilateral political and economic contacts as possible across ideological and military boundaries — has often angered the Soviet Union, Romania's foreign policy is guided by *Realpolitik*. This is nowhere more apparent than in its relations with China since the Sino-Soviet split. The Soviet Union's proximity and China's remoteness have in any case limited China's value to Romania even as a purely tactical ally. This fact has been recognized on both sides, as reflected in Zhou Enlai's oft quoted remark that 'distant waters cannot quench fire'. Perhaps making something of a virtue out of necessity, Romania has gone to considerable lengths to remain strictly 'above' the politics of the dispute, even to the point of occasionally offending the Chinese as well as Moscow.[10]

Although Romanian party leader Ceausescu has worked hard to prevent international condemnation of China, he has done so primarily in defence of Romanian domestic and foreign policy objectives and the principle of party autonomy. China, on the other hand, has seen and occasionally tried to use Romania as a back door through which to foment discord in Eastern Europe. Romania offered the Chinese far better opportunities in this respect than did Albania, China's formal ally but isolated foothold in the Balkans. Chairman Hua's visit to the Balkans in 1978 was aimed in part as a stab at the Soviet Union. Although Ceausescu remained unrepentant, the Soviet Union was clearly annoyed at the cordial reception Hua received in Romania during the course of his trip. Yet relations between China and Romania have fluctuated too. What appear to be parallel interests and, occasionally, common causes should not disguise the fact that the two countries are often pursuing different goals.[11]

Yet despite the fact that they have been at times uneasy allies, Romania has gained some practical advantage from its continued good relations with China. Although China's declarations of solidarity — for example, following Soviet threats to Romania after the Soviet invasion of Czechoslovakia in 1968 — can have only psychological impact, the Chinese have been known to step in with timely material aid. Chinese economic aid to Romania following the disastrous floods in 1970, not only brought some swift relief to the Romanian economy, it also enabled the RCP to avoid becoming entangled in any political strings that might otherwise have been tied to aid from the Soviet Union. Ceausescu's visit to Peking in 1971 was a graphic gesture, both of defiance in the face of earlier Soviet pressure and the practical benefits of temporal, as opposed to ideological, allies.

Thus Romania's original defence of national autonomy in its relations with Moscow had been given increasingly active support by an adventurous and imaginative foreign policy. In this respect China has provided only one, if occasionally a crucial, component in Romania's global strategy. But this strategy has had wider repercussions than simply the successful defence of Romanian autonomy *vis-à-vis* the Soviet Union.

As an avowedly independent-minded member of the Soviet bloc, Romania had already caught the attention of policy-makers in the United States and Western Europe. As with China, Romania could count on only indirect support, if at all, from Washington: President Johnson's warning to the Soviet Union in 1968 not to 'unleash the dogs of war' by pursuing further its interventionary policy in Eastern Europe, was designed primarily to deter any Soviet move against independent Yugoslavia. The warning could have only a symbolic value to Romania, as a member of the Warsaw Pact. All the same, in 1969 Romania registered another first by becoming the first Communist country to receive a visit from Richard Nixon as president. Itself only a symbolic gesture, the Nixon visit was nonetheless a welcome demonstration that Romania continued to enjoy moral support from outside the Soviet bloc. Ceausescu subsequently became the first East European leader to visit Washington.

In more practical terms, Romania saw its relationship with the United States as a way of obtaining vitally needed technology, of increasing trade to build up home industries and of staving off dependence on the CMEA beyond the limits deemed acceptable to Bucharest. One major political obstacle across this path was the Vietnam War and the RCP's support for the Hanoi regime. Yet this is precisely where the separate strands of Romania's maverick foreign policy could weave together fortuitously. As the only country simultaneously on speaking terms with Hanoi, China, the Soviet Union and the United States, Romania was excellently placed — and indeed was said to have been used by the United States — not only to facilitate contacts towards ending the war, but also to serve as a back-channel for the re-establishment of more normal relations between the United States and China.[12] By the time President Nixon made his historic trip to China in 1972, Romania had received tangible reward for this and other efforts by being granted Most Favoured Nation status by the United States Congress in 1971.

But having assisted at the birth of a tripolar world, the Romanians were soon to find that three centres of power were potentially no less dangerous to smaller powers than two. By 1972 the United States had found larger fish to fry, both in its developing relations with China and also in guiding the emergent process of détente in Europe. The stage was set for improved East-West relations by the partial resolution of the German problem (the Moscow and Warsaw treaties of 1970, the Berlin agreement of 1971 and the Basic treaty of 1972, and in particular West Germany's formal acceptance of the inviolability, if not immutability, of post-war borders in Europe). Romania's services, such as they were, as a back-channel between the major powers were now less in demand.

And the fact that they now numbered three rather than two did not remove the temptation on the part of the major powers to settle the world's problems among themselves — in the Middle East, in Asia or indeed in Europe. The Chinese leadership had in the past been highly critical of superpower dominance of world politics. The theory of the three worlds in the 1960s had been specifically intended to tar both the United States and the Soviet Union with the same 'hegemonic' brush. China, it was always implied, would never act in such a fashion and was therefore a natural ally of small states, particularly in the Third World. Yet as one of the world's few nuclear powers, China's political and strategic interests could not help but lead it in different directions from its smaller friends. And whereas in the 1960s and early 1970s China, like Romania, had argued that the existence of a leading centre of world socialism was no longer either desirable or possible, in practice the CPC appeared again to be pushing its claim to the socialist crown.

Similarly on the Western front, the 1975 Helsinki conference on security and co-operation in Europe gave Romania the opportunity to reaffirm in public and at an international forum its principles of national sovereignty and party autonomy. Yet as the subsequent deterioration in East-West relations has since shown, the arrangements actually agreed at Helsinki are just as dependent on the preservation of good superpower relations as was the less formalized system which preceded them.

From Romania's perspective the changing balance of power in the world has if anything narrowed its scope for political initiative. Such developments in the West as EEC integration and Western economic recession have narrowed the scope for expanded trade relations. Consequently in the past few years Romania has again found itself fighting a rearguard action in defence of its national economic independence, and in particular against increased Soviet pressure to return to the political and economic fold. The limits of Romania's previous semi-autarkic industrial policy have lately become increasingly apparent. The result has been a shift on the part of the RCP back towards selective co-operation in the CMEA.[13] Yet seen from a Romanian perspective this latest policy shift towards greater co-operation within Eastern Europe, like the earlier one away from it, has been inspired by domestic priorities. So far, these remain the cornerstone of Romanian foreign policy. There is nothing so far to suggest that Romania would be less capable in the future of utilizing increased opportunities for exercising political autonomy than she has in the past.

As a small power Romania has always seen its interests best served by maximizing its options in world politics and in the process minimizing its dependence on all the major powers, particularly the Soviet Union. This has frequently brought it into conflict with Moscow, the power with the most direct claim to its ideological allegiance. The East German regime, on the other hand, has always seen close alliance with the Soviet Union as the only reliable route to both physical self-preservation and national self-determination (that is, continued existence and international diplomatic recognition). Its existence having been officially ignored for more than 25 years by the West, there was no alternative for the GDR to alliance with the Soviet Union. Yet East Germany, too, has at times found itself very much a prisoner of great power rivalries.

For the entire 25 years or more the GDR spent in the diplomatic wilderness, the German problem was the sole preoccupation of its foreign policy. To the extent that the East German regime was able to pursue foreign contacts outside the socialist bloc, for example in the Third World, these were quite deliberately bent to serve the goal of breaking the diplomatic blockade imposed by West Germany against the international recognition of the GDR. To the extent that the GDR had a policy towards the Western alliance, it was characterized by acute hostility. Indeed, the GDR's only consistent channel to the outside world remained the socialist bloc; its only effective advocate on the international stage remained the Soviet Union. Therefore close alliance with Moscow was not only unavoidable for the GDR, it was essential.

But the Soviet Union was involved in the German problem at several different levels. It is the GDR's major ally and the channel through which the GDR was obliged to conduct its relations with the outside world. Yet the Soviet Union is also one of the four powers with continuing responsibilities for 'Germany as a whole'. This gives it a useful political lever against West Germany and ensures a continuing Soviet involvement in the political development of the Western alliance. At the same time, the Soviet Union is a global power with interest to promote and defend well beyond the confines of Germany or Europe.

Inevitably there have been times when these various levels of policy have come into conflict. Much to the chagrin of the East German regime, their Soviet ally has often been unwilling to allow GDR national priorities in the German question to override Soviet foreign policy objectives at all other levels. From time to time such differences between the GDR and the Soviet Union have afforded China some additional opportunities for mischief-making in Eastern Europe. Similarly, East Germany's relationship with both China and the Soviet Union has been conditioned by its own attitude towards the German problem. East Germany's more confined role in international politics has meant that the impact of great power relations has been felt differently there than in Romania.[14]

As a loyal ally in the 1950s, China added strength to the socialist camp and hence indirectly to the East German cause. In October 1949 the two states established diplomatic relations and in 1955 China became the first country to sign a treaty of friendship with the GDR.[15] But as in the rest of the Soviet world in the Stalin era and the early post-Stalin years, such good fraternal relations assumed no profound political meaning. The important links were still the ones channelled through Moscow.

Of all the East European states, East Germany, still struggling for international recognition, was the least likely to depart from the Soviet political and ideological line in the Sino-Soviet dispute. The GDR would probably have preferred to prevent an open split in the world Communist movement. A rift with China could only exacerbate internal divisions within the Communist parties of Eastern Europe. But more important, a weakening of the unity of the world Communist movement could only undermine East Germany's hopes for a united Communist front in its pursuit of international recognition. It was also bound to deflect Moscow's attention at least partially from the all-important ideological enemy in the west to the new ideological enemy in the east.

Once it became impossible to stay on good terms with both Peking and Moscow, the GDR sided firmly with the Soviet Union. Yet despite the increasing seriousness of the dispute and the GDR's close dependence on the Soviet Union, the East German party seemed reluctant to take any initiative in the war of words. Press coverage of the dispute was limited to the reprinting of Soviet statements, without additional comment. And in 1962 the GDR was still signing trade agreements with China which included the exchange of specialists, despite the fact that Soviet specialists and advisers had been abruptly withdrawn from China in 1960. Not until the sixth SED congress in East Germany in January 1963, when the dispute could no longer be papered over in public, did East German party leader Walter Ulbricht launch a bitter attack on the Chinese. But having presumably fulfilled its responsibilities as host to the fraternal delegations that attended the congress, East Germany then reverted to its previous tactics, simply publishing Soviet statements without comment.

It was not until the possibility arose of a *rapprochement* of sorts between Peking and the GDR's arch-rival, Bonn, that the SED began to take a more active part in criticizing the CPC. The 1964 GDR-China trade agreement was delayed as China awaited the outcome of economic feelers put out to Bonn.[16] East German concern at the prospect of improved relations between Bonn and Peking was obvious. As far as the SED was concerned there was to be no distinction between United States 'imperialism' and West German 'revanchism' — and both had to be opposed resolutely. China, on the other hand, operating on the basis of its theory of the three worlds, seemed intent on merely irritating either superpower by meddling in the affairs of both halves of Europe.

As it turned out, West Germany was in any case not yet ready to follow up this China option. But any relief felt in East Berlin was short-lived. For reasons of its own, the Soviet Union in 1964 was also interested in improving its relations with Bonn. Some kind of new political initiative was being hatched by Krushchev in the months before his fall from power in October. There is some evidence, too, that in 1964 the East Germans sought to mediate in some fashion between China and the Soviet Union, presumably to counter any further setbacks in the fight against 'imperialism'.[17] But whatever was being considered in Moscow at the time, the initiative collapsed along with Krushchev's political downfall — and Ulbricht, for one, was not sorry to see him go.

Yet the activities of both China and the Soviet Union in 1964 highlighted East Germany's basic weakness. Unlike Romania, which could preserve some distance from Moscow and hence draw some benefit from balancing its relations with both Communist super-powers, East Germany's preoccupation with the national problem meant that it was caught in a cleft stick — at the mercy of friend and foe alike.

China found that recurrent differences between the GDR and the Soviet Union over the German problem afforded excellent opportunities to make mischief in Eastern Europe. In 1964, when the Soviet Union backed down from its threat to conclude a separate peace treaty with the GDR (and thereby confer full international legitimacy on a separate East German state in defiance of Western policy), the Chinese accused Moscow of 'selling out' the interests of its erstwhile ally. And in 1970, when Moscow negotiated a treaty with West Germany which failed once again to make full and unrestricted recognition of the GDR a precondition of improved East-West relations in Europe, the Chinese were again quick to score a point off Moscow at East Germany's expense. As Soviet-West German relations rapidly improved in the early 1970s, Chinese accusations of a 'betrayal' of the GDR could do little to help the East German regime off the political hook onto which it had been hoisted by Moscow, but on the other hand they did give the East Germans a means of making their feelings public. This time the Chinese accusations were printed in full in *Neues Deutschland* with no comment attached — but none was needed.[18] The point was underlined at the 25th CPSU Congress in Moscow in March 1971. Walter Ulbricht conspicuously avoided echoing the criticism of the CPC which had peppered the speeches of Brezhnev and other Communist Party leaders. Thus, like Romania, East Germany has occasionally found itself able to make use of the deterioration in Sino-Soviet relations to score a point or two against Moscow. However, unlike Romania which at times was able to pursue parallel interests with both the United States and China, the GDR's hands had been tied for all practical purposes by the unresolved national problem.

This pattern has changed slightly for the GDR regime since the mid-1970s and its admission into the international fold. In principle the German problem remains unresolved: Berlin is still a city divided between the four powers; and West Germany still insists on a 'special' relationship between the two German states and refuses to acknowledge the full and unrestricted sovereignty of the GDR. From time to time, therefore, East Germany still finds itself under pressure to conform to Soviet policy preferences — particularly in its relations with West Germany — at the expense of its own. To that extent there is still room for conflict in East German-Soviet relations and East Germany is still effectively tied to Soviet apron strings.

Yet the wider international recognition and scope for foreign policy initiative which followed East Germany's admission to the United Nations in 1972 has produced a more obvious change in East Germany's relationship with China. Freed from the need to preserve the unity of the world Communist movement, East Germany now seems happy to project its foreign policy through the Warsaw Pact. East Germany, more than any of its East European allies in the Warsaw Pact, has devoted considerable energy to extending the influence of the narrower socialist community in Africa, Asia and Latin America. Unlike the experience of Romania with its diverse foreign contacts outside the Soviet bloc, this has inevitably brought the GDR into more direct conflict with China. In 1979, following the Sino-Vietnamese border conflict, the GDR for the first time took the initiative and printed its own condemnation of Chinese aggression against Hanoi. Similarly in Angola and Zimbabwe, East Germany found itself supporting a different domestic faction from the Chinese. Although this more assertive foreign policy enables the GDR to project a stronger image abroad, its close identification with Soviet foreign policy initiatives throughout the rest of the world still prevents the East German regime from using the great power triangle to its own advantage.

Eastern Europe in the Balance of World Power

China's re-entry onto the world stage in 1972 may have had a considerable impact on relations between the United States and the Soviet Union — or at least their perceptions of the balance of power in the world — but its impact on Eastern Europe has been muted. Considerations of geography and ideology, and the Soviet Union's continued strategic stake in its East European alliance, have all conspired to limit considerably any freedom of manoeuvre the individual East European regimes might otherwise have hoped to enjoy as a result of this change in the balance of international fortunes.

That is not to say that the great power triangle has had no impact on Eastern Europe. Both China and the United States have maintained their interest in Eastern Europe in the 1970s. For one thing, neither of the Soviet Union's two main rivals claims to accept the political *status quo* (i.e. Soviet hegemony) in Eastern Europe.

However, for all practical purposes their interest in the region remains very much a reflection of their relationship with Moscow rather than any intrinsic concern for the fate of the region itself.[19] On the other hand, because of the ideological strings which attach them so closely to the Soviet Union, the East Europeans do feel the force of superpower relations. But from their point of view it has been the smaller triangles — linking the Soviet Union, Eastern Europe and China, and the Soviet Union, Eastern Europe and the United States — which have dominated over any larger, superpower triangle. Consequently from an East European perspective the new triangular balance of world politics could be said to have added to, rather than alleviated, the pressures on the East European regimes, both from Moscow and from the challenge to their own domestic security posed by a more open relationship with the West.

On the one hand, the continuing Sino-Soviet dispute, together with the formal establishment of diplomatic relations between the United States and China, is likely to have reinforced Soviet fears of a developing anti-Soviet axis involving China, Japan and the United States. This, in turn, can be expected to reinforce Soviet pressure on the East European regimes to extend the commitments of the Warsaw alliance beyond Europe to Asia, and specifically to the defence of the Sino-Soviet border. This the East Europeans have so far refused to do, although all remain committed to mutual assistance against undefined external threat in their bilateral treaties with the Soviet Union.[20] However, Soviet pressure on its allies seems unlikely to diminish in the foreseeable future.

On the other hand, the improved climate in East-West relations in the early and mid-1970s never quite lived up to its promise. Trade, released from its earlier artificial political constraints, soon ran up against its natural economic limits. Bilateral levels of trade between East and West vary, but certainly from a Soviet perspective the level of exchange has fallen well below expectations. This would seem to reduce still further any hopes for modifying influence on Soviet policies in general and policy towards Eastern Europe in particular.

On the contrary, imports of Western technology and goods into Eastern Europe have proved a mixed blessing. Having contributed little in the short term to alleviating the pressure for higher consumption, such trade instead pushed up dramatically the level of East European financial indebtedness to Western credit institutions and governments. To counteract this trend, in the second half of the 1970s both the East European states and the Soviet Union scaled down their imports from the West, thereby further depressing the levels of trade. By the early 1980s assumed Eastern dependence on Western technology seemed to be increasingly offset by Western dependence on raw materials imports from the East, particularly energy imports.

Nor can the prospect of imminent financial collapse in Poland, in debt to the tune of some $25 billion to Western banks and governments, be said to offer opportunities for Western leverage. Quite the contrary, since the Polish crisis broke in the summer of 1980, Western governments bent over backwards not to appear to be exercising leverage in Poland's affairs for fear of the likely Soviet response. With a danger of a Polish default in prospect, the only option left appears to be to reschedule existing loans and lend yet more money to stave off financial disaster.

After a decade of détente in Europe, disquiet over its impact on Eastern Europe is not confined to the Kremlin. The Helsinki accords of 1975, offering enhanced security and increased trade in return — it was hoped in the West — for the greater permeability of ideological boundaries in Europe, have proved to be a mixed blessing in Eastern Europe itself. In the event of a crisis, few in Eastern Europe would in any case have put much faith in the authority of an international document to fend off unwelcome Soviet fraternal assistance. Rather than promoting the loosening up of the East European alliance, the Helsinki conference and the wave of dissent which spread through Eastern Europe in 1975 and 1976 in its wake, tended to have the opposite effect. Faced once again with a challenge to their domestic security and power, all the East European regimes, including the otherwise maverick Romanians, responded by reinforcing trends towards ideological consolidation and integration. And despite the attraction felt by some regimes — notably the GDR, Hungary and Poland — for some practical alternatives to the increasingly arthritic Soviet model of economic development, a similar response could be expected too to any spread of Eurocommunist ideological heresies in Eastern Europe. From a Soviet point of view recent contacts between the CPC and both the Italian and Spanish Communist Parties can only have reinforced the need for closer ideological co-operation and discipline in Eastern Europe in defence against both challenges. Thus, as in the case of China, developments in East-West relations in general and détente in particular have clearly had an impact on Eastern Europe, but that impact has not always been welcomed by the regimes concerned.

But the impact of détente in Eastern Europe has not been all negative. East Germany has its own special reasons for wanting to wall itself off ideologically and physically from the West in general and West Germany in particular. On past experience, no matter how chilly relations in Europe become, the GDR will continue to enjoy a preferential trading relationship with Bonn. However Polish and Hungarian concern over the health of East-West détente in the months following the Soviet invasion of Afghanistan in December 1979 was obvious. Both states have allowed their economies to become increasingly intertwined with those of the capitalist West. And both were apprehensive lest their improved economic and political relations with Western Europe suffer as a consequence of Soviet actions. The different responses to the Soviet invasion of Afghanistan reflected clearly these divergent interests within the Warsaw alliance. Whereas East Germany, Bulgaria and Czechoslovakia fully endorsed the Soviet action with what seemed at the time unseemly haste, Hungary and Poland remained critically silent. Romania, not surprisingly, called openly for a withdrawal of Soviet troops.

While this mixed response from Eastern Europe suggests that East-West détente is seen by some East European states as worth preserving, the invasion itself was just as clear an indication that the balance of costs versus benefits comes out differently in Moscow. The Soviet Union is quite prepared to disregard the wider interests of its allies when it feels the stakes are worth playing for.

However, if there was a suspicion by the late 1970s that the Soviet Union felt a sufficient degree of stability had been achieved in East-West relations for it to turn its attentions elsewhere, and particularly towards Africa and Asia, then the Polish crisis has dispelled that illusion. It has also highlighted Eastern Europe's position in the force field of superpower relations. Unlike 1956, this time China has had no role to play in the upheavals of the Soviet camp. Instead the PRC had used the opportunity presented by the crisis to take pot shots at both the 'mistakes' of the Polish Communist Party and their guiding — Soviet — model of development. The Western alliance, its resolve stiffened since Afghanistan, has made clear that a Soviet intervention in Poland would destroy any hopes of improved East-West relations for the foreseeable future. But if the Soviet Union stops short of military intervention there is little the West can do to aid the cause of stability in Poland that will not in the long run promote the stability of an increasingly distrusted, Moscow-oriented

Communist Party leadership. And when it comes to priorities in Western policy, the goal of security in Europe has always taken precedence over the promotion of autonomy and change in Eastern Europe.

The Soviet Union, for its part, has made clear that as a last resort to prevent the defection of Poland from the socialist camp or the overthrow of Party authority and control in Poland, it can again be counted on to render full 'fraternal assistance'. And the Polish example is a lesson to all other East European regimes that domestic rather than foreign policy issues must remain at the top of the political agenda.

In the meantime, although the emergence of a Moscow-Washington-Peking triangle may have created some additional headaches for Moscow and increased still further the burdens of empire in Eastern Europe,[21] the evidence available so far suggests that in some respects it has had a similar effect on the East European regimes themselves. Until the Soviet Union is prepared to modify its strategic stake in Eastern Europe and allow the individual Warsaw Pact states to develop a full range of contacts with the outside world, there seems little prospect that the more independent-minded East European regimes will be able to take serious advantage of Moscow's occasional embarrassments at the hands of its two chief ideological and political rivals.

Notes

1. In February 1955 Molotov spoke of China's 'co-responsibility' for the internal cohesion and external aims of the bloc. K.H. Pringsheim, 'New Dimensions in China's Foreign Policy', *China Quarterly,* October-December 1960, p. 44.

2. In particular in 1956 Mao is reported to have lent moral support to the Poles and the Hungarians in their pursuit of national autonomy. He spoke in support of the 'just demands' of the Hungarian reformers and against 'big power chauvinism'. Yet, once Hungary crossed the rubicon and declared its 'neutrality' and withdrawal from the socialist camp, the Chinese fully supported the use of force by the Soviet Union in the second intervention in Hungary. Anton Logoreci, 'China's Policies in East Europe', *Current History,* September 1972, pp. 118ff.

3. In a speech in November 1957 in Moscow Mao is quoted as saying: 'Our socialist camp should have a leader, and that is the Soviet Union. The Communist and Workers' Parties of all countries must also have a leader and that leader is the Communist Party of the Soviet Union'. Pringsheim, 'New Dimensions'.

4. Zbigniew K. Brzezinski, *The Soviet Bloc* (rev.ed.), Cambridge, Mass.: Harvard University Press, 1967, chapter 12.

5. Alexander Dallin, 'Long Divisions and Fine Fractions', *Problems of Communism,* March-April 1962, pp. 7 – 16.

6. Little has changed since. The point is put bluntly in Sarah Meikeljohn Terry, 'External Influences on Political Change in Eastern Europe', in J.F. Triska and P. Cocks (eds.), *Political Development in Eastern Europe,* New York: Praeger, 1977, p. 286.

7. Richard Löwenthal, 'China's Impact on the Evolution of the Alliances in Europe', in 'Western and Eastern Europe: The Changing Relationship', *Adelphi Papers,* No. 33, March 1967, pp. 20 – 29. The author argues that while Eastern Europe was not a priority for China (or for that matter the United States), for the Soviet Union at the time the East-West confrontation was still the prime focus.

8. The origins and development of Romania's dispute with the Soviet Union in the 1950s are sketched out in Michael Kaser, *Comecon: Integration Problems of the Planned Economies,* London: Oxford University Press, 1965; Robin A. Remington, *The Warsaw Pact: Case Studies in Communist Conflict Resolution,* Cambridge, Mass.: MIT Press, 1971, pp. 54 – 63.

9. Romania's 'Statement of Principles' was issued in April 1964. For an analysis of its theoretical underpinnings see Robert L. Farlow, 'Romanian Foreign Policy: A Case of Partial Alignment', *Problems of Communism*, November-December 1971, pp. 54–63.

10. This was demonstrated quite clearly and to the considerable annoyance of the Chinese during Zhou Enlai's visit to Romania in 1966. The Romanians took the liberty of editing out the more offensive passages in Zhou's speeches. R.R. King, 'Romania and the Sino-Soviet Conflict', *Studies in Comparative Communism*, Winter 1973, p. 379.

11. For example, Romania and China eventually both found themselves supporting the same side in the Angolan civil war — against the MPLA which had the support of the Soviet Union and, ultimately, Cuban troops. But this was more a result of Romania's consistent backing for the OAU line in the conflict than any bilateral collusion with China. Arthur Jay Klinghoffer, *The Angolan War: A Study in Soviet Foreign Policy in the Third World*, Boulder, Colorado: Westview Press, 1980, pp. 104–8.

12. For Romania's services to President Nixon's opening to China see Henry Kissinger,, *The White House Years*, London: Weidenfeld and Nicolson, 1979, p. 181. Poland also had a role to play as the country which hosted the confidential — but widely reported — talks between the United States and China before formal contact was established.

13. Jeanne Kirk Laux, 'Socialism, Nationalism and Underdevelopment: Research on Romanian Policy Making', in H. Adomeit and R. Boardman (eds.), *Foreign Policy Making in Communist Countries*, Saxon House, 1979.

14. The conflicts which arose in Soviet-East German relations are an important subject in themselves. For a lengthy analysis see N. Edwina Moreton, *East Germany and the Warsaw Alliance: The Politics of Detente*, Boulder, Colorado: Westview Press, 1978.

15. Relations in the early years are examined in M.J. Esslin, 'East Germany: Peking Pankow Axis?', *China Quarterly*, July-September, 1960. The value accorded by East Germany to such inter-state contacts was revealed in 1979. In celebration of its thirtieth anniversary as a state, the GDR gave a dinner for representatives of the states who had recognized the GDR in 1949, including the Chinese.

16. This period in Chinese-East German relations is documented in Carola Stern, 'East Germany', in W.E. Griffith (ed.), *Communism in Europe*, Vol. 2, Cambridge, Mass.: MIT Press, 1966.

17. David Childs, *East Germany*, London: Ernest Benn, 1969, p. 267.

18. Moreton, *East Germany and the Warsaw Alliance*, pp. 128 and 159.

19. Robin A. Remington, 'China's Emerging Role in Eastern Europe', in C. Gati (ed.), *The International Politics of Eastern Europe*, New York: Praeger, 1976, makes the point for China. For the United States see Bennett Kovrig, 'The United States:

"Peaceful Engagement" Revisited', in Gati, *The International Politics of Eastern Europe*, chapter 7.

20. The issue appears to have come up repeatedly since at least 1969. Romania effectively walked out of the November 1978 PCC meeting in Moscow over this and the issue of increased defence spending.

21. Vernon Aspaturian, 'Has Eastern Europe Become a Liability to the Soviet Union?', in Gati, *The International Politics of Eastern Europe*, p. 20.

Part Three
An Assessment of the Great Power Triangle

7   AN ASSESSMENT OF THE GREAT POWER TRIANGLE

Gerald Segal

What is the great power triangle, and is the answer to that question the same in Peking, Moscow and Washington? Clearly the answer is not identical, but in all three capitals they will recognize the political configuration under discussion. To a large extent the source and nature of the differences in understanding of the great power triangle can be traced to the varying ways in which the triangle's development was seen in each capital.

For Peking triangular politics was not unaccustomed. As Michael Yahuda has shown, China had faced tripolar situations well before 1949 and thus was not immediately averse to accepting a triangle composed of itself and the superpowers. As the power that sought to break a US-USSR condominium it was not surprising that China should be the first of the three powers to grasp the importance of nascent tripolarity. The decade or so of Sino-Soviet alliance stands out as the exception more than the rule in the relations between these two states and by the early 1960s China had regained much of the independence that it might have had in the first years of the revolution.

Since it was China that broke away from the Soviet camp (or if you will the Soviet Union that deviated from China's correct path), it was only reasonable that the jilted ally, the USSR, would be the next state to appreciate the dawning of a great power triangle. Moscow's difficult, and mostly futile, attempt to sail the choppy waters between the US Scylla and the Chinese Charybdis, eventually was manifest in the 1963 Sino-Soviet split and the limited Test Ban Treaty with Washington. The Soviet Union, as the power with the most to lose in the case of China emerging as a third pole, fought the hardest to prevent the development of the triangle. Moscow also faced the most difficult pressure in the first period of the triangle in the 1960s and was perhaps the first to learn the intricacies of three-way great power relations.

The US, on the other hand, was the slowest to sense that bipolarity had broken down and was the most unwilling to accept the role of

China as an independent force. The canons of containment that misperceived a monolithic Communist world were a long while in dying.
For most of the period when Moscow was struggling as the pivot
power between the competing demands of the US and China,
Washington was oblivious that a type of great power triangle was
already in operation. But when Sino-Soviet relations erupted in
significant border clashes and China made overtures to the US,
the new Republican administration suddenly discovered the China
factor and the great power triangle. The resulting American-centred
view of the triangle, as if it were a power configuration that
Washington had invented and it alone could manipulate, must have
been greeted with somewhat of a jaundiced eye in a USSR that had
previously struggled with the pivotal pressures in the triad.

The US' youthful zest for a new game in international politics is
well documented by Banning Garrett. His description of the rapidly
growing sophistication in scenario building in Washington highlights the critical problem of ethnocentrism in strategic analysis. The
fact that the US only 'discovered' the triangle in the 1970s, does not
mean that is when it first became important. The already well
developed Chinese and Soviet abilities to deal in triangular politics
while the US was still teething on the triangle, make it clear that
tripolarity meant different things to different people. We can speak
of a great power triangle in a general sense as a relationship among
three crucial states, but the actors could probably not agree on the
origins and development of the triad, let alone what was the best
policy to pursue under those conditions.

The different roles that each power played in the development of
the triangle, not to mention the different policy objectives of the
three states, meant that they all reacted differently to the question of
how important the triangle was for their foreign policy. Much like
any number of international issues, for example détente, states can
agree that it is a feature of foreign relations, even if they are far from
agreed as to the precise definition and rule book for the new state of
affairs. The contributors to this book have made it abundantly clear
that all three powers perceived the importance of triangular relations
in very different ways.

For Peking, there was no great difficulty in seeing a great power
triangle even if it did not sit evenly with ideological conceptions of a
Manichean world view. As Yahuda has suggested, there is much in
Mao's thought to incorporate a view of the world where 'contradictions' can be both primary and secondary. Chinese coalition theory

allowed for unity with one contradiction against the other, more primary threat. Thus Peking was permitted to 'lean to one side' (Moscow) in the 1950s and to the other (US) in the 1970s without fundamentally negating a view of the world that assumed the primary need to struggle against capitalism. Mao's coalition theory, and no doubt deeper historical traditions of tripolar balancing, meant that China could become a most astute player of the great power triangle if it so chose.

The USSR seemed to have more trouble in accepting the importance of the triad. Perhaps because it had the most to lose, or perhaps because it lacked China's revolutionary flexibility, Moscow persisted the longest in officially rejecting a triangular perception of international politics. As Peking split the Communist bloc and handed the Soviet Union its most devastating strategic loss of the post-war world, the USSR came to engage in effect in tripolar politics, all the while denying that it was doing so. The incessant Soviet efforts to forge 'united action' with Peking against the US, or the repeatedly stated belief that China would eventually return to the fold, may have ensued as much from wishful thinking as a deeply held belief that the world should be clearly divided between the forces of light (socialism) and the forces of dark (capitalism).

The role of ideology in states' foreign policies should always be approached cautiously, but the fashionable habit of denying any validity for it in foreign relations is to misunderstand at least a basic and long-term foreign policy objective. To view Moscow and Peking's analysis of the great power triangle without reference to ideology is to miss the point that they both share a common belief that struggle is essentially a Manichean process. Where the two Communist states differ is in an analysis of who is to be placed in which category and who upholds the true church dogma. Peking has found it easier to adapt itself to the triangle because its particular variant of ideology makes greater provision for coalitions. Perhaps this is because in the particular Chinese revolutionary process such suppleness was required, but whatever the case it has meant that Peking had initially fewer problems with tripolarity. Moscow's refusal to bend so far not only points to the enduring role of ideology in its foreign policy, but also helps explain a great deal of the hesitation and confusion in Soviet attitudes towards the triangle.

The US has had many of the same hesitations and confusions in its policy, and as Banning Garrett has shown there has been incessant factional politics as a result. Where the US has an advantage over its

Communist rivals is in the relative absence of ideological complications. Garrett has suggested that US policy has long been governed
by assessments of balance of power, and this is no doubt a major
component of Washington's policy even if it has been improperly
applied at times. But even so, the US has not escaped the problems of
coping with a tripolar system. For example, the US seems to have
developed no more persuasive answers to the dilemmas of the pivotal
position between the contradictory pressures of triangular rivals,
than did the USSR when it was the pivot in the 1960s. It may appear
that the US is the most sophisticated actor in the triangle merely
because it theorizes most openly and at length about the triad and its
possible permutations, but in reality Washington has been hampered
by the need to satisfy and not completely alienate both Peking and
Moscow.

It is apparent that all three powers do accept the centrality of the
China factor in international relations, but all define the importance
in different ways. For Peking the essential importance of the triangle
clearly lies in assuring national independence and security. China's
assessment of the most important global threat has changed in the
three decades since the revolution, and hence its triangular alliances
have changed. But there can be little doubt that tripolarity helps
ensure China's position in a world in which it would otherwise be
very vulnerable. Most foreign policy is above all concerned with this
dominant desire for security, and China is no exception. If the
triangle and the balance of power games it incorporates are useful in
pursuit of this objective, and if no basic ideological precepts are
violated, then tripolarity will be an important factor in Chinese
foreign policy.

Similar calculations apply for the USSR, but the implications of
the importance of tripolarity are different in significant ways. The
China factor is crucial to Soviet security, second only to the role of
the US. The 'loss' of China did serious damage to Soviet national
security, and the very concept of a 'two-front' war that it introduced
made it plain that tripolarity was a central factor. Now Soviet
security had to consider at least 'two wars' and to this extent even if
officially Moscow refused to accept the triangle, at least the military
planners were more realistic. As Krushchev once said about the
hidden nature of Sino-Soviet differences, 'even if you cannot see
your nose, that doesn't mean it doesn't exist'.

This is not to argue that Moscow gets around the ideological
problems by pretending that triangular relations do not exist. This is

not the first time that the USSR has had to face two enemies of different types. Soviet attempts in the 1930s to ally with the West against Germany, then with Germany in the Nazi-Soviet pact and finally against Hitler with the Allies, is a useful example of Moscow's ability to play triangular politics with overall success. This was not a case as many have suggested of an abandonment of Soviet ideology, but rather it was a choice between equally unacceptable ideological partners as the 'primary contradiction' changed. If necessary, even the Soviet Union can play tripolar games openly. What may be keeping it from doing so at present is its assessment of the most important axes of relations. For the Soviet Union its superpower ties remain pre-eminent, despite the growing power of Peking. The China factor may be the next most important aspect of Soviet policy, but it is still not on a par with US-USSR relations. While the Soviet Union tries to contain and indeed assimilate the Chinese problem, it stresses that the management of superpower relations is too important to be jeopardized by triangular games. As significant as China may be for Soviet security, it is not nearly as salient as the superpower balance.

Washington seems less concerned about the China factor in national security terms, although this assessment may now be changing. For the meantime, the US stands in contrast to the two Communist members of the triad in not seeing crucial changes in its security created by the emergence of triangular politics. Despite official designation of China as the cause of an ABM, or an Indochina conflict in the 1960s, Peking was not seen as posing a major threat to US security prior to the Sino-American détente of the 1970s. Where there has been an American perception of changed national security, interest has been in the way Soviet security has been threatened by US-China ties. This secondary effect is not to be dismissed as unimportant, but as Banning Garrett has shown few American decision makers have thought that China could fundamentally tip the strategic balance. Although US policy is far from coherent in all aspects of triangular policy, most Washington actors have not seen a Sino-American alliance as reason enough to reduce US military spending. China's importance has generally been seen as a way of pressuring, or in some cases inducing the USSR to act in a certain fashion, but few people have thought that the essential superpower balance could be tilted by China. To this extent the superpowers share the assessment that their bilateral axis is of overriding centrality and that while some aspects of international relations can be tripolar, or that China can affect the superpower balance in some meaningful way, in the end only Moscow and Washington retain the devastating nuclear destructive power. Both share the view that there is a China factor, but they also agree that there are only two super-powers.

Specific Realms of Triangular Policy Differences

Apart from the essential and overarching questions of the three powers' views of tripolarity, there are various other, more specific, realms of triangular politics where Moscow, Peking and Washington have differed in their assessments. The impact of the triangle on ideology shows perhaps the most complex pattern of relations.

For Peking, the ideological implications of its split from Moscow and manoeuvring in the triangle have been mixed. In the early 1960s China was largely successful in portraying itself as a true opponent of superpower machinations and Peking's campaign against US-USSR 'hegemony' earned it a new and important international role. However, domestic aspects of the Chinese campaign that had labelled the USSR as 'revisionist' developed in to the Cultural Revolution. The radicalism of that period merely increased China's isolation and lost it much credibility as a revolutionary force in world politics. The damage that China had done to Communism's appeal as an inevitable and scientific historical force could be managed for a time by claiming that the ideology was perverted by the USSR. But the Cultural Revolution further undercut the appeal of the Chinese model and delivered a further body blow to Communist ideology. China's declining concern with the US threat, and a rising one with all manner of Soviet challenges (including ideological) in the 1970s dealt further damage to Peking's revolutionary posture. The obsessive domination of Chinese foreign policy by the alleged global Soviet threat made Peking into a strange political bedfellow with some notoriously counter-revolutionary states. Policies in Africa and Latin America in the 1970s were reinforced by ambiguous Chinese reactions to the conflict in Afghanistan in the early 1980s. What these cases all had in common was China's confusion in analysing events because the necessities of worldwide anti-Sovietism conflicted with a clear-cut support for revolutionary forces.

For China, enmeshed in triangular politics where it was frequently allied with US-supported reactionary regimes, the ideological component of policy clearly diminished. Not that ideology ceased to be important in analysing Chinese foreign policy, but rather the ideological imperatives now seemed to be concerned far more with the distant future than the pressing present. There were both gains and losses for Peking in this process, for anti-Sovietism put China on the right side in Zimbabwe but on the wrong one in Angola. The advent of tripolarity did not so much assist or hinder China's ideological efforts as it made them far more complex. The adoption of the less principled policy of anti-Sovietism put China far more at the mercy of local states than it had been in the past, a lesson the superpowers had been learning for a while about the Third World.

The emergence of the China factor clearly also damaged Soviet ideology, if only for the most basic reason that the 'scientific principles' of a political system that was supposed to 'inevitably' march forward, were badly undercut by the Sino-Soviet split. The ideological fabric, once torn asunder, could never be returned to the same strength that it had before the tear. Moscow's concern with fighting Peking as much as Washington around the world, and especially in the Third World, further undercut the cause of those seeking Communist ideals. With competing Communist claimants to the hearts and minds of the developing world, Moscow found its ideological and political task far more complicated by China and the triangle.

The ideological split and the eventual alignment of China with the US did not fundamentally challenge Soviet control in East Europe, but it did undercut Moscow's influence in West Europe, especially in recent years regarding the Eurocommunists. The main damage to Soviet ideological interests was however to be seen in the Third World. Local states now found that they had yet another great power to play off in their successful game of obtaining what they could from outside powers without suffering political control. What tripolarity did from the Soviet perspective was similar to what it did to China, i.e. confuse and render more complex an assessment of conflict in the developing world. Tripolarity was of use to the local states, but was not positive from the point of view of Communist powers.

The US on the other hand could look favourably upon this trend. When your enemies are rent apart and begin fighting among themselves, this can only be to your advantage. The damage done to Communist ideology or a concerted Moscow-dominated political campaign could not harm the US position. The problem from the US position was to think that it either was responsible for that gain, or that it could control the process. The advantages accruing to the US were passive ones, and problems set in when some American decision makers thought they could manipulate the great power triangle to their advantage. Especially in ideological terms, it should have been clear to the US that they no more could control local states' reaction in tripolarity than they could in a more direct bipolar world. The curious and convoluted doctrines of 'linkages' between the great power triangle and developing states' affairs became a dominant US perspective on the triangle, but it was derived from an erroneous view that Washington was responsible for the emergence of the China factor.

Thus apart from the passive gains of a rival ideology split in two, there were few ideological and political gains for US policy. Cases of Sino-American alliance did not help US policy to any significant degree (e.g. Angola) and nothing much had happened to alter the assessment that the local states manipulated, more than were manipulated by, the three powers. Thus the ideological and political realm of tripolar relations was a crucial one in helping to understand the impact of the great power triangle, showing in part a relative US gain. But what it shows most clearly is that the world had become more complex and confusing, and therefore far less subject to any one power's machinations.

The more narrow realm of economics in the triangle shows far less of a significant change from the bipolar era. From Peking's perspective the triangle has given it few if any economic benefits that were not available in any case. It is not possible to substantiate that Sino-Soviet economic relations have been harmed or assisted by changes in attitudes towards the US. The changes that have resulted have been due far more to domestic policies, and bilateral relations. Moscow-Peking trade has by no means ceased even during the period of closest Sino-American relations. While Moscow denounced US sales of military related equipment to China, the Soviets sold Peking helicopters of their own.

The Chinese have greatly increased their trade with the US in recent years, but it is difficult to pinpoint any aspects resulting from the Soviet factor. The rise and now the fall of Sino-Western trade has far more to do with domestic economic plans in China than any tripolarity. These internal factors may eventually lead China to increase trade with the more compatible Soviet economy, but while that is clearly related to political and triangular considerations, the

economic changes are likely to follow rather than cause such alterations. What is more, there is very little evidence that there is an
economic dimension to the triangle in the developing world. In those
cases it is the local states and their various conditions that determine
the nature of economic ties. In any case, China seems to be retreating
from this area as it finds that as a member of the Third World itself,
it cannot afford a significant economic aid programme to the
developing world.

For the USSR, the economic dimension of the China factor is also
the least important. Moscow's China trade is higher now than it has
been for many years, even though the Soviets do make an effort to
warn the US about trade with China. Moscow also warns of the false
hopes of the vast China market, perhaps from its own personal
experience, but seems relatively unconcerned with most Western
trade with Peking. The exception on this issue relates far more to
Japan than to the US and in any case following China's economic
retrenchment the Soviets are likely to be even less worried.

The China factor and the triangle has had some secondary economic effects on the Soviets, if only in the realm of increased pressure
on limited resources due to military spending against China. Also,
the need to support states such as Vietnam or Kampuchea, who are
involved in Moscow's anti-China containment schemes in Asia but
are economically weak, has added to Moscow's financial concerns
with the triangle. But these efforts, as with other Soviet anti-China
moves around the world, have as much to do with bilateral relations
as they have with any calculation of the China factor or the triangle.

The US on the other hand has been at times under an illusion that
the economic dimension of the great power triangle is significant.
Much like the ill-fated US efforts to link Soviet behaviour with economic arrangements, for example on grain, so the US has seen its
Sino-American trade as a tool for pressuring the USSR. The optimistic talk in Washington of the 'limitless China market' was also a
prime motivation for increased Sino-US trade, but as Garrett has
shown in his chapter, the lure of the China market also had a tripolar
dimension. In a decision making process where every possible policy
tool is scrutinized for its relevance, economic trade was no exception.

However, the reality of tripolar politics did not reveal any useful
economic dimension. The rise in Sino-American trade, if it came at
the expense of anyone, was that of Western Europe and not the
USSR. Nor was Moscow forced to alter its policy toward Washington
because of US trade relations with China. Thus despite US hopes to

the contrary, economic relations in the triangle were not important. As with the Soviet and Chinese perspective, it is clear that bilateral, and above all domestic Chinese financial affairs determine economic ties and not anything more complex such as the great power triangle.

This low key conclusion is however not possible regarding the much discussed issue of the military dimension of the triangle. This component has figured prominently in each of the three chapters in Part One, but the conclusion on the importance of military aspects is not as uniform as it was regarding the economic dimension. As has already been pointed out the triangle has been important for Peking in assuring its national security. To that extent the military dimension in tripolarity is central. The debate develops when considering other military aspects of the triangle for China.

The much discussed issue of arms sales to China is perhaps the most contentious aspect. From Peking's perspective these arms are not necessarily part of an anti-Soviet campaign. Despite fervent US hopes to the contrary, there is little evidence that China will take an active military role against Moscow. China wants arms so as to modernize its forces, but it is unlikely to become the tool of anyone's policy. To the extent that triangular calculations in Washington help Peking obtain weapons, then China incorporates the triangle in its arms buying policy. But this is a different argument from the one suggesting that China wants arms because of the triangle. In any case, the issue of arms sales suffers from similar problems to the economic aspect, i.e. the inability to appreciate the severe constraints upon China's ability to purchase either large numbers of US weapons or even produce them in China on a massive scale.

The military dimension is also not to be found in triangular politics in the Third World. China's military factor has always been weak outside of Asia and therefore it should come as no surprise that China's military has little effect on global tripolar politics. Neither in cases of Chinese success (Zimbabwe) or failure (Angola) in Africa where tripolar factors were present, was China's military force in anyway significant. Thus it seems that the military dimension of tripolarity for China is far more important than the economic one, but it is not as critical as some might suggest. The three chapters on the policies of the powers have shown the limited albeit still important impact of the military dimension of tripolarity for China.

A similar pattern is apparent in the Soviet view of this issue. Clearly the most important military component of the great power triangle for Moscow is the necessity to plan for a two-front war.

As already pointed out, the conventional and nuclear Soviet forces have had to be adapted to cope with the China factor in a way that US forces were never designed, even in the 1950s. The superpowers'military relationship is still dominant for the USSR, but in triangular terms the military dimension is as crucial as any other issue.

This concern is also related to another aspect of the military issue: arms sales to China. Not that Peking is necessarily an offensive threat to the USSR, but as China's military strength grows the Soviets become less able to pressure the Chinese. Soviet concern with China is very much oriented towards the future, and it is precisely in that time scale that arms sales to Peking may have an effect. Moscow seems to be most perturbed that the US tries to circumvent arms control agreement by building up Chinese forces. The view of China as the sixteenth member of NATO is perceived as evidence of the extended impact of the military dimension of tripolar politics. Unlike the Chinese who perceive arms sales in bilateral terms, the USSR sees them in relation to the great power triangle.

Where the two Communist powers do share a view of military issues in the triangle is regarding the Chinese military factor outside Asia. The Soviets have not shown any significant concern with the PLA beyond Asia and China's frontier states. In Africa and the Middle East, for example, Chinese political influence is said to be a problem in tripolar terms, but the military dimension is virtually nonexistent. Bipolar, superpower relations remain pre-eminent.

The US attitude to these military issues is far more difficult to ascertain, for as Garrett has shown, the American points of view are constantly in flux. In general the US view is closest to that of the USSR in seeing the Chinese military factor both in general national security terms (adding to the Soviet security concerns) and as regards arms sales. The discussion about arms sales to China has been a process of waxing and waning ardour, but almost all discussions have been couched in terms of the great power triangle. The USSR shares this view, but China does not. The Chinese have taken advantage of this American desire to sell arms as part of the triangular diplomacy, without accepting the premise behind the US desires. Much as was evident in the case of the economic dimension, the US has read more into the China trade relationship than Peking was prepared to accept. China would be likely to accept any arms, but would not be likely to play the kinds of tripolar games that the US wants. The failure to understand Chinese motives led to a misunderstanding of China's approach to trade relationships, and may well happen again in the military sphere. To that extent the Soviet warnings to those who would blindly arm China and hope to control it in the future, are well spoken.

Where all three powers do agree regarding the military dimension is on the issue of Chinese military impact beyond Asia. Not even the most adventurous of the US military planners seems to conceive of China as taking a military part in anti-Soviet manoeuvres around the globe, let alone in the Gulf or any other hot spot. In sum, the military dimension of tripolarity is crucial, but it is largely restricted to the immediate triangular relationship concerning the three bilateral axes. Policy questions posed by alterations in national security or attitudes towards arms sales are some of the most crucial aspects of the triangle, and although the three powers may differ as to what should be done about them, they all mostly agree on the centrality of these military issues.

By way of summary of these more specific dimensions of tripolarity it is useful to make several points. First, the three powers have found that the emergence of the China factor and tripolarity has made international relations more complex. None of the powers have found it easier to manipulate their foreign policy in a triangle, indeed they have found it harder. The room for manoeuvre for each power is certainly not enhanced, and is probably reduced. Certainly the pivot powers have found the dual pressures of satisfying both other states a difficult task. In the 1970s the US need to retain working relations with both Moscow (e.g. on SALT) and Peking (e.g. on the extent of a Soviet threat) gave Washington little room to manoeuvre. This was especially so when the US sought to mix its policy of 'carrots' and 'sticks' in relations to both powers. It is less so on the surface in an era when the US merely seeks to 'punish' the USSR by the use of the China card, but the reality indicates only deterioration in superpower relations that in the final analysis cannot be allowed to disintegrate completely. Sino-American détente cannot be a real substitute for Soviet-American détente.

Second, it is difficult to suggest clear gains or losses for any of the three powers as a result of tripolarity. It is probably true that the US has benefited from the very existence of the Sino-Soviet split, both in ideological and military terms. But this was a passive gain and one not subject to manipulation to US ends. Much like the US' own 'loss of China', the Soviet case a decade later was due to domestic Chinese factors and not an event that one power could use against the other. Furthermore, the pre-eminence of domestic or local factors largely immune to 'linkages' or grand strategies, is evident when the triangle is analysed in the Third World context. Strategic analyses of the empyrean level frequently miss this point.

Third, relationships in the triangle are composed of both con-flictive and co-operative aspects. Simplistic views of playing cards or zero-sum gains and losses also miss this point. Thus the most effective policy in the triangle is a subtle and cautious one, in large measure because of the new complexity in relations. These aspects will be analysed in greater detail below, but first some points should be made about the factional politics in each power regarding tri-angular issues. The complexity of policy is merely enhanced by divergent domestic views of tripolarity.

Domestic Politics and the Triangle

One of the more notable aspects of the chapters analysing the policies of the three powers in the triangle is the less than monolithic attitude towards the question of how to manoeuvre in a tripolar world. Even in the Communist states where information is so much harder to come by, it has been apparent that differences of opinion have developed on this crucial policy question. In many respects the existence of these differences should come as no surprise. It is only natural that the move from bipolarity to tripolarity should be marked by such factional politics if only because now there were more foreign policy options. The question was no longer whether to have friendly or hostile relations with one main adversary, but rather whether to be friendly or hostile to two main powers. The way in which these new options were balanced within each state, as well as the way one domestic group interacted with another one in a rival state, is an important question in considering the policies of the powers in the triangle.

From the analysis in the three chapters on the policies of the powers it is possible to divide the spectrum of opinion in each state regarding tripolar politics into three main groups. They can be con-ceived of as lying on a continuum where at one extreme there are those wanting détente with the power seen as the main threat, and at the other extreme those seeking an alliance against the power seen as the main threat. In the middle lie those who seek to play a balanced and even-handed game. Before describing these groups in detail it should be pointed out that these categories are not solid and unchanging. They share the same benefits and drawbacks as does any arbitrary division (e.g. hawks and doves) but are useful primarily for the analytic purpose of distinguishing important differences of opinion, even if they are merely of degree. It should also be pointed out that in each state there tends to be a consensus of opinion on tripolar issues that seeks to moderate between the extreme views. The precise nature of that consensus changes in response to both domestic and foreign events and therefore should be seen as very fluid. The pulling and hauling of opposing forces is best documented in Banning Garrett's study of the US case.

The first group, those favouring détente, have probably been most dominant in the US and USSR, although at present they are encountering serious setbacks. In the US these forces seek an acceptance of the fact that the two superpowers must live with each other and that everything possible must be done to reduce tension with Moscow. They see playing the China card as dangerous and irresponsible, although accepting that Peking should be included as an important actor in great power relations. In Moscow this group is generally known as the 'moderates': those desiring to manage and stabilize relations with Washington. These people share the view with their US counterparts that China is an important power, but they also emphasize that superpower relations are pre-eminent. They view attempts to play off China against the USSR as undermining their argument that the US is a serious negotiating partner and that Washington is more realistic and sensible than the hardliners suggest. In China these détente forces are those leaders who now argue for some sort of *rapprochement* with Moscow. They see no point in exaggerated reaction to the Soviet challenge and feel that Chinese policy would be better served by more flexibility and less dogmatic anti-Sovietism. These forces are not so much anti-American, but they do feel that Chinese policy has become unbalanced and therefore there should now be far more co-operative aspects to Sino-Soviet relations.

The opposite end of the spectrum is also represented in each of the three powers. In Washington there are powerful voices urging a close alliance with China, including in the military sphere. They see the Soviet threat as paramount and any co-operation in that crusade is acceptable, even if it is with another Communist power. These tough balance of power advocates accept that 'the enemy of my enemy is my friend' and that most other views are ignoring these 'hard realities' of international politics.

The USSR on the other hand seems less subject to this kind of alliance position, tending to see superpower relations as too pre-eminent to be manipulated in this way. However there is evidence of some voices calling for 'united action' with forces of socialism against the US. These people are not necessarily the same as the 'hardliners' often discussed in the context of US-USSR relations, but they are a component of such a loose faction. Needless to say there are various other reasons for Soviet leaders to assume a hard-line posture against Washington, but one of the reasons appears to be related to tripolarity.

In China these alliance forces are the dominant voices in policy making in the triangle. The analysis that the USSR is the main con-tradiction has set the tone for much of the recent Chinese foreign policy in a way that not even the US proponents of similar sentiments dare articulate. Peking's position has not always been so much to this extreme of the continuum, but by the early 1980s it seemed clear that these alliance forces were continuing in the sharp anti-Sovietism as articulated by Mao in the latter part of his life.

The centrist voices on our continuum obviously combine aspects of both the extreme views. In the US these balanced decision makers see the need to mix co-operative and conflictive relations in tripolar politics. Especially with the US as the pivot power they see the need to retain working relations with both Communist powers. This delicate and difficult policy requires careful and incremental man-oeuvring in the triangle. Wielding a huge stick or brandishing massive carrots in an age of tripolarity is seen as counterproductive. These centrist views however are not necessarily the product of a determined or well-articulated group of advocates. Garrett has shown that many of these compromise positions develop as much from default due to clashing extremists, as from a coherent desire to be balanced in triangular policy. The lack of policy planning and the tendency towards decision by default tends to result when the détente and alliance voices clash over policy in the great power triangle.

The Soviet Union's policy in the triangle is also very much influ-enced by this type of consensus politics. Much work has been done on the subject of Soviet decision making and a great deal of it coin-cides with the assessment of the US bureaucratic policy making in the triangle. The resulting domination of the centre positions is as much due to a clash of extremes or the relative ease of settling on the median as it is due to a clear-cut policy choice to balance co-operative and conflictive relations as a rational option. For the two superpowers these centrist positions tend to dominate more than any other extreme, despite the fact that the radical postures may get more wide publicity from time to time. Perhaps the two superpowers, both having been pivot powers in the triangle, recognize the necessity to assume a balanced posture. More probably they both find it extremely difficult to reconcile the myriad of their interconnected global interests and therefore the bureaucratically acceptable middle path is the easiest to pursue.

Whatever the case it is significant that the superpowers' position resulting from its balance of domestic forces is different from that in Peking. For China the centrist option has been tried from time to time, but at present they are in a more extreme phase. The above analysis has emphasized the present balance of forces in the triangle and their internal implications, but it should be made clear that these configurations have changed in the past and are unlikely to remain immutable. The apparent fact that the two superpowers hold broadly the same views of tripolarity is perhaps the greatest source of stability at present for the triad. However, it is easy to contemplate various alterations that could either destabilize or reinforce the stability of the system. A growth in power for US alliance forces or the succession of supporters of 'united action' in the USSR would mean greater conflict and uncertainty in the triangle. On the other hand the more there is movement towards the balanced or even the détente end of the continuum the greater the chance of stability in the triangle. A moderation of China's anti-Sovietism or the resur-gence of détente forces in the superpowers would all assist this process.

It is therefore apparent that an analysis of the great power triangle must carefully consider the implications of domestic politics and dif-fering views of tripolarity. This is not merely an academic exercise in model building or category creation, for the three chapters on the policies of the powers make it clear that actual policy in the triangle has attempted to make use of these policy divisions. In the US case there have clearly been attempts to 'support' pro-US forces in Peking in times of domestic Chinese unrest. While it would be folly to suggest that any such clear-cut policy could hope to have a deter-mining effect upon a much more complicated factional political struggle, it is important to keep in mind that there are implications for states' actions in tripolarity that extend to forming at least tacit cross-national links with forces in another states' policy making. This is a phenomenon already studied in greater detail in super-power relations where some have suggested the need for US moderates to encourage fellow moderates in the USSR. While this relationship of political forces is inadequately understood, and decidedly more complicated in the three-way interaction of the tri-angle, nevertheless it is one of several useful ways of understanding tripolar interaction.

Apart from this point that factional politics in the triangle is crucial to an understanding of this relatively new great power relationship, it is also possible to make several other points pertain-ing to the decision making process. First, it seems clear that the change of leadership in any of the three powers does not necessarily bring about instability in the triangle. Neither the various change-overs of US administrations, nor the death of Mao have meant much change in tripolar policy. The strength of entrenched positions on an issue of international politics that assumes greater and greater permanancy, has meant that it becomes increasingly difficult to make radical change in a state's policy in the triangle. Thus the Soviet succession will not necessarily bring about changes in the great power triangle, nor will a further Chinese power struggle. There are examples of such changes (removal of Krushchev or the change to Nixon/Kissinger foreign policy) but the tripolar system on balance seems more stable than many give it credit for.

Second, and a related point, is that change in the triangle is likely to be incremental rather than sudden and dramatic. In part because of the complexity of decision makers and their delicately balanced coalitions it is difficult to make radical alterations. Such changes are possible, but in general it seems more likely that the most effective policy for all three powers will be to move carefully and in a step-by-step manner.

Third, this complexity and incrementalism is made more likely by the apparent lack of policy planning in tripolar policy making. The *ad hoc* reaction to changing events is perhaps a more reason-able approach to an international system that has far more possible permutations than did a relatively more simple bipolar system.

Fourth, the best policy for powers uncertain about how to man-oeuvre in the triangle seems to be one that mixes co-operative and conflictive relations and avoids excessive reliance on either carrots or sticks. The various axes of relations in the triangle work most effectively in a stable manner when they are moving in the same direction. This is evident when Sino-American relations are not pitted against Soviet-American relations, but rather when they are both improving at the same time. Not only would such a policy be more likely to appeal to a broader coalition in the other states' decision making process, but it would also not result in dramatic and destabilizing actions in the triangle. It is apparent that we now must pause to consider in greater detail the implications for tactics in tripolar politics.

Card Playing

The lack of understanding of the incremental nature of change in the triangle has led observers to view the playing of cards in only the crudest forms. However, in order to play the sensitive card games the more intricate aspects should be understood. In essence a state B has two key tactics when playing off A against C. If B perceives, rightly or wrongly, that A is more dangerous and aggressive than C, then it can adopt a 'strong' or 'soft' policy. The 'strong' tactic would be to play the C card against A, including such steps as military cooperation or major economic arrangements between B and C which A and B do not have. The 'soft' tactic would be for the pivot B to 'tilt' or lean slightly toward C in order to offset A. This tilt is accomplished by a subtle and sophisticated process of signalling including policy statements biased in favour of C and small-scale economic agreements between B and C. This delicate game is one of the principal ways in which a state can cope with its sensitive position in between its two adversaries and make incremental changes as required. A careful policy of moderate tilts to one power or the other will probably allow B to continue without unduly upsetting either A or C. This will be made easier if B avoids having its policy regarding A made in C's capital or vice versa. Both A and C will attempt to do so, but B must resist if it is to be successful.

This theory of playing cards and tilting can be applied to contemporary great power history. In the 1960s the USSR did not play the US or PRC card but it did engage in a good deal of tilting. This could be seen most vividly in the two parts of the 1962 Sino-Indian war. In the first period of the Indian subcontinent conflict when the Cuban missile crisis was at its height, the USSR tilted to China in order to maintain Communist bloc solidarity. In the second period when the Caribbean crisis had passed, Moscow then tilted to India (and by association to its US supporters) in order to stop the Chinese attack. Thus Moscow tilted rather than played cards in order to retain its pivotal position in the great power triangle.

In the 1970s the relations in the triangle were dominated by the fundamental imbalance caused by the fact that Peking was clearly the weakest member of the triad. Hence the US is more likely to tilt to China rather than the USSR, but it is not inconceivable for Washington to threaten to improve US-USSR ties in order to win concessions from Peking, for example on the Taiwan issue. Such a judicious and careful context-dependent use of tilts (as opposed to the strong tactic of card playing) was apparently seen in Washington as the way in which the US could retain and expand its pivotal position in the great power triangle. Washington's tilting in the India-Pakistan war of 1971 was a case in point and although in terms of the US' relations with India and Pakistan the results were less than positive, in great power terms, and especially for Sino-American ties, the tilting was successful.

As we have seen in various chapters in this book, the states have pursued variations of the 'hard' and 'soft' tactics in the triangle. There seems to be little evidence for the success of the hardline policy. The important distinction between card playing and tilting is also related to a more general problem of placing undue emphasis on the alignment of two powers against a third.

The extreme policy of forming alignments in the tripolar system appears to be very limited. The alignments formed in the 1960s were severely restricted by the conflicting, not to say changing nature of the great powers' interests. For example, the discussion of whether the USSR and PRC should engage in united action against the US in Vietnam in 1964–6, revealed the extreme difficulty which the Soviet Union as the pivot had in forming an alignment. China's national interests in the Vietnam War were fundamentally different from those of the USSR and the PRC's dominant leadership feared Soviet 'revisionism' at least as much as US 'imperialism'. In the end there was a limited degree of tacit united action against the US in that Moscow sent aid to Hanoi via the PRC, but one need merely reflect on the intense tone of the Vietnam-Cambodia conflict with the not so behind the scenes support from the PRC and USSR for opposing sides, to understand the limited nature of even such mild forms of great power alignments. In the 1970s there were also those in the US urging a Sino-American alignment against the

USSR, but despite dire Soviet warnings that such a coalition is indeed imminent, there is little evidence that a US-PRC alignment is possible, let alone desirable. In the full flush of warmth following the normalization of Sino-American relations, one should not lose sight of the fact that Peking has its own reasons for playing the US card against the USSR which are not necessarily co-terminous with US reasons for playing a China card. It is only necessary to mention the basic US desire for a SALT agreement and the reduction of tension in Europe, two goals which are not entirely to the Chinese liking. Thus card playing is unlikely to shape the long-term pattern of great power relations.

Those who favour card playing in the triangle and the formation of alignments also seem to argue that it is good for one power to foment conflict between the other two. However, such a policy of sitting back to watch tigers fight was not, at least in the triangle of the 1960s, advantageous. All three powers, to differing degrees, were apprehensive that one member of the triad wanted the other two to engage in conflict and so all three refrained from playing on that fear and creating instability. As the triangle developed in the mid-1960s, the US and USSR in particular went out of their way to clarify to each other the nature of their respective relations with the PRC. In the 1970s, Washington has been finding it increasingly difficult to negotiate the *tertium quid* between the Soviet Scylla and the Chinese Charybdis and the US might well find it advantageous to encourage at least a degree of Sino-Soviet *rapprochement*.

A reduction in Soviet-Chinese tension to a certain extent, as long as it was not on an anti-American basis, would mean that both Communist states were less suspicious (and critical) of US relations with the other Communist state. The sophistication in policy making required to bring this about appears to waning rather than waxing, especially in the West. As Banning Garrett has shown, there is a need to mix both co-operative and conflictive relations in triangular politics, and not merely wield the 'stick' of card playing. Nevertheless there is evidence that such a complex triangular process is possible. For example, in the 1960s and indeed much of the 1970s, there developed a complex trilateral communication pattern. This is evident in Henry Kissinger's trip to China following the 1974 Vladivostok summit, or Carter's discussions with Deng Xiaoping in January 1979 about US-USSR relations. Thus playing cards, forming alignments and provoking conflict in the tripolar system are ambiguous tactics rarely beneficial and with few clear and predictable consequences.

Other Tactics in the Triangle

One of the major problems in the playing of cards in the triangle is the failure to take into account what can be called triadic response or the multiplier effect. This effect essentially describes the spiral escalation caused when the action of A regarding B causes B to react, which forces C to act, which in turn provokes the other two. As with some of the other problems resulting from card playing which do not adequately consider the complications of the great power triangle, all too often the notion of playing cards only considers one step in the reaction process and does not fully take into account triadic response and feedback. The signalling pattern in particular needs to be sophisticated and discriminating. For example, the discussion in the US in the mid to late 1960s of deploying an anti-China ABM system failed properly to assess the effect of such an action on the USSR. Some American decision makers attempted to make it clear to the Kremlin that the ABM system was not directed against the Soviet Union, but often the signals were confusing. Moscow naturally enough viewed the US decision to deploy ABMs as a threat to its ability to deter the Americans and so *inter alia* the arms spiral escalated.

Thus actions in the triad have complex effects. However, this phenomenon can also be harnessed to positive purposes if certain perspectives are adopted by the decision makers. For example, on the one hand the Soviet Union's expansion of the size of its armed forces can simply be seen in Washington as evidence of the USSR's aggressive intentions necessitating a US escalation in its own arms procurement. On the other hand, these developments could be understood in tripolar terms, as measures designed to cope with the USSR's perception of the Chinese threat. If seen as such, the US might refrain from developing new weapons and escalating the arms race, thereby lowering Soviet fears of Washington's intentions and easing the escalation process. Triadic response can be positive, for as with many aspects of great power relations, so much depends on the perception of intentions. If cards are played instead of a more sophisticated policy of tilting, this intricate negotiating process in the triangle as manifest in the triadic response model, is less likely to be effective.

The playing of cards in many respects also distorts the changed nature of the pattern of deterrence in the tripolar as opposed to bipolar system. In the great power triangle, powers no longer deter only one power but rather they now deter two at the same time. Deterrence commitments are issued against two powers; the initiation of action to challenge deterrence must consider two not one deterrence postures; and the response of two powers to such initiation is different from the response of only one power. Most strikingly, there is a tendency for one power to incorporate, as part of its own deterrence, the deterrence posture of another power against the initiator. For example, in the Sino-Indian war of 1962 and the India – Pakistan conflict of 1965 the USSR made use of the US deterrence posture in order to help deter PRC action. With the new concept in mind it is clear that at the present time the talk of playing the China card against the USSR gives the distorted impression that the US now ceases to have a need to deter the PRC as well as the USSR. If American strategy is formulated and forces are deployed in such a way that the dual requirements of deterrence in the triad are ignored, the US will be failing adequately to consider the implications of the tripolar system. If a pivot power is to be able effectively to wield a carrot and a stick against both of the other members of the triad, its deterrence posture must be properly formulated. The necessity to tilt or play cards on the part of the pivot may vary and the options to credibly deter both powers should be available. The talk of card playing, and to a lesser extent tilting, tends to overly simplify the complexity of the great power triangle.

The Chinese for their part do seem to appreciate this problem of deterrence of two powers rather than one. Recent trends in Chinese defence policy, and pre-eminently the 1980 ICBM test, indicate China's desire to develop a capability against the US as well as the USSR. This costly programme was undertaken and carried out despite growing Sino-American *rapprochement*.

The above is not an argument for higher defence budgets, for there are aspects of tripolar deterrence that can reduce military spending. Firstly, as noted above, a sympathetic US perception of the Soviet's need to deploy forces to meet a perceived (or misperceived) Chinese threat will not mean that Washington must match every Soviet rouble spent on its armed forces. Furthermore, the US might consider the Chinese forces as part of its own anti-Soviet deterrence in Europe just as the PRC apparently perceives the US and NATO in Europe as a supplement to the Chinese anti-Soviet posture. This second concept of relying on another power's deterrence may appear to some to contradict the view expressed in the previous paragraph that the US should build a dual deterrence posture even if Washington is, in the short term, playing the card of one power against the other. However, there is no such contradiction. What needs to be stressed here is that the US requires both an anti-PRC and anti-USSR deterrence (alignments are after all only temporary) but America does not need to match every aspect of its rival's military posture. The total US force facing the USSR need only match a portion of the Soviet force as it can be reasonably assumed that a large segment of the USSR's military forces are anti-PRC. In addition, the US can assume that the PRC's forces ranged against the USSR form a part of the deterrence against Soviet actions.

Therefore card players in the triangle must be careful how their actions affect the pattern of deterrence. By overplaying the cards, one power may distort its perception such that it assumes merely a short-term perspective and fails to see the need to deter two powers rather than only one. Furthermore, the playing of cards may destroy the opportunities for reducing military expenditures as a result of the peculiar nature of tripolar deterrence. Once again short-term calculations of gain may upset a longer-term stable pattern of deterrence. For example, if the US overly plays the China card against the USSR (e.g. by selling arms to Peking) in an attempt to build up the PRC element of Washington's anti-Soviet deterrence, the USSR may well feel the need to expand its defence budget to such a degree that the US can no longer restrain its own budget. This will assist the PRC in frustrating the joint superpowers' goal of strategic arms limitation and negating any value to the US that might be gained from using the PRC's anti-Soviet deterrence posture. Because of the complex nature of the triangle, the playing of cards may be too harsh a tactic when what may be required is a more cautious tilt to one side. Those who suggest playing the card of one power against the other power, tend to oversimplify and distort the nature of the great power triangle and the possibilities inherent in the system.

The Triangle in Europe

While there are some important effects of the China factor and the great power triangle on the policies of the three powers in general, it is much more difficult to suggest aspects of European policies that have been similarly affected. When comparing the evidence analysed in the chapters by Lawrence Freedman and Edwina Moreton, the absence of a coherent pattern of foreign policies is apparent. The pre-eminence of local factors and domestic determinants of policy cannot be overestimated.

The development of the triangle in Europe did not appear to follow a consistent course as the importance of events differed significantly between East and West, let alone among specific countries. In the era of Sino-Soviet unity the eastern part of Europe was on balance more interested in the role of China in foreign policy. Precisely because it was more permissible to deal with China as it was a Communist state, some East Europeans found that Peking could be useful in their foreign and domestic policies. At a time in the 1950s when virtually no analyst could conceive of a great power triangle, the China factor was perhaps at its peak of influence in East Europe.

The opposite was true in West Europe, for reasons derived from the same Cold War conditions. China, as a Soviet ally in a time of reasonably sharp East-West lines, was not seen as a suitable partner for West Europeans. Peking was perceived to be merely a radical aspect of an antagonistic Soviet bloc. Far from offering potential for new foreign policies in Europe, China was seen as nearly beyond the pale. Although it is true that some West Europeans were less critical of China than was the US, nevertheless there were relatively few people prepared to suggest China as an important actor affecting the Cold War divisions of Europe.

The focus of the Cold War in Europe had meant that East and West Europe maintained diametrically opposed views of the role of China in the 1950s, but the thawing of the frozen East-West ties in the early 1960s brought some important changes. For East Europe the melting of the Cold War meant that potentially they now had more room for manoeuvre, but new problems specifically linked to the China problem minimized any such advantages. The open Sino-Soviet split led Moscow to concentrate on tightening its basic support in East Europe which meant less freedom for East European foreign policy. In some senses détente was cancelled out by the Moscow-Peking rift. For West Europeans the early 1960s was only important in one sense, that of East-West détente. To the extent that West Europeans were interested in the Sino-Soviet split it was in the way it would perhaps make the USSR more amenable to deals with the West. Some sympathy was felt in West European capitals for the plight of Kremlin leaders struggling to control a radical influence in their bloc. But still there was little perception of new policy options opened for West Europeans because of the emerging independence of Chinese foreign policy.

Another interesting development in the mid-1960s highlighted by Freedman and Moreton is the emergence of relatively independent policies by crucial states in Europe. Freedman pointed to the French role in particular as being independent of the Cold War framework of relations. De Gaulle, nearly alone among West European leaders in the mid-1960s, saw the potential for ties to China as being important in establishing an independent foreign policy. Indeed many initial comparisons were drawn between the problems France caused for the Western bloc and problems caused by China for the Eastern coalition.

This appeal to greater independence in policy was also elaborated upon by Moreton in her discussion of Romanian foreign policy. Bucharest's attempt to mediate both the Sino-Soviet rift and even Sino-American relations suggests some parallels to France's desire to serve as some kind of roving international broker. Even East Germany's less than total obeisance to the Moscow line at this time supported this trend, and can be put down to specific local determinants of policy. Both Freedman and Moreton have stressed that these local factors make any drawing of a detailed pattern of importance for the China factor in Europe relatively futile.

Perhaps the most important role for China in Europe came later on, well into the 1970s. Once again it was a case of a change in Sino-Soviet relations that had different implications in both the Eastern and Western parts of the continent. The open hostilities along the Ussuri in 1969 and the crucial strategic changes when Sino-American détente got underway, caused very different repercussions in East and West. In the East the USSR saw the need to draw its European allies closer together and room for manoeuvre was further reduced. In the West the effect was opposite. Europe was now freed to consider open ties to China that had been held back because of NATO and COCOM restrictions on 'dealing with the enemy'. A flood of speculation ensued in the West as to the new role for China in Europe as well as East-West relations.

While much of the scenario building on the role of the China factor has proven to be illusory, it is still true that China assumed greater importance in Europe than it had ever done before. This role was almost exclusively in West Europe as in the words of General Alexander Haig 'China could become the 16th member of NATO'. This was a role for China that clearly would not appeal, nor be allowed to appeal, to East Europeans. Thus as the China factor and the great power triangle was at its peak of influence in West Europe in the late 1970s, so it was at its lowest ebb in the eastern part of the continent. Much as the mirror image conditions 25 years previous, so it became apparent that there is no pattern to the times at which China and the triangle was important in Europe. But what of the specific issues concerned? When China was important, was it in both East and West; was it for the same reason and in the same fashion?

It seems only logical to suggest that in a place where there is extreme conflict between two parties, the appearance of a strong new third party will be of great importance to the competing states. Thus it should not be surprising that the advent of the China factor was important for the two parts of Europe focusing on a Cold War. However, it is because of the centrality of the Cold War for Europeans that the importance of the China factor was not over-estimated. Both East and West Europe find themselves forced to get along with the USSR, for Moscow is central to European politics. No extreme solutions to political problems that would exclude the Soviet voice are possible.

In East Europe the importance of the China factor was felt at times, but primarily in terms of bilateral relations or as part of Communist bloc politics. Peking rarely had importance in a triangular sense. Unlike some Third World countries, East Europeans were never really able to play off Moscow and Washington by use of the Peking card. China's influence was primarily as another Communist voice, with the legitimacy to speak out on a wide range of issues precisely because it was Communist. At the point that China was seen as 'splittist', its power for East Europeans waned.

What is worse from the East European point of view, was that the very fear of a great power triangle in the area led Moscow to tighten the screws and cut off any hope for actual tripolarity in East Europe. Thus if there was a role for the triangle it was negative, i.e. it placed added restrictions on the room for manoeuvre of the already circum-scribed East Europeans' foreign policies.

This was not the case in West Europe, for here the role of China and the triangle followed a more conventional and expected pattern. The importance of China, such as it was, never reached major pro-portions, but it is possible to speak of a positive effect on the policies of West European states. This was especially true at the time of tran-sition from Sino-American rivalry to détente. The Europeans were able to get out ahead of US policy and consummate the relations with China that it long urged on American decision makers. However, the major gains that these states had hoped would accrue were in the realm of East-West relations, and this did not turn out to be the case. Because Sino-American détente went hand in hand with Sino-Soviet rivalry, the USSR was not pleased with growing West European ties to China. Whereas in the 1950s and 1960s the West Europeans may have gained some room for manoeuvre between East and West, by the early 1970s the ties to China did them relatively little good. Much like the states of the Eastern part of Europe, they found that relations with the USSR remained too important to be sacrificed for whatever marginal gains China could offer. By the beginning of the 1980s, both East and West Europeans had come to appreciate that the China factor had some importance for them, but not to any great degree and not without important costs in other aspects of their foreign relations.

Effect on Ideology, Economics and Military Affairs

If the advantages and disadvantages of the China factor are broken down into three aspects, ideology, economics and military affairs, the difficulties in drawing a European-wide pattern become apparent. The importance of the ideological realm in East Europe should by now be obvious. Unlike events in West Europe, ideology in the East affected crucial aspects of both domestic and foreign policies of those states. Because of the significance of ideology in Communist politics in general, it should not be surprising that China's formulation of alternative ideological 'rules' for Communist societies, including those of East Europe, had at least a potentially important impact. The Chinese model was however only relevant in the period of Sino-Soviet unity, and played virtually no part in the period after the open Moscow-Peking rift. In West Europe there was no significant Chinese impact on domestic politics, in any period.

The China factor in the ideological realm did have a broader appeal in foreign policy issues. At the time in the 1950s when Peking argued for a tighter Communist bloc, its independent foreign policy role was limited. As China began to formulate a more independent line and argued that there should be no single centre of the Communist world, the impact of China and triangular factors increased in both East and West Europe. In the East the more nonconformist states such as Romania were pleased and sought to take some advantage of the change. Most other states in East Europe found that the ideological reins were tightened as a result, and especially the GDR felt that a weakening of the bloc would harm its own interests. In West Europe more recently this Chinese ideological appeal has gained it some new friends and influence, especially among Eurocommunists in Italy and Spain. While China and the Eurocommunists differ on a vast range of other ideological principles, they do seem to be able to unite on the issue of opposition to a dominant centre of the Communist movement. The days are now over when China and the Italian Communist Party stood at the opposite ends of the Communist political spectrum, and thus the ideological dimension in West Europe has taken a new twist. It is paradoxical that Peking's ideological influence may become greater in West Europe than in the Communist East, a development that mirrors the importance of local conditions and Moscow's role as indicated above.

The overall judgement on the ideological aspect of the China factor is however one of minimal importance. Especially in the past 20 years Peking was seen as a radical state out of touch with what was a reasonable ideological attitude to both domestic and foreign problems. China's extremism of the Cultural Revolution made it plain that Peking was not a useful model for domestic politics either in East or West Europe. In foreign policy the appeal to national liberation struggles and carrying the Sino-Soviet conflict into the furthest reaches of Chinese diplomatic activity, meant that Peking was also unlikely to find anything but fringe adherents to its foreign policy ideology. This radical legacy has until recently served to limit China's ideological role in Europe. Perhaps the longest lasting ideological doctrine of this kind was regarding the 'inevitability of world war'. This was a view abandoned in the early 1950s by the USSR and one that never found favour in West Europe. It was an extremely convenient stick with which the Soviet Union could beat the Chinese in propaganda exchanges and one that fell on receptive ears in West Europe. In late 1980 when China dropped the doctrine and suggested that war could be prevented if there was 'unity against hegemonism', a degree of moderation was returned to the ideological component of China's role in the triangle. The appeal to West Europe would no doubt be increased by this move, although the critical view of Chinese ideology in East Europe was unlikely to be much changed by this development.

Where recent changes in Chinese ideology might mean an increase in the China factor in ideological terms in East Europe, may be in the realm of domestic politics. The de-radicalization of the Chinese economy and adoption of aspects of moderate East European models could be an important beginning for the process of bringing China's and East Europe's ideologies closer together. The incorporation of elements of the Yugoslav and Hungarian models as well as the virtual cessation of Chinese attacks on the Soviet domestic scene have brought the Chinese and East Europeans potentially closer together. The USSR is no longer called 'revisionist', as China itself seems to have adopted a similar model.

It is however difficult to see how Chinese influence is increased by these changes. Far from East Europe converging with the Chinese model, it is the Chinese that are moving closer to the Soviets and East Europeans. Peking's influence and triangular factors are not increased as a result. Compare the role of China in the Polish events of 1956 and 1980/81 and one can see a reduced Chinese impact in this crucial ideological sphere. Peking now sits on the sidelines.

In summary of the ideological component, it seems clear that it has relatively little impact on West Europe except in some narrow aspects of Eurocommunist policy. In East Europe the foreign policy impact of Chinese ideology is even less. Although in domestic terms Chinese and East European ideologies now seem more compatible, that is by and large because China has adopted the European model. In this crucial realm of ideological matters, Moscow's influence remains dominant, even though it faces continuing challenges and confusing prospects, such as those posed by the Sino-Eurocommunist link.

The economic aspect of the China factor and the triangle in Europe has perhaps fluctuated more wildly than any of the three aspects. The seemingly eternal dreams of a vast China market have proven as illusory in the present as in the past. The economic dimension has neither been crucial in either the East or West European cases. For the Soviet bloc states their trade has by and large followed the trends in USSR trade with China: strong in the 1950s, declining sharply after the split and rising once again in the 1970s. Although there were some divergences from the Soviet pattern of trade, the broad trends remain the same. It is Moscow's relations as well as the East Europeans' with China that have determined the rise and fall of economic relations. It is however a very different pattern from that in the western portion of Europe.

Sino-West European trade did not begin to take off until the détente in Sino-American relations. As with the pattern of broader political events, trade generally mirrored the improvement in political relations. Despite the growth of economic relations in the 1970s, the myth of the massive China market was once again punctured. As Lawrence Freedman has suggested in his chapter, by 1979–80 the Chinese were revealed as 'industrial voyeurs'. Their trade missions were thick on the ground in Western Europe in the last part of the 1970s, but few major deals were in fact agreed and implemented.

Economic aspects have not turned out to be a great success in either East or West European relations with China and certainly do not serve as a third force anywhere equal to the trading power and economic punch of the two superpowers. This is the case in part because of continuing political problems — witness French and Dutch trading problems with China in 1980 — but especially because of domestic Chinese economic developments. The rapid and repeated abandonment of Peking's new economic plans in the post-Mao era has made it plain that China is in no position to become a major trading partner. The retrenchment in massive deals arranged with Western companies, especially in Japan and West Germany, has meant that the economic potential for the China factor is only likely to decline for Western nations. China simply cannot afford to enter the Western economic system on a massive scale and its recent withdrawal from contracts will at least stave off Poland-like problems of overcommitment to Western economic arrangements.

China's economic weakness and its inability to absorb Western goods may bring the day closer when economic ties with Eastern Europe are improved. It has been suggested that the Soviet Union and East Europe are more likely trading partners in the long run with China as their economies can be more easily meshed. Both the type of goods available and the nature of long-term economic planning models make Chinese trade with East Europeans a more sensible policy. Thus we may once again be watching yet another rise and fall of trade with China that has a rising East European role and a declining West European one.

The military aspect of the China factor is in some senses an opposite relationship from that in the ideological realm. In terms of Peking's military effect on Europe, the emphasis is mainly in West Europe and virtually absent from the Eastern portion. As Edwina Moreton pointed out, 'distant water cannot quench fires', and thus the Chinese are of little military use for Eastern Europe in seeking independence from Moscow. With the exception of Albania there has been no important Chinese military presence in East Europe, and even the Albanian connection provided little real protection from or threat to the USSR. The significance of the Sino-Albanian ties lay in the political realm, and indeed Albanian independence was guaranteed by political calculations rather than some sense of tangible Chinese deterrence of the Soviet Union. Neither is it possible to see a successful Soviet policy of incorporating the anti-China struggle in the Warsaw Pact framework. Attempts to link Asian, and especially Vietnamese, defence policies to that of the Pact met with a distinctly cool attitude in East Europe.

The role of the Chinese military factor in Europe is however far more complex. There has been a great deal of discussion in the West about China serving an important task in the anti-Soviet struggle, but it is unclear how important Peking has really been. From the Chinese point of view Europe is still seen as the main centre of Soviet expansionist designs and Peking's rhetoric on the need to take a united stand against 'Soviet hegemonists' and avoid the 'appeasement of détente' is a mainstay of China's rhetorical policy. It is unclear whether Peking's desires for co-ordination of policy are real, or whether they are merely willing to fight 'to the last European'. Either way, at least in rhetorical terms there is a military dimension to China's involvement in West Europe.

Alexander Haig's view that China can be considered the 'sixteenth member of NATO' has been seized upon by Moscow as evidence of real links between its two main adversaries and thus would substantiate the view that there is a Chinese military factor in Europe. But as Lawrence Freedman has pointed out, the military relationship is more ambiguous than Soviet statements or 'hawks' in the West would have us believe.

It is possible to suggest important military dividends for West Europe (unlike East Europe) in terms of the Chinese military impact. The Soviet Union's necessity to plan for conflict on two fronts has had real military implications, especially in the 1970s. At least for a time the pressure was taken off Europe as the USSR concentrated on building its Asian forces.

For this reason alone there has been a military dividend from the China factor. There also have been liabilities, for example in terms of the deployment of the SS-20. This new and more sophisticated system might not have been deployed, let alone developed, if not for the China threat and thus it can be argued that West Europe might have faced a lesser threat if not for the Chinese factor.

This complex but important verdict on the role of the military dimension of China's influence in Europe is also evident on the related topic of arms sales. While East Europe has never been involved to any great extent in arms sales to China, the topic was a crucial one with West Europe in the latter part of the 1970s. Some people thought that the West Europeans were eager to break out of the COCOM straitjacket limiting arms sales to Communist states, and launch into a massive arms deal with Peking. This was not the case when many restrictions were lifted by 1979–80. The West Europeans perceived themselves to have different objectives than the crude one of 'the enemy of my enemy is my friend'. The West Germans in particular understood the necessity to retain decent ties with the Soviet Union and saw little purpose in antagonizing them by selling weapons to China. The British lay at the opposite end of the spectrum: more willing to sell arms, but even they were not making open-ended deals. The complexities of the specific domestic and bilateral politics of West European states make it impossible to suggest a coherent pattern of reaction to the issue of military deals with China.

The salience of domestic factors is also crucial from the Chinese side in explaining why arms deals never developed anywhere near the high levels of early expectations. Peking was neither able nor willing to buy massive numbers of weapons. In the second phase of retrenchment in military modernization China was also not willing or able to buy specimens of equipment for production at home. Such a policy would have been expensive and essentially purchasing a dated technology for the future. Thus the military aspect of the China factor in Europe does have some important components, but they are limited to West Europe and only certain vague areas, such as the provision of a 'second front'.

The Position of the Three Powers in Europe

The relative position of the three powers in Europe does not seem to have improved in the period of China's changing impact on the states of the area. From Peking's point of view the balance sheet is not positive. In general China's position has changed in a direction in keeping with the transition from Sino-Soviet unity to dual opposition and then to Sino-American détente. Friends in one place were exchanged for friends in another part of Europe, but with little apparent advantage for Peking.

In the ideological realm China's position in Europe became more confused and less self assured. The period of influence in the 1950s gave way to isolation from both East and West Europe and in the 1970s was replaced by a generally declining role of Chinese ideology in both parts of Europe. East Europe had taught China a thing or two about domestic ideological principles and Peking had abandoned the doctrine of the 'inevitability of war' rather than having been able to convince the Europeans of its relevance. Some limited gains were made regarding links to Eurocommunists but once again that was a matter of China changing its view rather than Eurocommunists coming around to Peking's position.

China's economic balance sheet in Europe also is not positive. It has gone from a period of important relations with East Europe through a period of low trade generally and finally ended up with disappointment in the prospects of economic ties to West Europe. Peking has not been able to serve as an important trading partner for either East or West, with the lone exception of isolated Albania, and even that tie is now lost. Continuing problems of an economic type with West Europeans do not bode well for Chinese policy in this respect.

The overall Chinese military attitude towards Europe is also not pleasing to Peking. The extent of military links with the USSR and East Europe in the 1950s was stronger than it is now with the US and West Europe. The desires for détente and coexistence with the USSR among West Europeans have not been dampened despite Chinese attempts to do so. The essential realities of power in Europe, the confrontation between the US and USSR, have not really changed in Europe, despite various changes in Chinese attitudes.

It is however difficult to suggest that any of the three powers is terribly pleased with the impact of China in Europe. This is not a zero-sum game. From the Soviet Union's point of view Peking has been and continues to be a problem in Europe, albeit of a different sort. In the ideological realm China did pose major problems for Soviet control of East Europe, but by the early 1960s these difficulties were by and large controlled. Indeed the unity of the Soviet bloc against the Chinese challenge was probably assisted by the Peking threat. The new connection between China and Eurocommunism may pose a new problem for the USSR, but one that will probably be open to exploitation. China's unity with the Italian and

Spanish parties has more to do with certain narrow agreements (for example that there is no centre to Communism) but there remain important areas of disagreement between the two.

The economic sphere has not been a problem for the USSR as Chinese trade with East Europe has not significantly affected Moscow's ties of a similar nature. In the military realm the China factor has only been a secondary problem. The USSR's main problem with China concerns bilateral relations. It is true that Moscow might have spent more on East European military matters if not for the Chinese threat, but it is equally possible that the resources might have been diverted to non-military areas of the Soviet economy. By and large the USSR appears to have learned to cope with the China factor and latent triangular aspects in Europe, but essential Soviet security is not challenged.

Both Moscow and Peking might wish to lessen the difficulties facing their European policies by engaging in a modicum of détente, but the gains in either case would not be dramatic. From the Chinese point of view some doors in East Europe might open that otherwise are shut, especially in economic terms, but there are unlikely to be major changes in relations. From the Soviet point of view some conflict may be taken out of its relations with East Europe, especially in the areas where Moscow seeks a more forthright anti-China stand from Warsaw Pact states. However, the changes would unlikely be great, for the essential roots of Soviet-East European differences lie in more fundamental aspects of their relationship and China policy disputes, such as they are, are more of an effect than a cause.

If it is possible to point to a 'winner' from the changing China factor in Europe, some might suggest that it is the US. While this may be true in certain respects, it is by no means an unqualified success. The Reagan administration may well be more pleased than a more 'dovish' set of American leaders if only because of the potential for incorporating China into an anti-Soviet front. The formulator of the 'sixteenth member of NATO' slogan is now the US Secretary of State, but there do exist important cleavages in the American administration on China policy.

In the ideological sphere the US was greatly pleased with the implications of the Sino-Soviet split. The rending asunder of what was perceived as a uniform enemy bloc was counted as a major victory, as was the damage done to the sense of 'historical momentum' claimed by Communist parties and states in Europe. But the

Communist unity and historical force were more a figment of American misperceptions in the first place and probably never were as much of a challenge to the US as first thought. In any case, the resulting tightening up of Soviet control in Europe on ideological grounds after the Moscow-Peking split could not have pleased the US. Nor can Chinese ties to Eurocommunists be satisfactory to Washington, for legitimation of parties seen by the Reagan administration as Trojan horses, is not a positive development.

The China factor in economic terms in Europe may have initially been seen as a positive development, but not recently. When the US was unwilling to pursue an open relationship with China for fear of antagonizing the USSR, European economic ties to Peking were seen as useful. But now that the shoe is on the other foot and the West Europeans are trying to hold back the Americans from sewing up the China market, the Europeans are not pleased with the US on economic grounds. The economic aspect of the China factor probably now damages US-West European ties more than it helps.

The military factor is by and large the most successful from the American point of view. The assistance to efforts in building a strong China against the USSR is generally welcomed. However, now it is more likely that the US will be urging closer ties on military issues to China than the West Europeans are willing to accept. Once again as in the economic sphere, the US is less likely to find Europeans enthusiastic about antagonizing the USSR by arming China. Where the US can be more unambiguously pleased about the Chinese military factor in Europe is in the provision of a second front that relieves the pressure on its European allies.

A possible further change in the China factor in Europe towards some sort of Sino-Soviet détente will not necessarily meet with opposition in Washington. So long as that détente is not on an anti-American basis (and it need not be), then the US may be quite pleased with the changes. For example, the conflict with West Europeans about whether to arm or trade with China might well be reduced. In sum, the China factor in Europe has had some important effects on the policies of the three powers, but they are limited in place and duration. There can be no unambiguous balance sheets in assessing the great power triangle in Europe.

The trends, such as they are in the policies of the local states or the great powers, are pre-eminently limited by the domestic and local sources of change. Europe is less subject to the manipulation of triangular politics because of the primacy of these bilateral and internal factors.

Nor is it possible accurately to point to long-term trends in the policies in Europe, for much seems to hinge on a complex pattern of change derived from local factors. There clearly are some triangular aspects to international relations in Europe, but they are by no means dominant. The classic bipolar model is also not applicable (if it ever was), but more is to be gained in an analysis of great power relations with Europe by concentrating on this level than on the tripolar one.

Concluding Remarks

As we come to the end of this collection of analyses of the contemporary great power triangle, it is hoped that at least some points have been made clearly enough to merit a brief recapitulation. There can be little doubt that at least some aspects of the international system are characterized by a great power triangle. While there can be no suggestion that China is an equal of the superpowers, it has overall achieved the status of the next most important power. This is also not meant to imply that all aspects of contemporary international politics are shaped by a great power triangle, but some issues of importance do seem to be affected by tripolarity. While the triangle in Europe, or indeed most multilateral cases, do not seem to be the dominant configuration, there are crucial aspects of the three-way relationship between the powers themselves that do exhibit important triangular patterns.

What should be equally apparent is the different meanings of the term 'triangle'. While all three powers and the Europeans understand the meaning of such words, and do in part conceive of international politics in that way, they do not always mean the same thing by the use of the triangular metaphor. This essential problem of ethnocentrism is a common one in strategic analysis. It also requires a careful analysis on a case-by-case basis so as to ascertain whether all sides are speaking the same language or have an effective translator.

Various dimensions of triangular politics now have more than a 20-year history. Certain basic aspects are emerging as increasingly relevant for any analysis of the tripolar relationship. The role of the pivot power, first the USSR and then the US, is perhaps the most useful notion brought out as it highlights the complex and conflicting pressures faced by states in the triangle. Other concepts, such as deterrence in the triangular world and its need to deter two powers rather than one, should also be evident. This is also associated with the changes in crisis management that have a complex three-way process of communication. The task of the analyst therefore has become more difficult when studying those elements of the international system characterized by a great power triangle.

This difficulty should therefore make us wary of those who would have us believe that triangular politics is a simple process. Those who suggest that 'cards can be played' or indeed that the triangle is a masterful American invention to cope with two different Communist powers confuse more than they clarify. Tripolarity, in some respects developed before the US was even aware of the process and has defied any attempt to categorize it in neat analytical frameworks. 'Card games', as with other sporting models (e.g. billiard balls), simply do not do justice to the complexity of the problems associated with relations between the three great powers.

The complexities that render any rigid analytical pattern difficult to ascertain have a great deal to do with the powerful force of domestic and local elements. The motivations for making triangular policy in the three powers are distinctly different. China does not share US motives, either in ideological terms or power political terms. Certainly the USSR has approached tripolarity with very different motives. The location of a conflict also fundamentally affects the way in which triangular relations are played out. As we saw in the case of Europe, but also in other areas of the world, the domestic and local events are more powerful than any putative master-plan of a great power. Various other aspects render any triangular pattern building a dubious pastime, pre-eminently the role of personality and their own particular misperceptions. Factional politics and leadership changes have proven as crucial to triangular politics as they have to the rest of international relations.

Therefore when one is presented with assertions that triangular politics can be effectively manipulated by a skilful diplomat, the response should be extreme suspicion. For example, those who would argue that 'linkage politics' can be a finely-tuned tool of policy are deluding themselves as much as their audience. While there are clearly some relationships in the triangle that are linked, it is difficult to suggest that these linkages can be manipulated, let alone controlled. Those who would suggest that there are 'rules' to the tripolar game that can be utilized to coerce an opposition, will be sorely disappointed.

This is not to suggest that we must throw up our hands in despair and let international events pass us by without an attempt to analyse them. To argue that analysis is difficult is not to say that it is fruitless. It has been the purpose of this book to point to the areas where there is at least some degree of regularity and a nascent pattern of relations. It is hoped that some of the key aspects and motivations have been studied, because it is felt that the triangle is likely to be with us for quite some time to come. China is not about to collapse despite recent retrenchments, and therefore will be the third most important power to affect the superpowers and their basic interests at least in the near future. Prediction of that future is impossible, but it is hoped that the functioning of at least some of the more important triangular aspects will now be better understood.

BIBLIOGRAPHY

Addy, Premen, 'South Asia in China's foreign policy: a view from the left', *Journal of Contemporary Asia 2*, no. 4, 1972, pp. 403–14

Adie, W.A.C., 'China, Russia and the Third World', *China Quarterly*, July-September 1962, pp. 200–13

____ ' "One-world" restored? Sino-American relations on a new footing', *Asian Survey 12*, no. 5, May 1972, pp. 365–85

Andelman, David, 'China's Balkan Strategy', *International Security*, Vol. 4, No. 3, Winter 1979/80

Armstrong, J.D., *Revolutionary Diplomacy*, Berkeley: University of California Press, 1977

Ashley, Richard, *The Political Economy of War and Peace: The Sino-Soviet-American Triangle and the Modern Security Problematique*, London: Frances Pinter, 1980

Barnds, William J., *China and America: The Search for a New Relationship*, New York: New York University Press, 1977

Barnett, A. Doak, *China Policy — Old Problems and New Challenges*, Washington, DC: Brookings Institution, 1977

____*China and the Major Powers in East Asia*, Washington: Brookings Institution, 1977

Blum, Robert, *U.S. Policy Towards Communist China*, New York: Foreign Policy Association, 1966

Bobrow, Davis *et al., Understanding Foreign Policy Decisions: The Chinese Case*, London: Collier Macmillan, 1979

Borg, Dorothy and Heinrichs, Waldo (eds.), *Uncertain Years: Chinese-American Relations 1947–1950*, New York: Columbia University Press, 1980

Borisov, O.B., and Koloskov. B.T., *Soviet-Chinese Relations 1945–1970*, Bloomington, Indiana: Indiana University Press, 1975

Brown, Leslie H., *American Security Policy in Asia*, Adelphi Papers, No. 132, London: International Institute for Strategic Studies, 1977

Brown, Roger Glenn, 'Chinese politics and American policy', *Foreign Policy*, No. 23, Summer 1976, pp. 3–23

Buchan, Alistair (ed.), *China and the Peace of Asia*, London: Chatto and Windus for the Institute for Strategic Studies, 1965

Caplow, Theodore, 'A Theory of Coalitions in the Triad', *American Sociological Review*, 21, 1956

_____'Further Developments of a Theory of Coalitions in the Triad', *American Journal of Sociology*, Vol. 64, No. 3, March 1959

_____*Two Against One: Coalitions in Triads*, New Jersey: Prentice Hall, 1965

Chai, Winberg (ed.), *The Foreign Relations of the People's Republic of China*, New York: Putnam, 1972

Chari, P.R., 'US-USSR-China interaction: the strategic plane', *China Report 12*, No. 1, January – February 1976, pp. 33–42

Chen, King C. (ed.), *China and the Three Worlds*, New York: M.E. Sharpe, 1979

Choudhury, Golam W., 'Post-Mao policy in Asia', *Problems of Communism 26*, July – August 1977, pp. 18–29

_____*Chinese Perceptions of the World*, Washington, DC: University Press of America, 1977

Clemens, Walter C. Jr., *The Arms Race and Sino-Soviet Relations*, Stanford, Calif.: Stanford University, 1968

Clubb, O. Edmund, *China and Russia: The 'Great Game'*, New York: Columbia University Press, 1971

_____'China, Russia and East Asia', *Pacific Community*, No. 4, July 1972

_____'China and the Superpowers', *Current History 67*, No. 397, September 1974, pp. 97–100

Coffey, J.I., 'The Chinese and Ballistic Missile Defense', *Bulletin of the Atomic Scientists*, Vol. 21, No. 10, Dec. 1965

Cohen, Jerome Alan (ed.), *The Dynamics of China's Foreign Relations*, Cambridge, Mass: Harvard University Press, 1970

Cohen, Stephen P., 'Security issues in South Asia', *Asian Survey 15*, No. 3, March 1975, pp. 203–15

Crankshaw, Edward, *The New Cold War. Moscow vs Peking*, Harmondsworth: Penguin, 1963

Davies, Derek, 'China's foreign policy: idealism versus reality', *Pacific Community 1*, No. 4, July 1970, pp. 564–78

Deutscher, Isaac, *Russia, China and the West: A Contemporary Chronicle – 1953–1966*, London: Oxford University Press, 1970

Eckstein, Alexander, *China's Economic Revolution*, Cambridge: Cambridge University Press, 1977

Fairbank, John King (ed.), *The Chinese World Order. Traditional China's Foreign Relations*, London: Oxford University Press, 1969

____*The United States and China*. Cambridge, Mass.: Harvard University Press, 1971

____*China Perceived: Images and Policies in Chinese American Relations*, New York: Alfred A. Knopf, 1974

Feis, Herbert, *The China Tangle*, Princeton, NJ: Princeton University Presses, 1972

Fingar, Thomas (ed.), *China's Quest for Independence: Policy Evolution in the 1970's*, Boulder, Colorado: Westview Press, 1980

Fitzgerald, C. P., 'The Sino-Soviet border conflict', *Pacific Community*, January 1970, pp. 27–83

____*China and Southeast Asia Since 1945*, Melbourne: Longman, November 1972

Floyd, David, *Mao Against Khrushchev*, New York: Praeger, 1963

Freedman, Lawrence, *The West and the Modernization of China*, Chatham House Papers No. 1, London, RIIA, 1979

Garrett, Banning, 'The China Card: To Play or not to Play', *Contemporary China*, Vol. 2, No. 3, Fall 1978

____'China Policy and the Strategic Triangle', Kenneth Oye *et al.* (eds.), *Eagle Entangled; U.S. Foreign Policy in a Complex World*, New York: Longman, 1979

Gass, Oscar, 'China, Russia and the U.S.', *Commentary 43*, April 1967, pp. 39–48

Garner, William, 'SALT II: China's Advice and Dissent', *Asian Survey*, Vol. 19, No. 12, Dec. 1979

Garver, John, 'Chinese Foreign Policy in the 1970's; The Tilt Towards the Soviet Union', *China Quarterly*, No. 82, June 1980

Gelber, Harry C., 'Strategic Arms Limitations and the Sino-Soviet Relationship', *Asian Survey*, Vol. 10, No. 4, April 1970

____'The United States and China: the evolution of policy', *International Affairs* (London), *46* No. 4, October 1970, pp. 682–95

____'The Sino-Soviet relationship and the U.S.', *Orbis 15*, No. 1, Spring 1971, pp. 118–33.

____*Technology, Defense and External Relations in China, 1975–1978*, Boulder, Colorado: Westview Press, 1979

Gelman, Harry, 'Outlook for Sino-Soviet relations', *Problems of Communism 28*, September-December 1979, pp. 50–66

Ginneken, Jaap van, *The Rise and Fall of Lin Piao*, New York: Avon Books, 1977

Gittings, John, *The World and China, 1922–1972*, London: Eyre Methuen, 1974

_____*Survey of the Sino-Soviet Dispute: a commentary and extracts from the recent polemics, 1963–67*, London: Oxford University Press, 1968

_____'The great power triangle and Chinese foreign policy', *China Quarterly*, No. 39, July – September 1969, pp. 41–54

_____'China between the superpowers', *New Society 79*. No. 3, 10 October 1974

Godwin, Paul, 'China and the Second World: The Search for Defense Technology', *Contemporary China*, Vol. 2, No. 3, Fall 1978

Gottlieb, Thomas, *Chinese Foreign Policy Factionalism and the Origins of the Strategic Triangle*, Santa Monica: Rand Corp. R-1902-NA, Nov. 1977

_____'The Hundred-Day Thaw in China's Soviet Policy', *Contemporary China*, Vol. 3, No. 2, Summer 1979

Griffith, William E., *Sino-Soviet Relations 1964–65*, Cambridge, Mass.: MIT Press, 1966

_____*Cold War and Coexistence: Russia, China and the U.S.*, Englewood Cliffs, NJ: Prentice-Hall, 1971

_____'Peking, Moscow and beyond: the Sino-Soviet-American triangle', *The Washington Papers*, No. 6, Georgetown University Washington, The Center for Strategic and International Studies, 1973

Gurtov, Melvin, *China and South East Asia: The Politics of Survival*, Lexington, Mass.: Heath Lexington Books, 1971

_____'Sino-Soviet relations and S.E. Asia: recent developments and future possibilities', *Pacific Affairs 43*, No. 4, Winter 1970–71, pp. 491–505

Halperin, Morton. and Perkins, Dwight, *Communist China and Arms Control*, New York: Praeger, 1965

_____(ed.), *Sino-Soviet Relations and Arms Control*, Cambridge, Mass.: MIT Press, 1967

Halpern. A.M. (ed.), *Policies Toward China: Views from Six Continents*, New York: McGraw-Hill, 1965

Harding, Harry and Gurtov, Melvin, *The Purge of Lo Jui-ch'ing:*

The Politics of Chinese Strategic Planning, Santa Monica: Rand Corp. R-548-PR, Feb. 1971

Harrison, Selig S., *China, Oil and Asia: Conflict Ahead?*, New York: Columbia University Press for the Carnegie Endowment for International Peace, 1977

Hinton, Harold C., *China's Turbulent Quest*, New York: Macmillan, 1972

____*Communist China in World Politics*, Boston: Houghton Mifflin, 1965

____*The Bear at the Gate: Chinese Policy Making under Soviet Pressure*, Washington, DC: American Enterprise Institute for Public Policy Research, 1971

____*Three and a Half Powers: The New Power Balance in Asia*, Bloomington, Indiana: Indiana University, 1975

____'The U.S. and the Sino-Soviet Confrontation', *Orbis*, Vol. 19, No. 1, Spring 1975

____ *Peking and Washington: Chinese Foreign Policy and the United States*, Beverly Hills, Calif.: Sage Publications, 1976

Holbraad, Carsten, *Superpowers and International Conflict*, London: Macmillan, 1979

Holsti, Ole, 'East-West Conflict and Sino-Soviet Relations', *Journal of Applied Behavioural Science*, Vol. 1, No. 2, April – June 1965

Horn, Robert C., 'China and Russia in 1977: Maoism without Mao', *Asian Survey 17*, No. 10, October 1977, pp. 919–30

Hsiao, Gene T. (ed.), *Sino-American Détente and Its Policy Implications*, New York: Praeger, 1974

Hsieh, A. L., *Communist China's Strategy in the Nuclear Era*, Englewood Cliffs, NJ: Prentice-Hall, 1962

____'The Sino-Soviet nuclear dialogue, 1963', *Bulletin of the Atomic Scientists 21*, January 1965, pp. 16–21

____'China's Nuclear-Missile Program: Regional or Intercontinental', *China Quarterly*, No. 45, June 1971

Hsiung, James C., 'U.S. relations with China in the post-Kissingerian era: a sensible policy for the 1980's', *Asian Survey 17*, No. 8, August 1977, pp. 691–710

Hsüeh, Chun-tu (ed.), *Dimensions of China's Foreign Relations*, New York: Praeger, 1977

Huck, Arthur, *The Security of China: Chinese Approaches to Problems of War and Strategy*, London: Chatto and Windus, 1970

Hutchinson, Alan, *China's African Revolution*, Westview: Boulder Co., 1976

Jencks, Harlan W., 'China's 'Punitive War' on Vietnam: A military assessment'. *Asian Survey 19*, No. 8, August 1979, pp. 801–15

Jonsson, Christer, *Soviet Bargaining Behaviour*, New York: Columbia University Press, 1979

Kaplan, Morton, 'Variants on Six Models of the International System', in James Rosenau (ed.), *International Politics and Foreign Policy*, New York: Free Press, 1968

Kim, S.S., *China, the United Nations and World Order*, Princeton, NJ: Princeton University Press, 1979

Kinter, William R. and Copper, John F., *A Matter of Two Chinas*, Philadelphia: Foreign Policy Research Institute, 1979

Kirby, Stuart, *Russian Studies of China*, London: Macmillan, 1975

Kun, Joseph C., 'Peking and world communism', *Problems of Communism 23*, No. 6, November-December 1974, pp. 34–43

Larkin, Bruce D., *China and Africa 1949–70,* Berkeley: University of California Press, 1971

Lawrence, Alan, *China's Foreign Relations Since 1949*, London: Routledge and Kegan Paul, 1975

Levine, Steven, 'The Devils Alliance; Soviet Perspectives on US-China Relations', *Contemporary China*, Vol. 2, No. 2, Summer 1978

____'Some Thoughts on Sino-Soviet Relations in the 1980's', *International Journal*, Vol. 34, No. 4, Autumn 1979

Lieberman, Bernhardt, 'Experimental Studies of Conflict in Some Two-Person and Three-Person Games', in Jean Criswell, Herbert Solomon, Patrick Suppes (eds.), *Mathematical Methods in Small Group Processes*, Stanford: Stanford University Press, 1962 ·

____'The Sino-Soviet Pair: Coalition Behaviour from 1921 to 1965', paper presented to the Conference on Sino-Soviet Relations and Arms Control. Airlie House, Warrenton, Virginia, 30 Aug. – 1 Sept. 1965

____'Not an Artifact', *Journal of Conflict Resolution*, Vol. 15, No. 1, March 1971

____'Coalitions and Conflict Resolution', *American Behavioural Scientist*, Vol. 18, No. 4, March/April 1975

Lieberthal, Kenneth, 'The foreign policy debate in Peking as seen through allegorical articles 1973–76', *China Quarterly*, No. 71, September 1977, pp. 528–54

____ *Sino-Soviet Conflict in the 1970's*, Santa Monica: Rand Corp.

R-2342-NA, July 1978

Liu, Leo Yueh-Yun, *China as a Nuclear Power in World Politics*, London: Macmillan, 1972

___'The People's Republic of China as a nuclear power: a study of Chinese statements on global strategy', *Asian Studies 10*, No. 2, August 1972, pp. 183–95

Louis, Victor, *The Coming Decline of the Chinese Empire*, New York: Times Books, 1979

Löwenthal, Richard, 'Russia and China; Controlled Conflict', *Foreign Affairs*, Vol. 49, No. 3, April 1971

Luttwak, Edward, 'Against the China Card', *Commentary*, Vol. 66, No. 4, Oct. 1978

Maillard, Pierre, 'The Effect of China on Soviet-American Relations', *Adelphi Papers*, No. 66, March 1970

Maxwell, Neville, *India's China War*, London: Jonathan Cape, 1970

Mendl, Wolf, *Issues in Japan's China Policy*, London: Macmillan, 1978

Middleton, Drew, *The Duel of the Giants: China and Russia in Asia*, New York: Scribner, 1978

Mills, Theodore 'Power Relations in the Three-Person Group', *American Sociological Review*, Vol. 18, No. 4, Aug. 1953

___'The Coalition Pattern in the Three-Person Group', *American Sociological Review*, Vol. 19, No. 6, Dec. 1954

Newhouse, John, *Cold Dawn: The Story of SALT*, New York: Harper and Row, 1973

Nogee, Joseph, 'Polarity: An Ambiguous Concept', *Orbis*, Vol. 18, No. 4, Winter 1975

North, R.C., *The Foreign Relations of China*, Belmont, Calif.: Dickenson, 1974

Ojha, Ishwer C., *Chinese Foreign Policy in an Age of Transition: The Diplomacy of Cultural Despair*, Boston, Mass.: Beacon Press, 1969

Oksenberg, Michel and Oxnam, Robert B. (eds.), *Dragon and Eagle: United States-China Relations: Past and Future*, New York: Basic Books, 1978

O'Leary, Greg, *The Shaping of Chinese Foreign Policy*, London, Croom Helm, 1980

Peterson, Sophia, *Sino-Soviet-American Relations: Conflict, Communications and Mutual Threat*, Denver: University of Denver Press, 1979

Pillsbury, Michael, *Soviet Apprehensions About Sino-American Relations 1971 – 4*, Santa Monica: Rand Corp. P-5459, June 1975
_____'Future Sino-American Security Ties', *International Security*, Vol. 1, No. 4, Spring 1977
_____'U.S.-Chinese Military Ties?', *Foreign Policy*, No. 23, 1977
_____'The Military-Security Dimensions of Recent Sino-American Relations', *Contemporary China*, Vol. 2, No. 1, Spring 1978
Pollack, Jonathan D., 'The logic of Chinese military strategy', *The Bulletin of the Atomic Scientists 35*, No. 1, January 1979, pp. 22 – 33
_____'The Implications of Sino-American Normalization', *International Security*, Vol. 3, No. 4, Spring 1979
Pye, Lucian W., 'The puzzles of Chinese pragmatism', *Foreign Policy*, No. 31, Summer 1978, pp. 119 – 36
_____'Dilemmas for America in China's Modernization', *International Security*, Vol. 4, No. 1, Summer 1979
Ra'anan, Uri, 'Peking's Foreign Policy Debate 1965 – 1966', in Tang Tsou (ed.), *China in Crisis*, Vol. 2, Chicago: University of Chicago Press, 1968
Reardon-Anderson, James, *Yenan and the Great Powers*, New York: Columbia University Press, 1979
Riker, William, 'Bargaining in a Three-Person Game', *American Political Science Review*, Vol. 61, No. 3, Sept. 1967
Robinson, Thomas W., 'The view from Peking: China's policies toward the United States, the Soviet Union and Japan', *Pacific Affairs 45*, No. 3, Fall 1972, pp. 333 – 55
_____'Detente and the Sino-Soviet-U.S. Triangle', in Della Sheldon (ed.), *Dimensions of Detente*, New York: Praeger, 1978
_____'Chinese-Soviet Relations in the Context of Asian International Politics', *International Journal*, Vol. 34, No. 3, Autumn 1979
Rogers, Frank, 'Sino-American Relations and the Vietnam War, 1964 – 66', *China Quarterly*, No. 66, June 1976
Rothenberg, Morris, *Whither China: The View From the Kremlin*, Miami: Center for Advanced International Studies, n.d.
Rubinstein, Alvin Z. (ed.), *Soviet and Chinese Influence in the Third World*, New York: Praeger, 1975
Rustin, Michael, 'Structural and Unconscious Implications of the Dyad and Triad: An Essay in Theoretical Integration, Durkheim, Simmel, Freud', *Sociological Review*, Vol. 19, No. 2, New Series, May 1971
Salisbury, Harrison E., *The Coming War between Russia and*

China, London: Seckeṙ and Warburg, Pan, 1969

Scalapino, R.A., 'China and the balance of power', *Foreign Affairs 52*, No. 2, June 1974, pp. 349–85

Schiebel, Joseph, 'The Soviet Union and the Sino-American Relationship', *Orbis*, Vol. 19, No. 3, Fall 1975

Schurmann, Franz, *The Logic of World Power*, New York: Random House, 1974

Schwartz, Harry, 'The Moscow-Peking-Washington triangle', *Annals of the American Academy of Political and Social Sciences 414*, July 1974, pp. 41–54

Schwartz, Morton, *Soviet Perceptions of the United States*, Berkeley: University of California Press, 1978

Segal, Gerald, 'Chinese Politics and the Soviet Connection', *Jerusalem Journal of International Relations*, Vol. 2, No. 1, Fall 1976

____'China and the Great Power Triangle', *China Quarterly*, No. 83, Sept. 1980

____'China's Strategic Posture and the Great Power Triangle', *Pacific Affairs*, Winter 1980–81

____'China's Nuclear Posture in the 1980's', *Survival*, Jan. – Feb. 1981

____*The Great Power Triangle*, London, Macmillan, 1982

Sergeichuk, S., *Through Russian Eyes: American-Chinese Relations*, Arlington, Virginia: International Library, 1975

Shichor, Yitzhak, *The Middle East in China's Foreign Policy*, London: Cambridge University Press, 1979

Shishko, R., *Defense Budget Interaction Revisited*, Santa Monica: Rand Corp. P-5882, June 1977

Shubik, Martin, 'Does the Fittest Necessarily Survive?', in Martin Shubik (ed.), *Readings in Game Theory and Political Behaviour*, Garden City NY: Doubleday, 1954

Simmonds, Robert, *The Strained Alliance*, New York: Free Press, 1975

Simon, Sheldon W., 'China, the Soviet Union and the subcontinental balance', *Asian Survey 13*, No. 7, July 1973, pp. 647–58

____The Japan-China-U.S.S.R. triangle', *Pacific Affairs 47*, No. 2, Summer 1974, pp. 125–38

____'New conflict in Indochina', *Problems of Communism 27*, September – October 1978, pp. 20–36

Solomon, Richard H., 'Thinking through the China problem',

Foreign Affairs 56, No. 2, January 1978

Sonnenfeldt, Helmut, 'The Chinese Factor in Soviet Disarmament Policy', in Morton Halperin (ed.), *Sino-Soviet Relations and Arms Control*, Cambridge: Harvard University Press, 1967

Subcommittee on Asian and Pacific Affairs, Committee on Foreign Affairs of the US House of Representatives, *Playing The China Card: Implications for United States-Soviet-Chinese Relations*, Washington: USGPO, 1979

Subcommittee on National Security and International Operations, Committee on Government Operations, US Senate, *The Great Power Triangle*, Washington: USGPO, 1971

Sutter, Robert G., *China Watch: Toward Sino-American Reconciliation*, Baltimore, Md.: Johns Hopkins University Press, 1978

Tatu, Michel, 'The Great Power Triangle: Washington-Moscow-Peking', *Atlantic Papers*, No. 3, December 1970

Taylor, Jay, *China and South East Asia: Peking's Relations with Revolutionary Movements*, Praeger Special Studies in International Politics and Government, New York: Praeger, 1974

Thomson, James, Jr., 'On the Making of US China Policy 1961–9: A Study in Bureaucratic Politics', *China Quarterly*, No. 50, April–June 1972

Van Ness, Peter, *Revolution and Chinese Foreign Policy: Peking's Support for Wars of National Liberation*, London: University of California Press, 1970

Vinacke, Edgar and Arkoff, Abe, 'An Experimental Study of Coalitions in the Triad', *American Sociological Review*, Vol. 22, No. 4, Aug. 1957

Waller, D.J., 'Chinese perception of Soviet-American relations 1962–1970: a pilot study', *Political Science Review 9*, Nos 3–4, July–December 1970, pp. 258–69

Weinstein, Warren (ed.), *Chinese and Soviet Aid to Africa*, New York: Praeger, 1975

_____and Henriksen, Thomas (eds.), *Soviet and Chinese Aid to African Nations*, New York: Praeger, 1980

Whiting, Allen S., *China Crosses The Yalu*, New York: Macmillan, 1960

_____*The Chinese Calculus of Deterrence: India and Indochina*, Ann Arbor: University of Michigan Press, 1975

Wight, Martin, *Systems of States*, London: Leicester University Press, 1977

Wilcox, Francis (ed.), *China and the Great Powers — Relations with the United States, the Soviet Union and Japan*, New York: Praeger, 1974

Wilkinson, David, *Conflict and Cohesion*, London: Frances Pinter, 1976

Willis, Richard and Long, Norma, 'An Experimental Simulation of an International Truel', *Behavioural Science*, Vol. 12, No. 1, Jan. 1967

Wilson, D., 'Sino-Soviet rivalry in South-East Asia', *Problems of Communism 23*, No. 5, September – October 1974, pp. 39–51

Wolfe, Thomas, *Soviet Strategy at the Crossroads*, Cambridge: Harvard University Press, 1964

Yahuda, Michael B., 'Chinese Foreign Policy After 1963: The Maoist Phases', *China Quarterly*, Oct – Dec. 1968

____'China's Nuclear Option', in *China After the Cultural Revolution*, New York: Random House, 1969

____'China's new foreign policy', *The World Today 28*, No. 1, January 1972, pp. 14–22

____'Kremlinology and the Chinese Strategic Debate, 1965–1966', *China Quarterly*, Jan. – March 1972

____'China's new era of international relations', *Political Quarterly 43*, September 1972, pp. 295–307

____'Chinese Conceptions of Their Role in the World', in William Robson, Bernard Crick (eds.), *China in Transition*, Beverly Hills, California: Sage Publications, 1975

____'Problems of Continuity in Chinese Foreign Policy', *Asian Affairs*, Vol. 8, Part 3, Oct. 1977

____*China's Role in World Affairs*, London: Croom Helm, 1978

Yalem, Ronald, 'Tripolarity and the International System', *Orbis*, Vol. 15, No. 4, Winter 1972

Yu, George T., *China's Africa Policy: A Study of Tanzania*, New York: Praeger, 1975

____'Peking's African diplomacy', *Problems of Communism 21*, March – April 1972, pp. 16–24

____'China and the Third World', *Asian Survey 17*, No. 11, November 1977, pp. 1036–48

____'China's impact', *Problems of Communism 27*, January – February 1978, pp. 40–50

Zagoria, D.S., *The Sino-Soviet Conflict 1956–61*, Princeton, NJ: Princeton University Press, 1962

_____*Vietnam Triangle: Moscow, Peking, Hanoi*, New York: Pegasus, 1967

_____'The Strategic Debate in Peking', in Tang Tsou (ed.), *China in Crisis*, Vol. 2, Chicago: University of Chicago Press, 1968

_____'Averting Moscow-Peking Rapprochement; A Proposal for U.S. Foreign Policy', *Pacific Community*, Vol. 8, No. 1, Oct. 1976

_____'The Soviet Quandary in Asia', *Foreign Affairs*. Vol. 56, No. 2, Jan. 1978

Zimmerman, William, *Soviet Perspectives on International Relations 1956–1967*, Princeton: Princeton University Press, 1969

NOTES ON CONTRIBUTORS

Lawrence Freedman is head of the Policy Studies Unit, The Royal Institute of International Affairs, London. He is the author of *U.S. Intelligence and the Soviet Strategic Threat* (London: Macmillan, 1977); *Britain and Nuclear Weapons* (London: Macmillan, 1980); *The Evolution of Nuclear Strategy* (London: Macmillan, 1981) as well as various other works in the strategic studies field. Dr Freedman would also like to thank the Ford Foundation for financial support for his chapter. The Foundation is funding a larger project on Sino-Soviet relations led by Dr Freedman at the RIIA.

Banning Garrett is a Research Associate, Institute of International Studies, University of California, Berkeley and Senior Foreign Policy Analyst, Harold Rosenbaum Associates, Arlington Virginia. He is the author of *The 'China Card' and its Origins: U.S. Bureaucratic Politics and the Strategic Triangle* (Berkeley, California: University of California, Institute of International Studies, forthcoming) as well as various other articles on US foreign policy and the triangle.

Edwina Moreton is a specialist on Soviet and East European affairs and a member of the editorial staff of *The Economist* (London). She is the author of *East Germany and the Warsaw Alliance: The Politics of Detente* (Boulder, Colorado: Westview Press, 1978) as well as various other articles on Soviet foreign policy, East European affairs and East-West relations.

Gerald Segal is a Lecturer in Politics at the University of Leicester. He is the author of *The Great Power Triangle* (London: Macmillan, 1982), co-editor of *Soviet Strategy* (London: Croom Helm, 1981) as well as various other articles on the great power triangle and Chinese foreign and defence policy.

Michael Yahuda is a Senior Lecturer in International Relations at the London School of Economics. He is the author of *China's Role in World Affairs* (London: Croom Helm, 1978) as well as various other articles on Chinese domestic and foreign policy.

INDEX